The Philosophy of Art

The Philosophy of Art

An Introduction

THEODORE GRACYK

polity

First published in 2012 by Polity Press
Reprinted 2012, 2013, 2015, 2016, 2018 (twice)

Polity Press
65 Bridge Street
Cambridge CB2 1UR, UK

Polity Press
350 Main Street
Malden, MA 02148, USA

ISBN-13: 978-0-7456-4915-3
ISBN-13: 978-0-7456-4916-0 (pb)

A catalogue record for this book is available from the British Library.

Typeset in 9.5 on 12 pt Utopia
by Servis Filmsetting Ltd, Stockport, Cheshire
Printed and bound in the United States by LSC Communications

The publisher has used its best endeavours to ensure that the URLs for external websites referred to in this book are correct and active at the time of going to press. However, the publisher has no responsibility for the websites and can make no guarantee that a site will remain live or that the content is or will remain appropriate.

Every effort has been made to trace all copyright holders, but if any have been inadvertently overlooked the publisher will be pleased to include any necessary credits in any subsequent reprint or edition.

For further information on Polity, visit our website: www.politybooks.com

Contents

Preface

This book is genuinely introductory. It is intended for college and university students who have no previous exposure either to philosophy or to the specific subfield of philosophy of art. My overall aim is to present a basic overview of the field, balanced by an exploration of topics that are of interest to beginning students (such as the topics of creativity, authenticity, and popular art). My selection of topics and their relative emphasis is informed by three decades of classroom experience.

Philosophy has numerous subfields, such as logic, theory of knowledge, ethics, and philosophy of mind. Although they are unified by shared philosophical methods, these subfields diverge from one another in the core questions they address. Theory of knowledge explores the nature of knowledge, philosophy of mind raises questions about the nature of the mind, and so on. Philosophy of art is most readily understood as the philosophical pursuit of two fundamental questions:

What defines art?
What is artistic value?

However, this approach faces an obstacle. Philosophy of art is historically intertwined with a second discipline, aesthetics. The term "aesthetics" is often used as a shorthand way of designating philosophy of art. That equation is a mistake, because aesthetic concerns are not limited to art. (The tendency to equate the two inquiries may arise from the historical fact that the aesthetic theories of many philosophers have focused on art.) Another mistake is to think that aesthetics is limited to issues of beauty and ugliness. We will see that the field encompasses much more than that. Properly understood as a distinct philosophical subdiscipline, aesthetics can be provisionally understood to focus on these two questions:

What defines the aesthetic?
What is aesthetic value?

This book is an introduction to philosophy of art rather than aesthetics. However, the fields overlap, so a general guide to philosophy of art is, by default, an introduction to aesthetics.

Anyone with an interest in the arts will have encountered some of the issues discussed here. At the same time, it is likely that some of the issues explored here will be surprising. The very *range* of issues may be surprising. However, a moment's reflection on the wide range of activity called "art" does a lot to explain why there is such a range of topics. Painting and music and literature are obviously very different as art, involving distinct materials and appealing to distinct modes of sensory perception, so it is not surprising that different issues arise for the different arts. A second reason for the wide range of issues is that philosophy of art does not proceed in a philosophical vacuum. Many debates arise within philosophy of art as the result of debates in *other* philosophical subdisciplines. Developments in theory of knowledge, philosophy of language, and metaphysics have regularly influenced and redirected philosophizing about art. As a result, contemporary philosophy of art is not a particularly systematic field of inquiry. A glance at the table of contents will reveal that only three chapters of this book concentrate on the questions that I've just provided as indications of the central concerns of aesthetics and philosophy of art. To the extent that those questions stand at the center of the enterprise, the organization of this book reflects my conviction that some of the most interesting work is happening at some distance from that center.

Because this is an introduction, my primary goal is to outline major topics. A secondary goal is to outline debates within those topics. Philosophy is not just a set of theories. For practicing philosophers, philosophy is the activity of philosophizing. It is the active debate that arises in defending and criticizing theories. In addition to presenting the major theories on each topic, this book presents the most important arguments for and against those theories. For the most part, I avoid "taking sides" in these debates. However, decisions about what and who to cover can never be entirely neutral, so I owe it to you, the reader, to be honest about my basic prejudices. The general focus here is contemporary Anglophone philosophy, which is to say that the focus is philosophy of art as pursued in English in recent years. There is a strong emphasis on analytic philosophy and a lesser emphasis on its historical sources, with very little space devoted to a second stream of contemporary philosophy, the Continental tradition. It is extremely difficult to present Continental philosophy at the introductory level, and its general omission from this book will not surprise philosophy instructors in the Anglophone tradition. As a general rule, I have concentrated on the methodology and topics that one normally encounters at meetings of the American Society for Aesthetics and the British Society for Aesthetics, and in their respective publications, the *Journal of Aesthetics and Art Criticism* and *The British Journal of Aesthetics*. Therefore I have not excluded Continental philosophy entirely, because it does have supporters among British and American philosophers.

Newcomers to philosophy are often surprised by the nature of philosophical debates. Philosophical debate is seldom a matter of simply trying to prove one theory correct and another theory wrong. Instead, philosophical debates have multiple functions, including (1) identification of underlying issues, (2) clarification of key concepts, (3) identification of subtle reasoning errors, (4) exploration of the implications of adopting a position, and (5) exploration of a solution's consistency or "fit" with other theories. Progress in philosophical debate is often measured according to the degree of insight that is achieved. It seldom consists in the construction of some knock-out argument that settles things once and for all. Throughout this book, I have concentrated on displaying these five dimensions of philosophical engagement. There is no effort to declare winners and losers in the various debates. My neutrality is not an indication that I regard every "side" as equally plausible. It reflects the view that an introduction to philosophy is first and foremost an introduction to critical thinking directed at a particular topic. The starting point for critical thinking is a thorough understanding of the issues and competing positions. The first priority is to be clear about what is involved in endorsing or rejecting a position. You are invited to draw your own conclusions about the relative merits of different positions. How could I, or anyone else, stop you? But you won't know how strong your own position is if you haven't examined the competing views and competing arguments.

Although I try to maintain neutrality about most of the issues covered, I will not hide my sympathies for certain positions. Contextualism is a good example. Implications of accepting or rejecting contextualism arise in several chapters. Although there isn't much point to explaining what I mean by this until we move into the subject matter, it receives attention in several places. Yet the attention that I pay to contextualism is something more than a personal bias. Support for contextual theories is one of several key reversals in the last half-century of philosophizing about art. There have been others. The last half-century has proceeded without much concern for the aesthetic dimensions of art. Although it was a major topic in earlier eras, contemporary philosophy of art is no longer centered on art's aesthetic value. Given that philosophy of art and aesthetics were historically associated, and given that this association remains in many people's minds, the shift away from "aesthetics" deserves some attention in its own right. It is addressed in the book's later chapters. So is the recent renewal of the topics of aesthetic experience and aesthetic value. Fresh thinking is being directed at the aesthetic dimension of nature, environments, and our everyday activities and surroundings. Finally, I occasionally divert the discussion of a contemporary debate into a review of historically important philosophers. It can be useful to have some background on why philosophers have emphasized different aspects of art at different times. Many theories in contemporary philosophy are variations of older theories, and it is important to have a sense of their evolution and variation. If nothing else, a little history can show that labels like "aesthetic value" and "expression theory" have more than one meaning. As the book unfolds, it will become clear that "art" joins this list of contested words. It refers to the treasures of the world's great art museums, but it also applies to the activities of musicians and comedians and dancers and poets. And the musicians and dancers don't require the cultural status of Ludwig van Beethoven and the Bolshoi Ballet. Art is also produced when a mother sings a lullaby and when amateurs post their cool dance moves on Internet video sites.

Finally, the book's lack of visual illustrations deserves a comment. Many books of this sort contain illustrations of works of visual art that are discussed in the text. I have not provided them, largely because it is not possible to provide quality reproductions in a book of this size. I assume that anyone who reads this book will have access to the Internet, and I think you're better served by doing an Internet search for the images that figure in the discussion. For example, the first chapter discusses a particular figure in Rembrandt van Rijn's *Night Watch* (1642). Reproducing that immense canvas on a single page of this book cannot do it justice. Whenever the visual appearance of an example might be important to a reader, I provide the artist's name, the work title, and the year of creation, which is all the information that you need to locate adequate (and even excellent) reproductions of the artwork that I discuss. So, rather than select a small number of examples for reproduction, I have instead allowed myself to mention a very wide range of examples and I leave it to you, the reader, to locate the visuals that you think you ought to see. The same goes for musical examples. The major video posting sites should allow you to hear all of the music that I mention as examples. Most readers will find that an Internet search is far more useful than my inclusion of a few bars of musical notation.

There is nothing sacred about the order of the chapters. Although the order of topics reflects my goal of offering an integrated introduction, I have done my best to make each chapter an independent essay. There should be no great loss in comprehension if you impose your own order on them. The only exceptions are chapters 6 ("Defining Art") and 9 ("Artistic and Aesthetic Value"). Chapter 6 will make more sense after you've read all of 1 through 5, and chapter 9 works best after you have some sense of the wide variety of objects and practices that are at stake here, and after reading chapter 7. Where the discussion in one chapter is highly relevant to the material in an earlier or later chapter, the connection is noted in the text.

For purposes of readability, I've avoided cluttering the text with extensive references. Each chapter ends with a list of further reading that will guide you in finding additional material about a particular philosopher or philosophical position. Besides those recommendations, there are a number of general reference works about philosophy of art that are well worth consulting: *The Oxford Handbook of Aesthetics* (Levinson 2005), *The Routledge Companion to Aesthetics* (Gaut and Lopes 2005), *A Companion to Aesthetics* (Davies et al. 2009), *The Blackwell Guide to Aesthetics* (Kivy 2004), and the *Encyclopedia of Aesthetics* (Kelly 1998). (Interesting, isn't it, that none of them has the phrase "philosophy of art" in its title?)

Acknowledgments

I thank Emma Hutchinson for instigating this project. Although I have been immersed in aesthetic theory and philosophy of art for 30 years, it had not entered my mind to write an introduction to the field until she approached me with the idea. I also thank the three readers she secured to respond to my initial proposal. Their encouragement and advice influenced the book in numerous ways, most notably by recommending the inclusion of chapter 8. I particularly thank one of those readers, Julie Van Camp, for providing extensive commentary on the manuscript as it neared completion. Her parallel experience in teaching this material to undergraduates generated invaluable advice about keeping my explanations clear, and her detailed knowledge of the material saved me from more than one blunder. Finally, I thank William H. Bossart for guiding my graduate studies as I made the transition from would-be epistemologist to aesthetician. Looking at what I've assembled here, I recognize that his influence on my thinking is incalculable.

1 Meaning, Interpretation, and Picturing

Philosophy of art can be puzzling in many different ways. Unfortunately, these puzzles begin with the meanings of the most basic terminology. Offered without further qualification, "artist" refers to someone who produces visual art and "art" normally refers to visual art, the stuff that most people associate with art museums and art galleries. Some people refer to these objects as "fine art," or even "Art with a capital *A*." However, there is another standard use of these same words according to which Ludwig van Beethoven and William Shakespeare are great artists, and symphonies and tragedies are fine art, too. By including the performing and literary arts, we arrive at the broad category of the arts. Philosophy of art is interested in this very broad class of objects and activities. How broad is this class of objects? That issue is itself one of the most challenging issues in philosophy of art. Another puzzle or misunderstanding can arise from the way that some European languages and some legal contexts say "author" instead of "artist" when referring to someone who creates art. In this book, "author" will be restricted to poets, novelists, playwrights, and other literary artists. "Artist" will embrace anyone who creates any kind of art.

Philosophy of art tries to make sense of these broad general categories. However, philosophy of art should not be confused with art history, art criticism, or art appreciation. Generally, philosophy is less an exploration of things than an exploration of our shared conceptual frameworks for thinking about them. Applying this distinction, one philosophical task is to determine whether there is an underlying logic to what we include and exclude from the category of art. Are there criteria demarcating the line between what is art and what is not? For example, both photography and cinema were initially denied the status of art. Yet now there is very little resistance to the idea that at least some photographs and movies are works of art. At this early point in our investigation it makes no sense to try to decide why some photographs and movies might be art while others are not. We must leave that task to the later chapters that explore major criteria offered to distinguish art from non-art.

Until the twentieth century, most theorizing about art focused on pictures and literature. Because almost all pictures and literature were representational until the twentieth century, it was easy to over-generalize and adopt the thesis that fine art is necessarily representational. As a result, the *absence* of a clear representational function was sometimes offered as a reason why certain kinds of things cannot be art. Lack of representation was an important historical reason for saying that instrumental music is not art. At best, it might provide a very high level of entertainment. However, such arguments cut both ways. J. S. Bach, G. F. Handel, W. A.

Mozart, Joseph Haydn, and Richard Wagner wrote considerable amounts of vocal music. These composers achieved clarity in representation by incorporating verbal texts. They stand in contrast to Beethoven, who made his name with instrumental music. Early nineteenth-century music lovers who regarded Beethoven as an artistic genius therefore assumed that his piano sonatas and symphonies must possess some element of representation, however mysterious the precise nature of that representation might sometimes be. It was obvious to Beethoven's admirers that they should interpret his music – they should ask themselves what his various musical works are about – even if he seldom offered them explicit guidance through titles and other texts.

Despite the many complications, we must start somewhere. So let us begin with the intuition that ordinary, everyday usage of the term "art" refers to visual art. Here, then, are two obvious facts. First, visual art remains the paradigm of fine art. Second, photographs and films are like paintings and sculpture in that all of these are *seen* and *looked at*. Because the visual arts have played a central role in theorizing about art, we have good reasons to begin our philosophical inquiry into art and aesthetics by examining visual art. For the remainder of this chapter we will set aside literature and music in order to concentrate on visual representation. We will begin with pictures.

1.1 Visual representations and pictures

Just as the visual arts provide the traditional paradigm of fine art, pictures are the paradigm of visual art. But is this a legitimate basis for thinking about the nature of art?

As a provisional starting point, let us understand a picture to be a fixed, two-dimensional visual representation of the visual appearance of a three-dimensional object or arrangement of objects. It might seem redundant to say that pictures are visual representations of visual appearances, but this point distinguishes pictures from other two-dimensional surfaces that are visually marked to represent something non-visual. Examples include sheet music (where the marks on the musical staff visually represent musical sounds) and ordinary writing (where the marks visually represent language). Or consider a map shown on television during election night news coverage, gradually filled in with different colors to show which party is winning in which area. Although the visual pattern of colors *represents* how districts and regions voted, votes are not visual objects. So the colors on the map do not *picture* what they represent. (Some philosophers prefer to say that they represent but do not depict.) Arguably, no element of a map counts as a picture. The same goes for a schematic diagram.

Here are some other kinds of visual representations that are *not* pictures:

- representational sculptures and models differ from pictures by incorporating the third spatial dimension.

- "moving pictures," as films were once called, are something more than pictures. They employ a *series* of pictures in order to convey the dimension of time. Furthermore, they almost always have a soundtrack, and some are (relatively) three-dimensional in appearance.
- plays and other theatre productions are three-dimensional. Normally, they unfold in time and utilize sound.

It is important to locate pictures within this larger family of visual representation, because doing so focuses our attention on the unique manner in which pictures visually represent things beyond themselves. Starting at a very general classification and working our way down, we have the categories of communication, representation, visual representation, and pictorial depiction. If picturing is a unique method of visual communication, we must be careful not to assume that all other visual representation works in the same way.

On this approach, where should we locate the arts of painting and photography? Painting seems to be a species of picturing. Photographs are also pictures, for what strikes most of us as relevant about Dorothea Lange's famous photograph *Migrant Mother* (1936) is also present in a painting such as Rembrandt van Rijn's *The Militia Company of Frans Banning Cocq*, popularly known as *Night Watch* (1642). They both provide two-dimensional visual content in visually depicting how something looks. At the same time, these pictures are like all other representations in being communications that are subject to interpretation. Presented with a picture, it is reasonable to ask what it pictures – to determine its referent or "subject" – as well as to ask what it shows us about that referent. Who is the woman in Lange's photograph, and where was she? When was it taken? What misfortune was she so evidently suffering, and what should we think about her situation? Similarly, who are all these people in *Night Watch*, and what are they doing (both individually and collectively)?

Let's focus on the most basic requirement of communication, picking out a referent or subject. You might suppose that a picture achieves representational reference by visually imitating its referent. Among other things, Rembrandt's *Night Watch* depicts Willem van Ruytenburch holding a spear. It is tempting to say that the painting accomplishes this function by copying or imitating, in paint, the visual appearance of van Ruytenburch, the visual appearance of a spear, and so on. And this common view has a prestigious pedigree: the earliest philosophers to discuss art, Plato (2004) and Aristotle (1997), assumed that "mimesis" (imitation) is the essential relationship. Defending theatre productions against Plato's criticism that imitations are unhealthy distractions, Aristotle counters,

> To imitate is, even from childhood, part of man's nature (and man is different from the other animals in that he is extremely imitative and makes his first steps in learning through imitation); and so is the pleasure we all take in copies of things – as we can tell from experience, for there are things that we find painful to look at in real life – misshapen animals, for example, or corpses – and yet we take pleasure in looking at the most

accurate images of them. . . .The reason for this is that learning is a very great pleasure. (Aristotle 1997: 57)

This position on the psychological roots of representation is so intuitively appealing that it seems mere common sense, and early definitions of fine art simply took it for granted that art necessarily requires the production of simulations or likenesses. It is only relatively recently that philosophers have begun to challenge imitative or *mimetic* theories of visual representation.

Exercise: Does Aristotle's hypothesis about the natural pleasure of imitation explain our continuing interest in old paintings, such as Rembrandt's Night Watch, *where we have no preexisting reason to be interested in the people and events depicted? If so, how do you explain the boredom that typically arises when viewing someone else's vacation photos?*

If philosophy teaches us anything, it warns us not be too hasty when we generalize. *Night Watch* is a picture, but do all paintings fall into the category of pictures? (Is painting necessarily a pictorial art?) Art has an interesting history of resisting our expectations. Long-standing assumptions were disrupted early in the twentieth century when Wassily Kandinsky produced a series of paintings that art historians regard as the first genuinely abstract paintings. He denied that the meaning of his visual "improvisations" and "compositions" derives from the representation of the appearance of material objects (Kandinsky 1977: 57). Other painters followed him, as did sculptors. In a very short time, art critics and audiences became familiar with the possibility that a visual artwork might not function as a picture – that is, it might not provide a visual likeness of something beyond itself. Picturing no longer looked to be a good candidate for grasping the essence of art, visual or otherwise. As we proceed, it is important to remember that our exploration of the nature of picturing cannot be expected to provide a complete account of artistic meaning. Furthermore, we will see that the rise of photography and cinema generates additional questions about the basic nature of both visual representation and picturing.

1.2 Theories of picturing

Despite the rise of abstract art, picturing remains an important practice in the fine arts – most visitors to art museums prefer pictures to abstractions, and abstract cinema has never attracted much of a following. What, then, are pictures, and why do they interest people? These questions have generated much discussion, which can be broadly summarized in terms of two competing positions:

- visual resemblance is essential to pictorial representation, making it in some degree independent of symbolic conventions.
- all denotation is established by symbolic conventions, including cases of pictorial representation.

This section explains what these claims involve and how they differ. The significance of the disagreement rests on a standard philosophical distinction between *denotation* and *predication*. This distinction is a more precise way to capture our earlier contrast between what is pictured and what is shown about it.

Here are some basic ideas and terminology. Suppose I am walking my dog in the park and I cross paths with someone from the school where I teach. My co-worker is walking with a child. I recall that she told me that she has no children. We stop to talk but she does not introduce the child, so I ask, "And who is this?" Suppose she answers, "This is Pamela." What have I learned? Not much. In learning the child's name, I have learned how to refer to that child. In philosophical terminology, I now have a name. A name is a word that *denotes*. Although we did not use the term "denotation" in section 1.1, we discussed the idea. Denotation is a symbol's capacity to pick out a particular referent or subject, singling it out from among all the other things in the world. Thanks to our exchange, "Pamela" can now replace my context-sensitive denoting term, "this." I can now refer to Pamela without describing her. However, that is not the information I was seeking. I wanted to know about the nature of their relationship. I wanted help with the general descriptive category that captured the situation – I was asking for *predication*, rather than *denotation*. I was hoping for a complex communication that would clarify the state of affairs, such as, "This is Pamela, my niece."

As used here, *complex* does not mean that the communication is complicated or lengthy. Instead, it indicates that the communication combines the dual functions of denoting and predicating. In the sentence "Wassily Kandinsky is a painter," the name "Wassily Kandinsky" denotes the subject (in this case, a particular historical individual). The remainder of the sentence predicates the property of being a painter, something that holds for an unknown number of individuals. This level of complexity is regarded as the minimum level required for generating communications that are either accurate and inaccurate, or true and false. "Wassily Kandinsky was born in Helsinki" is false, because that historical individual was born in Moscow, not Helsinki.

So what does all of this terminology have to do with picturing? Ordinarily, pictures are complex communications involving the appearance of a two-dimensional surface. They are a species of representation. As explained in section 1.1, they differ from other representations in *depicting* their subject matter. In the present context, the important point is that we normally treat pictures as a species of complex communication. As such, a picture can be evaluated for accuracy. For example, Vincent Van Gogh's *Self Portrait with Bandaged Ear and Pipe* (1889) shows a man with a bandaged right ear. Van Gogh had cut off a portion of his *left* ear the previous month. The inaccuracy of the painting is explained by the fact that Van Gogh painted himself as he appeared in a mirror. Since the painting gives a false impression of which ear was mutilated, pictorial depiction is like language in its capacity to combine denotation and predication.

The central philosophical dispute about picturing emphasizes the question of whether the perceptual specifics of an image play an indispensable role in the complex representation. If the *look* of the picture captures a state of affairs, the work will succeed in pictorially denoting and pictorially predicating. A picture's accuracy (or inaccuracy) will depend on its *visual* accuracy.

Against this view, *conventionalists* maintain that pictures operate just like our ordinary verbal language. Like ordinary sentences, pictures are arbitrarily connected to their meanings. The sentence "Wassily Kandinsky is a painter" can be written on a page or said aloud. Either way, it refers to that one person and predicates something of him. While a competent English speaker might think it is simply obvious that the sentence means what it does, it is important to recognize that success in interpreting and understanding it depends on an acquired competency in a particular language. Furthermore, our "language" is actually several different symbol-systems. The sentence can be communicated either aurally or visually. Rendered into Braille, the mode of access is tactile. Thus, the perceptual presentation of "Wassily Kandinsky is a painter" plays no special role in its communication of the relevant information. There is no change of meaning when we change the medium of delivery. More radically, the choice of language is arbitrary. We can translate the sentence into another language, again preserving all of the information: "Wassily Kandinsky ist ein Maler." Rendered into German, only the denoting phrase remains the same. English speakers who hear or see it in German have no basis for recognizing that it says something about Kandinsky's profession. Linguistic competence is system-specific.

You are probably tempted to say that the situation is different with pictorial representation. Unlike reading Braille and understanding German, competence in picture interpretation is not an acquired competency. Success in recognizing pictorial depiction involves the same perceptual ability that lets you see and recognize ordinary objects. Pictures denote by showing. Aside from some very specialized cases, there is no "picture competency" along the lines of language competency. Very small children can follow the story in a picture book far in advance of learning to read words. And a small child who can visually recognize a dog will also recognize that same thing in a reasonably clear picture. Conversely, by learning to recognize a dog in a picture, a child acquires the ability to recognize dogs, because a competently rendered picture of a dog shows what a dog looks like. Let us return to Willem van Ruytenburch, one of the subjects of *Night Watch*. How does it represent him, and not someone else? The obvious answer is that it pictures him by showing what he looks like, and it accomplishes this by imitating his appearance. Anyone who could recognize him by looking at him should be able to pick him out in the painting, and if the painting is a good likeness, his historical contemporaries could have learned to recognize him by studying the painting.

Exercise: What is the purpose of placing photographs on passports and driver's licenses? Is this practice essentially different from providing a detailed verbal description?

Against the seeming common sense that pictures involve some degree of imitated appearance, a number of influential philosophers contend that pictorial depiction must depend on more than our innate perceptual capacities. These conventionalists insist that our grasp of denotation and predication always depends on acquired competence in a symbolic system. Rembrandt's painting of van Ruytenburch refers to him the same way that the words "Willem van Ruytenburch" do: they are established by conventional association within a language system. The same point holds for predication. Rembrandt put a spear into van Ruytenburch's hand by using paint in conformity with established conventions of depiction. The same information can be communicated verbally, by saying "Willem van Ruytenburch has a spear in his hand." In much the way that a detailed verbal description is regarded as highly realistic, the conventionalist thinks that a visual representation is thought to be more realistic – and so is easily confused with perceptual imitation – when it is in a familiar style and contains a significant amount of information about the details of the represented situation. In other words, we regard pictures as realistic when they are dense with information. Nonetheless, conventionalists deny that this sense of realism is based on visual likeness.

It's one thing to hold a view. It's another to offer reasons in favor of it. Philosophers want to examine those reasons. What evidence recommends pictorial conventionalism?

There are four strong reasons in favor of the position that pictures are like other conventional symbolic representations. (1) Pictures do not really resemble what they picture. For example, even when my cat holds still for a long time, no one would ever confuse a cat with a flat white sheet of paper with a few black lines on its surface. (2) Even if they do resemble one another in some respects, their resemblance does not establish the desired relationships. (3) Art history documents the appearance of successive, distinct styles of representation. However, this makes no sense if picturing is merely imitating. Art history should not traverse such a range of distinctive pictorial styles. (4) Consistent with the point about changing styles, people who can recognize an object cannot always recognize it when it is presented in an unfamiliar pictorial style, so picturing is more like conventional language use than imitating.

The first pair of these arguments is powerfully articulated by the American philosopher Nelson Goodman (1976). Resemblance alone cannot do the job, because "no degree of resemblance is sufficient to establish the requisite relationship of reference" (Goodman 1976: 5). A photograph of Rachel may resemble her twin sister, Raquel, just as much as it resembles Rachel. Nonetheless, it does not depict Raquel. Furthermore, nothing in the world resembles Rachel as much as Raquel does. Nonetheless, Raquel's appearance does not denote Rachel any more than Rachel's appearance denotes Raquel. Therefore denotation is independent of resemblance.

The next stage of the argument aims to show that a two-dimensional drawing cannot denote any particular thing unless its interpretation is directed by a particular symbol system. To secure his point that denotation is the product of a particular notational system, Goodman invites us to consider two objects that resemble one another while denoting very different things. Consider the visual depictions of Mount Fujiyama in *Thirty-six Views of Mount Fuji* (1826–33), a set of wood-block prints by the nineteenth-century Japanese printmaker Katsushika Hokusai. In many of them, the mountain is rendered with little more than a black line that ascends and then descends against a plain background. However, exactly the same line might be found on a hospital electrocardiogram (EKG, or ECG in the UK), a mechanically produced diagram of the electrical activity of a patient's heart. Although the two lines look the same, the EKG is not a picture of Mount Fuji. In fact, it's not a *picture* of anything at all. But why not? If Hokusai's line *looks like* Mount Fuji, then so does the EKG. Yet the EKG does not denote the mountain. Lacking that denotation, the EKG cannot be used to predicate information about Mount Fuji. Yet, looking at one of Hokusai's prints, it is perfectly plausible to say, "Look how isolated Mount Fuji is, and see how the thickness of the line communicates the mountain's mass." Something more than visual resemblance must be at work here if we are to account for this difference in capacity to denote, and to explain the additional fact that the thickness of the line is important to the print but not to the diagram. The difference, according to Goodman, is the difference between representational schemes, each of which involves distinctive conventions governing what is and what is not relevant to the interpretation of the marked surface in question. A cardiologist "reads" the EKG by understanding the rules for extracting information from an EKG. Visiting the art museum, the same doctor might "perceive" Mount Fuji in a Hokusai print, and this process is no less governed by an acquired understanding of how to extract information from pictures of this sort. The print depicts the visual mountain because it is properly "read" in a pictorial symbol system, and not vice versa.

Defenders of the uniquely *perceptual* dimension of picturing have an obvious response to Goodman's conventionalism. They concede that successful picturing involves something more than mere imitation or resemblance. No one is going to confuse Hokusai's picture with an actual mountain. Ink on paper does not resemble a mountain, nor does a mountain resemble a sheet of paper. Therefore Goodman is correct that pictorial denotation cannot require a genuine resemblance between a picture and its subject. Instead, successful picturing requires that the visual *experience* of looking at the one resembles the visual *experience* of looking at the other. When we recognize one line in the Hokusai print as the mountain, we do so quickly and without conscious thought. This is possible because our visual recognition of different types of things is based on surprisingly little information. Visual artists need only capture a few vital visual cues and viewers will "see" the mountain in the marked surface, by having a parallel experience. Vanilla and artificial vanilla are very different things, yet they produce similar experiences. Jadeite and nephrite are very different things, yet they produce very similar visual experiences. So it is with the mountain and Hokusai's line.

Robert Hopkins (1998) offers an important account of such cues. In keeping with Hokusai's ability to render the mountain with a single line, the appropriate visual mechanism is our experience of an object's outline shape as seen from a particular vantage point. We don't have X-ray vision, and each object normally blocks our ability to see some or all of whatever is behind it. This blocking effect has a boundary in the dimensions of width and height. Setting aside the question of depth perception, Hopkins argues that object recognition depends significantly on perception of the object's two-dimensional shaped outline relative to our specific position as a viewer. A successful picture is one that produces a visual experience like that of seeing the pictured object's outline shape from a particular vantage point.

Artists generally select outline shapes according to their communicative purposes. Suppose an editorial cartoonist wants to communicate something about Barack Obama. Rather obviously, the outline shape of Obama's head is more distinctive – and thus more recognizable – when viewed from the side (i.e., his profile) than when viewed from behind. Therefore a cartoonist who wants to depict Obama as the visual subject is unlikely to do so by picturing the back of his head. The shape is not specific enough to allow recognition of the intended referent. Depending on which and how many outline shapes are incorporated, a particular picture might be very imprecise, as are Hokusai's views of Mount Fuji, or it might seem highly realistic. Willem van Ruytenburch's spear provided Rembrandt with one outline shape; the feather on his hat provided a different one; his nose provided quite another. Viewed in this way, Rembrandt's *Night Watch* is actually a coordinated series of smaller pictures. By thus providing numerous outline shapes of great complexity, Rembrandt produced a realistic picture. Thus, a black-and-white drawing can look more realistic than a colorful painting – it largely depends on which does a better job with the experienced outline shapes. Finally, photographs can do mechanically what traditional artists did intentionally and by hand.

This "experiential" account of visual resemblance does not deny that convention plays some role in picturing, too. Returning to Goodman's question of why the line on the EKG is not a picture of the mountain, Hopkins allows that a visual design becomes a picture by the presence of a human intention to provide outline shapes that can be interpreted pictorially. Similarly, Richard Wollheim emphasizes that we often see objects in clouds and we see faces in tree trunks. However, clouds and tree trunks do not denote whatever we see outlined in them. In the absence of human intentions, there is no standard of correctness here. Although you might see a bunny in a cloud, you cannot complain – not seriously, anyway – that the cloud has done a bad job of representing the bunny. Yet it's appropriate to say such things about a picture that someone draws. The difference, Wollheim proposes, is that a standard of correctness "derives from the intention of the maker of the representation, or 'the artist' as he is usually called" (Wollheim 1980: 205). Hopkins and Wollheim agree that the mere look of something is insufficient for picturing, and that a human intention to picture one thing rather than another is required.

Lacking the proper intention, the EKG is not a picture. This theory becomes even more plausible when we make further concessions about the limitations of representational systems. For example, different pictures are intended to be understood in terms of stylistic conventions, and so applying the conventions of the wrong perspective system will produce serious misinterpretations of how one part of a picture relates to another. It is also important to admit that outline shapes are only one of many things that go into a picture. Therefore, many details of a picture's marked surface can complicate its proper interpretation. (Reading a graphic novel such as Art Spiegelman's *Maus: A Survivor's Tale*, you probably have no trouble in understanding that the speech balloons do not furnish the outline shapes of objects within the pictorial space. However, if you have no familiarity with medieval portraiture, you might confuse medieval speech balloons with pictured scrolls.) Finally, denotation and predication do not exhaust the information carried by a picture, for our visual attention can explore both what is pictured and *how* it is pictured. Looking at James Abbott McNeill Whistler's famous painting *Arrangement in Gray and Black No. 1 (Portrait of the Artist's Mother)* (1871), we can attend to the way that Whistler adopts asymmetrical organization and flattened spatial depth, two pictorial techniques that Whistler borrowed directly from his close study of Japanese woodblock prints.

Exercise: Look at a page of a comic book or graphic novel. Within the frames of the picture panels, locate coloring or markings that have a purpose other than delineating outline shapes. Does their presence contribute to denotation or predication? Do they contribute to the experience in some other way? Explain.

In saying that picturing is due to some limited resemblance in the *experience* of the visual information, we preserve the distinctively perceptual nature of picturing. Pictures communicate, yet they do not communicate like verbal descriptions. However, resemblance is not the only way to preserve this insight. We can endorse the visual nature of depiction without basing it on visual recognition of resemblance. Hopkins claims that artists exploit a particular resemblance (in experiences of outline shapes as viewed from a particular viewing position) in order to trigger visual recognition. A number of philosophers think that it's the other way around: visual recognition triggers our experience of resemblance. Paintings, drawings, and photographs encode information that involuntarily provokes the brain's visual recognition system. This view, called recognition theory, says that we literally recognize a spear when we see a certain area of *Night Watch*. We recognize the spear because we recognize selected aspects of a spear, such as the long handle and the pointed tip. As with ordinary object recognition, our ability to classify the object is based on a few pertinent aspects of it. Provided that the paint on the canvas is arranged to trigger recognition of relevant aspects, the act of visual recognition is the same as it is when we visually recognize the thing denoted by this patch of paint, and our sense of resemblance consists in this exploitation of the recognition process. In supporting this claim, the recognition theorist points to doctored photographs where outlines are preserved yet recognition routinely fails. These cases of failed recognition are then compared to visual examples where recognition of the subject must precede recognition of the relevant outlines. For example, there are a number of pictures used in psychological research that initially present an incoherent visual pattern. These pictures furnish an appropriate experience of resemblance *after* the viewer reads the caption and understands what is pictured. The random aspects of the visual experience suddenly fall into place. So the experience of resemblance depends on recognition, not the other way around (Lopes 2006: 165–8).

Against recognition theory, there is something rather strange about saying that recognition explains the experience of resemblance in a painting such as *Night Watch*. The recognition of the spear would have to be based on recognition of limited aspects – the handle, the point – as flattened into two dimensions. To see why this is a strange idea, consider your ability to see a spear in a sculpture, a three-dimensional representation. Consider James Earle Fraser's famous sculpture, *End of the Trail* (1915). It depicts a Native American sitting slumped on his horse, spear pointed to the ground. In creating the sculpture, Fraser had to place all represented aspects of the spear into the same spatial relationships that they would really have in three-dimensional space. As a result, the perceived visual relationships among the parts, such as the perceived distance from end to end, depend on the viewer's own spatial relationship to the sculpture. Seen from below, looking up, the spear's point would loom large. Seen from behind the horse's left flank, the point might not be visible at all. So it is plausible to say that recognition of the sculpted spear involves awareness of the same spatial relationships that permit recognition of a real one (Hopkins 2010). But does it really? Since our normal visual system involves three-dimensional vision, the painter's highly selective reduction of spear-aspects to two dimensions will introduce relationships that mean nothing to us except when pictured two-dimensionally. The recognition theorist will have to say that Rembrandt's painting succeeds in picturing van Ruytenburch with a spear by triggering our capacity to recognize a spear "seen two-dimensionally" (Hopkins 2006: 157). But what recognition capacity is that? A recognition skill developed to deal with pictures? But then what's happened to the insight that pictorial recognition creates an experience of resemblance by exploiting our ordinary recognition capacities?

1.3 Intentions and transparency in pictures and photographs

Let us examine how photography complicates the analysis. You have no doubt heard someone say, about a photograph, "Look at this picture I took." In contrast, no one talks that way about a drawing. You "make" a drawing, rather than "take" one. This linguistic distinction suggests awareness of a difference in the way that drawings and photographs relate to both their creators and their denoted subjects. At the same time, it is quite natural to think of photographs as a species of picturing. Therefore reflection on photographs may enrich our thinking about pictorial representation. Photos may invite us to reconsider how pictures denote, and what it means for a picture to represent a state of affairs. Dominic Lopes maintains that photographs reveal the key to understanding all picturing (Lopes 1996: 179). To make sense of Lopes' claim, however, it is necessary to understand how it contrasts with the position held by Kendall Walton (1984).

Walton is the best-known advocate of the *transparency thesis*, the position that photographs are unique among pictures in being transparent to their subjects. Against Lopes, Walton thinks that photographs are fundamentally different from non-photographic pictures. Think of the difference between an opaque brick wall and a transparent glass window. You can see through the window to objects on the other side. The process of seeing an object involves interaction with light reflected from it, and the light that passes through a window is coming from the object on the other side of the glass. The window might distort whatever you see through it, as when glass is of uneven thickness, but the distorted object that you see is the same one you'd see if the glass was not there. Consider, then, why you see what you see when you look at a photographic print, such as your driver's license or identification card photo. The print is a visual object because it absorbs and reflects light, and this pattern of reflection is determined by the pattern of light that reached the camera lens, which is light reflecting off whatever is in front of the camera. (Notice, furthermore, that the camera can be eliminated. Some photographers, such as Man Ray, make photographs using photographic negatives but no camera.) Next, consider a mirror. When you look at your face in a mirror, you see yourself and not a representation of you. Why? Because you see the pattern of light that reflects off your face, reflected back to you. A photographic print likewise reflects the pattern of light that reached the camera lens, and so to look at a photograph is to look *through* the piece of paper or screen to whatever was photographed. Looking at a photograph of your own face is no different from looking at yourself in a mirror. You literally see yourself. Like the mirror, the photo is a device for seeing what cannot be seen directly. Like a window or mirror, a photograph is transparent to its subject.

Walton's transparency thesis has the important implication that it makes photographs – and films, which involve a series of photographs – essentially different from drawings, paintings, and all other non-photographic picturing. Photographs provide "visual experiences which do not depend on the picture-maker's beliefs in the way that paintings do" (Walton 1984: 264). In contrast, you do not literally see Willem van Ruytenburch by looking at Rembrandt's *Night Watch*. You see a representation of him, and that representation inevitably presents Rembrandt's decision about what he wants to show. Therefore a non-photographic picture is always opaque with respect to its subject. It does not allow the viewer to see the thing it denotes. In contrast, photographs show whatever was there. If there are no unicorns and hobbits, then there are no photographs of them, either. Be very careful about this claim – it does not mean that photographs never *look like* fictitious things. What looks like a photo of a unicorn is probably a photograph of a horse with prosthetic make-up. An advertising photo of a bowl of cereal is probably a photograph of the cereal in white glue, not milk. So although photographs constitute evidence in a way that drawings and paintings do not, they have their limitations as evidence. Nonetheless, photographs furnish a natural realism in seeing that cannot be derived from other modes of picturing.

Exercise: Each year, more than a million tourists make their way to Grauman's Chinese Theatre in Hollywood to see the handprints and footprints that celebrities have pressed into cement. If you go to Grauman's Chinese Theatre and locate Charlie Chaplin's handprints, is your relationship to Chaplin essentially different from your relationship to him when you view a "print" of one of his films? How do these compare with John Doubleday's statue of Chaplin in Leicester Square, London?

Against Walton, Lopes (1996) contends that transparency is not the essential difference between photographs and other pictures. Every picture is transparent to its subject. Lopes argues that no picture denotes its subject visually unless its visual appearance depends on how the subject really looks: "All pictures, if they are information-transmitting devices, are causally linked to their sources" (Lopes 1996: 163). For example, *Night Watch* cannot contain a portrait of Willem van Ruytenburch if van Ruytenburch was beardless, 11 years old, and 4 feet tall in 1642, its year of execution. The mustachioed man with the spear is pictured as much older and taller than that. Similarly, a mere blotch or squiggly scribble is not a picture of any person, for it does not contain visual information facilitating visual recognition. It can represent something beyond itself, in the same way that mere dots on a map represent towns, but nothing *pictures* what it represents unless the causal mechanism of seeing guides the selection of marks that subsequently guide viewers to the visual recognition. Therefore every picture is transparent to its subject: every picture is causally linked to its subject by a causal process, just like photographs. Lopes' final step is to argue against Walton's claim that paintings are special because their patterns always depend on the picture-maker's beliefs about the subject. A "competent draughtsman" might render the visual aspects of something without forming beliefs about the nature of the object being drawn, and yet the result will be recognizable to those who can recognize the object (Lopes 1996: 186; a case study is provided by Sacks 1998:

ch. 24). Visual transparency is an essential feature of all picturing, not just photography.

Exercise: Stephen Wiltshire was diagnosed with severe autism at a very young age. He produces highly detailed drawings of buildings, from memory. It is doubtful that Wiltshire understands much about what he is drawing, for he often produces them very quickly after a brief exposure to the depicted subject. How would Walton account for Wiltshire's ability? How would Lopes? What does it mean to "understand" the object that one draws?

The debate over transparency raises an important question about the role of intentions in picture-making. A child's scribble can represent the family's dog in the same way that a line on a map represents a highway, by the mere intention to have it stand for that thing. However, neither the scribble nor the dot is a picture of what it denotes. So intention is insufficient for picturing. Now suppose that it is true that picturing is independent of a picture maker's beliefs (as Walton claims of photographs and Lopes claims about all pictures). In that case, intentions are not necessary for fixing denotation. Therefore intentions are neither necessary nor sufficient for denotation in visual representation. One implication is that Hopkins and Wollheim are wrong to claim that a visual design becomes a picture by the presence of a human intention to provide a design that is to be interpreted in a particular way. Another implication is that a mechanical copy of a picture will denote whatever the original picture denoted. Because this implication falls foul of the lesson of indiscernible counterparts, we will turn to that topic.

1.4 Indiscernible counterparts

Earlier sections of this chapter challenged imitative or *mimetic* theories of visual representation, the doctrine that pictures denote their subjects by successfully imitating how they look. Pictures are perceptually very different from the things they denote. Viewers are normally aware when they are viewing a picture instead of the thing pictured. As Wollheim observes, the experience of pictures involves twofold attention. Our visual attention is divided between two things, "what is represented and . . . the representation" (Wollheim 1980: 213). Seeing Willem van Ruytenburch in Rembrandt's canvas, we remain aware of the paint. Granted, there are times when the size and placement of a picture "fools" us, if only for a moment, but this misperception is rare and it seldom lasts for very long. In contrast, there is an interesting set of artworks that are to all appearances exactly like other things, "mere real things" that are not artworks. These cases raise interesting puzzles about artworks and their interpretation (Danto 1981: 1). These examples are relatively easy to locate once the basic situation is clear. Indeed, we've already considered such a case in Goodman's example of Hokusai's print of Mount Fuji compared with the line on the EKG.

Imagine two objects that are to all appearances the same: two white pawns from the same chess set; two cans of beer from the same six-pack; a simple line drawing and a photo-copy of it; Rupert and his identical twin brother, Robert. Such pairs of objects are known as perceptually indiscernible counterparts, meaning that we cannot discern or perceive which one of the pair is in front of us merely by looking. (Notice that the counterparts do not have to be visual. Perhaps you've been with a group of people when a cell or mobile telephone rings, and several people check their telephone because their ringtones are indiscernible counterparts.) Arthur Danto (1981) argues that indiscernible counterparts are philosophically important in demonstrating that otherwise identical objects can carry very different meanings. The meaning of an artwork involves consideration of its cultural context or artistic provenance – that is, of the time and place of its creation – where a counterpart "mere object" does not. Notice that, if true, Danto's contextualism implies that a picture's meaning cannot be reduced to its pictorial function. In fact, its meaning as a work of visual art might be completely independent of its pictorial dimension.

Danto's primary example is a set of boxes made and exhibited by Andy Warhol in New York City in 1964. They are not actual boxes, but rather three-dimensional replicas of cardboard shipping cartons, silkscreened with the visual designs found on commercially produced shipping cartons for several well-known household products: Brillo scouring pads, Heinz ketchup, Kellogg's cornflakes, Campbell's Tomato Juice, Mott's apple juice, and Del Monte peaches. Warhol fabricated many copies of each kind and then displayed them in stacks, just like the stacked boxes in a supermarket storage room. Ironically, given their subsequent fame, Warhol's boxes sold very poorly. But is that a surprise? Why pay good money for something that looks just like the boxes that supermarkets flatten and throw away? But that seems to be part of Warhol's point in making them. They look like the boxes that supermarkets throw into the dumpster. So why replicate these mass-produced, disposable objects? On a basic level, Warhol's replicas call attention to the visual designs that most people take for granted. Warhol was also contrasting contemporary commercial design with the kind of non-pictorial design that dominated New York art galleries at that time, namely abstract expressionist painting. By displaying groups of boxes in huge stacks, Warhol seems to be saying that there is no need for artists to produce unique, original objects. James Harvey created the actual design found on the surface of Warhol's Brillo boxes, and the design itself belongs to the Brillo Manufacturing Company. Art can be mass-produced, like any other consumer product, which further suggests that art is just another consumer product. In inviting us to think about these things, Warhol's boxes have a significance that their counterparts, "real" packing crates, lack.

A lot of critical interpretation has been directed at the boxes (particularly the Brillo boxes). They interest philosophers because they demonstrate the point that if mere resemblance is sufficient to establish denotation and thus meaning, then the perfect resemblance between Harvey's design and Warhol's design would ensure that each means exactly what the other means. However, no one thinks that Harvey and Warhol made the same "statement." Warhol made the boxes in order to call attention to this difference. For our purposes, it is sufficient to understand that Warhol's boxes are bearers of meaning, and one of those meanings seems to be the assertion, "In today's America, art is a consumer product." Stamped on disposable commercial cartons, Harvey's design did not carry any such message about art. To the extent that a Brillo carton had a message in 1964, it was, "This carton contains 24 packages of Brillo soap pads." Meanings depend on context, and correct interpretation depends on correctly understanding the time, place, and circumstances of the communication. Meanings are unperceivable, non-exhibited properties of things, and they constitute the interesting dimension of Warhol's creations. Generalizing, we might draw the lesson that the important properties of any artwork are non-exhibited.

Warhol was not the first artist to explore indiscernible counterparts. Marcel Duchamp's readymades are an important precedent. The most famous readymade is *Fountain* (1917), which is nothing more than a commercial porcelain urinal that Duchamp purchased from a plumbing supply store. He placed it on its back, painted a signature on it – the pseudonym "R. Mutt," derived from its purchase from the Mott Iron Works – and then, as Mutt, submitted it to an open-admission art exhibition that he had helped organize. This "sculpture," if that is the right category, was not the first commercial object that Duchamp had treated as an artwork. But it was certainly the first that was calculated to offend. (In 1915, he'd exhibited another readymade sculpture, an ordinary mass-produced snow shovel purchased in a hardware store, giving it the title *In Advance of the Broken Arm*.) As Duchamp no doubt intended, *Fountain* was rejected by the board overseeing the art exhibition. He then made sure that their act of refusal was publicized: he published a photograph of it in an avant-garde magazine along with a justifying explanation. He explains that choosing and titling an object attaches a meaning (Duchamp's text says "a new thought"), and these processes are sufficient to make something art (Duchamp 2003).

Like Warhol's Brillo boxes in the 1960s, Duchamp's readymades are generally understood to be statements about the nature of art in the modern, industrial world. It is likely that *Fountain* was intended to have a more specific meaning, directed to the board of the Society of Independent Artists, something on the order of "You think you're so avant-garde, liberal, and democratic? I dare you to display this!"

While Duchamp and Warhol explored non-exhibited differences between objects and artwork counterparts, indiscernible counterparts have also arisen where both the original and the counterpart are artworks. For example, in 1936 Walker Evans photographed individuals and scenes in rural Alabama. A number of these photographs have become well known, both as documents of poverty during the Great Depression and as art objects – he was the first photographer to receive a solo show at New York City's Museum of Modern Art (in 1938). However, because some of Evans' most iconic images were works commissioned by the federal Farm Security Administration, Evans was not entitled to claim copyright. Instead, the images are in the public domain and anyone can reproduce them. In 1981, a New York art gallery exhibited a show of photographs, "Sherrie Levine after Walker Evans." All of the photographs bore that title, and each was a photo that Levine had made by photographing the images in a book of Walker Evans photographs. Upon casual inspection, Levine's photographs are indiscernible counterparts of Evans' work. Unlike Warhol and Duchamp, Levine's artworks have other artworks as their counterparts. Furthermore, if you endorse the thesis that photographs are transparent to their subjects, then Levine's pictures are transparent depictions of the same individuals who appear in Evans' pictures – by photographing his photo of Allie Mae Burroughs (1936), Levine has also photographed the very same woman. The causal process ensures that her photograph denotes Burroughs, just as his does. (On the other hand, if photographs are not transparent in the appropriate sense, then we would have to say that Levine's photograph visually depicts Burroughs without being a photograph of her.)

Exercise: Is it plausible that you can photograph someone by photographing a photograph of them?

Despite their near-indiscernibility, the two photographs make radically different artistic statements. Where Evans is calling attention to the suffering of America's working poor in the 1930s, Levine's pictures are normally understood to make dual statements. On the one hand, they suggest that, economically, nothing has changed in America. On the other hand, her decision to appropriate the images of a highly respected male photographer is regarded as central to her message. Her act of copying is generally understood to be a feminist, transgressive gesture that calls attention to Levine's status as a woman artist in the late twentieth century, working in the shadow of male artists. What is the point, the photos seem to ask, of trying to be original when you cannot escape comparison to established artists? Where Warhol's appropriations aroused either puzzlement or amusement, Levine's art incited considerable anger in other (overwhelmingly male) artists. Her apparent lack of originality in photographing photos blinded many viewers to the originality of her strategy of calling attention to the very possibility of originality in photography, given the medium's inherent transparency. Although Levine herself denied having any such intention, they are additionally taken to be statements about women's access to property in a paternalistic society.

As Danto summarizes it, the philosophical lesson of indiscernible counterparts is that "you cannot define the visual arts in terms of anything that meets the eye when one looks at them" (Danto 1993: 197). This is because art appreciation is necessarily "a function of interpretation" (Danto 1981: 113). Simply *looking* at a Warhol Brillo box or a Levine photo in the "After Walker Evans" series will never reveal its most interesting features. Evans' photograph of Allie Mae Burroughs is stark and sad. Levine's photograph is equally stark and sad. But it is also both aggressive and playful. Evans' photograph, which is neither aggressive nor playful, is about conditions in rural Alabama in 1936. Levine's photograph is about the American economy

under President Reagan. The important point is that you cannot appreciate these aspects of Levine's work unless you know who photographed it,
and how she did so. However, these are not things that one can determine
simply by looking. Therefore art appreciation is contingent upon art interpretation, which in turn depends on knowledge of artistic provenance.
Ignorance of originating context will result in misunderstanding of what
one is encountering. To focus on the physical object, the artifact, is to
ignore what makes the artifact unique, what differentiates it from an indiscernible "real thing," and so it results in the misappreciation of the artwork.
In Danto's favored way of putting it, exhibiting something as art will "trans-
figure" an otherwise meaningless thing into an artwork, which is an object
for interpretation that "make[s] different statements depending upon a
variety of contextual factors" (Danto 1981: 133). To grasp the statement,
you must locate the work within the history of art. You must see how the
work is more than the artifact that embodies it. In Danto's own summary of
this view, "a work of art is an interpreted artifact" (Danto 1993: 200).

There are two obvious problems with Danto's position. In emphasizing
that knowledge of artistic origins is required to understand what an artwork
is really about and what it has to say, he thinks that his point extends to
all art. Against Danto, it is not clear that every work of art has historically
emergent properties of this sort. There is decorative art, some of which is
meant to be looked at, without concern for interpretation. Furthermore,
some abstract art appears to fall into this category, as does some instrumental music. These works involve aesthetic display, but they don't "say"
anything. The second problem is that it does nothing to distinguish artworks from many other visual images, such as photographs of particle trails
left in the wake of subatomic particles passing through a cloud chamber.
These images are "about" the world. Yet their interpretation is just as
theory-dependent as the photographs that make up "Sherrie Levine after
Walker Evans." You might be tempted to say that the crucial difference is
that the scientist's photographs require knowledge of theoretical physics
rather than of art history. However, that objection fails. It begs the question,
for it builds a reference to "art" into the very distinction that we are trying to
explain. (We'll revisit this issue in section 6.4.)

*Exercise: Most billboard and magazine advertisements employ pictures. Many
of these pictures are "stock" photographs, licensed from large photo libraries.
As a result, advertisements for two different products will occasionally feature
the same photograph. If the same photograph is used to advertise two different products, does it change its meaning so that it makes a different statement
each time?*

1.5 Fine art

Let us close by backtracking to the case of the EKG that looks like Hokusai's
rendering of Mount Fuji. The EKG is not a picture of the mountain.
Something more than the shape of the line is required to establish the

pictorial relationship. But what? Recognitional capacity? Visual transparency? Experiential resemblance? The artist's intentions? Notice that only one of these proposals, the last, refers to art. The other three proposals do not imply that pictorial representation is an artistic practice. Our survey of the major theories of pictorial representation encountered only one philosopher, Arthur Danto, who argued that the correct interpretation of some pictures depends on their status as artworks. Yet there is no reason to suppose, even here, that an object's status as fine art is relevant to its proper interpretation. At the same time, Danto's argument turns on the claim that "you cannot define the visual arts in terms of anything that meets the eye when one looks at them" (Danto 1993: 197). The *pictorial* dimension of visual art is irrelevant to Danto's argument.

This chapter started with the observation that the visual arts have been a central case for theorizing about fine art. Pictorial representation has long held center-stage in both art history and philosophy of art. Therefore it may strike you as a disappointing result to find that recent philosophizing about pictures does not shed any light on the nature of fine art. But is that really so surprising?

Someone hears a strange noise outside his apartment and looks out the window. He sees a bearded man wearing a blue sweatshirt pulling on the locked door to the building. The stranger in the sweatshirt walks away from the door when it does not open. The next morning, a police officer visits the apartment building and informs the residents that there was a burglary in the building the previous night. The police are seeking information about any recent prowlers. At least one other resident saw the man in the blue sweatshirt. Together, the two residents furnish enough information to allow the police to produce a sketch of the suspect. The next night, a prowler is caught trying to break into a nearby building. He closely resembles the police sketch.

Although it is likely that the "artist" who produced the police sketch received some formal art training, is the picture of the suspect an artwork? What difference would it make if it were?

In Philip Roth's early novella *Goodbye, Columbus* (1959), a librarian is surprised to find that a poor African-American child spends a great deal of time in the library looking at an oversize book about the art of the painter Paul Gauguin. The boy has no interest in art. Asking for the location of picture books, he does not even know to ask for art books. Yet he is drawn to Gauguin's beautiful images of Tahiti, which allow him to imaginatively escape the housing projects of Newark. Granted, the boy does not grasp the deeper meanings of the images. Yet Gauguin's pictures still function as pictures, and their status as artworks appears to be beside the point.

So the central philosophical issues of pictorial communication shed no light on the nature of fine art. Let me offer a more technical explanation of why this is so. When two categories overlap, so that neither is a subset of the other, there is only a contingent or accidental relationship between them. Neither category holds much promise of clarifying the other. For example, the categories of visual artist and taxpayer overlap; we might even discover that visual artists are typically taxpayers. But here it would be foolish to try to understand what a visual artist is by asking what makes someone a taxpayer. It would be a howler (a logical blunder) to infer that modern tax structures are important to the activity of creating visual art. Likewise, it would be a howler of an inference to suppose that insight into the pictorial function of Rembrandt's *Night Watch* holds the key to understanding fine art. Picturing gives us a category of objects that is not confined to art. Many things besides pictures are artworks. Furthermore, some very famous paintings do not depict anything at all. Like the categories of visual artist and taxpayer, the categories of picture and painting are merely overlapping categories. The same is true of the categories of fine art and pictures. So here is a bit of advice about philosophy of art. Given the wide range of things that can be artworks, philosophy of art explores many philosophical problems that tell us little or nothing about the general nature of art. Although it would be nice to think that philosophy of art is organized around a few core questions – What is art? What is artistic value? – that is not really true. Contemporary philosophy of art is just as likely to tell you something interesting about things that are not artworks.

Issues to think about

1. What are the important differences between visual representation and picturing?
2. Assuming that painters engage in imitation, Plato observes that you can make images of "yourself and the other animals, manufactured items, plants, and everything else" by holding up a mirror (Plato 2004: 299). What is the relationship between a mirror image and what it shows? Does Plato's point demonstrate that the ability to make pictures is a trivial accomplishment?
3. An architect is designing a building. Why does the architect construct a three-dimensional model of the building as a supplement to a series of drawings of it? How does the activity of model building suggest ways in which picturing is a unique mode of visual representation? Architects frequently use so-called "3d" (three-dimensional) computer software to create videos of simulated movement through their designs. To what degree can these videos replace three-dimensional models?
4. Choose a visual artwork that pictures a recognizable subject. Explain the difference between accounting for this relationship in terms of recognitional and in terms of experiential resemblance.
5. Does an artist's intention to portray one person rather than another impose a standard of correctness for interpretation of the resulting portrait? Are paintings and photographs different in this respect?
6. Are there any artworks that lack historically emergent properties, such that their appreciation does not require knowledge of the work's historical origins? As a test of this idea, select several examples of visual art and then decide whether their meanings would change if they came from different cultures or were created in different historical eras.

Further resources

Wollheim's account of the "twofold" thesis is a classic essay on the perceptual dimension of pictures (Wollheim 1980). It strongly contrasts with the position that all denotation is a matter of convention (Goodman 1976). However, it is generally agreed that Goodman cannot account for picturing; see, for example, the criticisms in Peacocke (1987) and Hopkins (1998). The contrast between the recognitional and experiential resemblance accounts of picturing plays out in greater detail in a published debate between Hopkins and Lopes; see Kieran (2006). Gaiger's *Aesthetics & Painting* (2008) provides a solid overview of all of these topics. Walton's essay on photographic transparency and his further reflections on the topic are collected in *Marvelous Images* (2008); there is no end of response to it, but you might have a look at Lopes (2003) and Gaut (2008), both of whom tie the debate to non-photographic pictures. Danto's discussion of indiscernible counterparts is found at the beginning of *The Transfiguration of the Commonplace* (1981), and also in Danto's widely reprinted essay "The Artworld" (1964). As with Walton on transparency, this topic has generated endless discussion (e.g., Rollins 1993). Finally, Dilworth (2005) has some interesting things to say about the complexity of representational content in art. His theory about "double content" contrasts with my concluding comments in this chapter.

The classic film on the question of photography and its content is *Blowup* (1966). For an extreme example of how historical context might play into the correct interpretation of a painting, consider *Rembrandt's J'accuse* (2008), Peter Greenaway's strange analysis of Rembrandt's *Night Watch*. In the course of this chapter there is mention of "abstract" cinema. An excellent collection is *Unseen Cinema: Early American Avant-Garde Film 1894–1941* (2005).

2 Art as Expression

Each time I teach philosophy of art, I begin by asking my students to iden-tify the defining features of art. The majority of students give me some variation of the answer that art is about emotion. Pressed for clarifica-tion, they mean that art is essentially a platform for emotional expression. However, this broad agreement obscures an underlying failure to agree, because what is meant by "expression" usually differs according to whether a student is thinking about an artist who is producing art or about a viewer who is viewing art. Depending on the point of focus, artist or audience, two very different assumptions about expression come into play. One is artist-centered and the other is audience-centered.

- The artist-centered theory of expression claims that artists express their own emotions in their art.
- The audience-centered theory of expression claims that audiences respond emotionally to art.

Let's call the first of these the *self-expression theory*, and the second the *emotional engagement theory*. In this chapter we will focus on the core ideas of these two proposals, as well as their plausibility as defining features of art.

The two proposals are generally asserted in order to justify two closely related positions on the value of art.

- The self-expression theory claims that art is valuable for permitting art-ists to express themselves.
- The emotional engagement theory claims that art is valuable when it elicits an appropriate emotional response.

Expression theories of art offer support for these two very common ideas about artistic value. However, we ought to decide whether we can make sense of the basic concepts of expression before we get caught up in a dis-cussion of their relevance to artistic value. So this chapter will set aside the question of value and will concentrate on exploring basic claims about art's expressive function. (The topic of artistic value is the focus of chapter 9.)

2.1 Overview of expression theories

It is important to note that there is no necessary connection between an artwork's serving as a vehicle for self-expression and an artwork's capacity to emotionally engage us. Although modern audiences are accustomed to associating audience engagement with artistic self-expression, this association has almost no historical precedent before the nineteenth century. For example, both Plato (2004) and Aristotle (1997) discuss the emotional engagement theory at considerable length. In the *Republic*, Plato criticizes art for stirring up the passions of audiences. Aristotle, who was Plato's pupil, disagrees. He endorses emotional engagement. In the *Poetics*, he offers detailed advice to playwrights about how to construct tragic plots that will produce the emotions of fear and pity. However, neither Plato nor Aristotle ever seems to consider the possibility that artists rely on self-expression (i.e., the expression of their own emotions). Plato thinks that artists can successfully imitate emotions that they do not themselves possess, and Aristotle thinks that basic plot strategies do most of the work of creating the audience's emotional response. Looking beyond the Western tradition, the Sanskritic tradition in India has similarly recognized that dancers, musicians, and other performing artists can convey distinct emotions by learning the proper forms and techniques for their expression. Each artwork is expected to have a dominant *rasa* or emotional flavor, yet there is no expectation that the writers, composers, and choreographers should engage in self-expression. (For more information on this tradition, see Keith 1924.)

Both Plato and Aristotle focus on representational art, particularly the narrative arts of epic poetry and tragic theatre. There were no Abstract Expressionist paintings in their day! Their culturally narrow focus might be taken as a reason to doubt that we should generalize from their positions. So perhaps we should not be overly hasty in thinking that their debate about the value of emotional engagement applies to all the arts. On the other hand, it is safe to say that some kinds of art, particularly narrative arts, engage people emotionally in every known culture.

Although such widespread phenomena are easily taken for granted, this emotional engagement has puzzled many philosophers. And not just philosophers: William Shakespeare, speaking through the character of Hamlet, observes that there is something strange about the expectation that audiences will respond emotionally to art, particularly fictional stories. It is "monstrous," Hamlet says, that an actor can construct "a dream of passion" and move the audience to tears. Using the example of ancient Greek stories about Hecuba, queen of Troy, Hamlet asks how a fiction can incite strong emotions in an audience member who has not experienced the same situation that is enacted in the fictional story:

> What's Hecuba to him, or he to Hecuba,
> That he should weep for her? What would he do,
> Had he the motive and the cue for passion
> That I have? He would drown the stage with tears. (*Hamlet*, Act 2, Scene 2)

Hamlet is proposing that the strength of the emotional response depends on the person's identification with the represented content. Since the character is not real, why should anyone weep at Hecuba's misfortune? It can only be because we identify with her situation. But, again, her situation was relatively unique, which generates the puzzle of why more than a handful of people would be moved by her story.

Hamlet's question is one version of a general problem, the problem of tragedy. The basic challenge is to explain how art can engage us emotionally when it lacks a necessary condition for such engagement. Emotion involves more than feelings. In order for an individual to be emotionally engaged, it is not enough to feel a certain way. It is also necessary to believe certain things about oneself in relation to one's circumstances. This cognitive requirement generates a *cognitive theory of emotion*. (It is sometimes known by its nickname, "thought theory.") For example, in order to experience fear, a person must believe that a threat is present. To experience pity, a person must believe that someone else has experienced misfortune. However, if Hamlet watches a play about Hecuba but does not believe that Hecuba existed – after all, he regards it as "a dream," a fiction – then his mental processes do not satisfy the belief-requirement for experiencing pity, because he does not believe that there was someone whose situation went from good to bad. Audiences for fiction are simply not in the correct psychological state to have the emotions that they report having.

This problem about psychological processes has implications for self-expression. It is commonly supposed that people are emotionally engaged with artworks *because* they involve self-expression. When people believe that an artist is not sincere – if they suspect that an artist is faking it – then they generally react with anger. But what if the audience lacks a basis for judging the artist's sincerity? And what if sincerity puts the artist in an adversarial relationship with the audience? Shakespeare's *Henry V* features a famous speech by Henry (Act 4, Scene 3) as he rallies his men before the battle of Agincourt (1415). This speech is the source of the phrase "band of brothers," which is often used to describe the close bond within military units. The play was written for an English audience, yet it offers no basis for evaluating Shakespeare's personal level of patriotism. Although we know that the words spoken in the play by King Henry are actually Shakespeare's words, not Henry's, there is not much evidence available about Shakespeare's life and beliefs. Audiences for *Henry V* have no reason to believe that Shakespeare was personally proud of the victory at Agincourt. Therefore, if positive emotional engagement requires sincerity, this speech should not emotionally move you unless you also believe that Shakespeare was extremely patriotic. And, if you think he was, shouldn't this interfere with Shakespeare's popularity? Specifically, why should this play meet with the approval of a French pacifist who has no reason to endorse British patriotism based on a fifteenth-century military victory in France? Yet people throughout the world are deeply moved by this scene, including some pacifists, and many of these same people would be offended by genuine self-expression that endorses the bravery of English soldiers engaged in the conquest of France.

There is a second problem here. Why would anyone *want* to experience fear or cry tears of pity in the theatre? We will return to this aspect of the problem when we consider the details of different versions of expression theory. Yet it seems to be the case that most people prefer emotionally expressive art, and that many visitors to art museums are put off by artworks that they find detached, "cold," or intellectual rather than emotional.

The two accounts of expression tell us distinct and perhaps even competing things about it. Although they are independent of one another, many people insist on combining the self-expression and emotional engagement theories. So one of the best ways to get a handle on expression in art is to examine influential theories that combine the two accounts of expression. Such accounts are offered by Leo Tolstoy and R. G. Collingwood.

Exercise: Before reading further, write down your own example of an emotionally engaging book or film that was created by a person (or persons) whose sincerity you cannot judge. What is it that you find emotionally engaging?

2.2 Tolstoy's account of expressive art

Tolstoy is one of Russia's most famous writers, yet after the publication of his novel *Anna Karenina* (1873–7) he experienced doubts about what he was doing to people by writing fictional literature. What real value, he wondered, does the audience receive from this emotional manipulation? Pleasure seems too trivial a justification. Furthermore, Tolstoy experienced repulsion and bewilderment in response to a great deal of highly regarded literature and visual art. (He is particularly critical of Shakespeare's plays and Impressionist paintings.) Committed to the position that art must serve a positive social function, Tolstoy became one of the primary defenders of sincere self-expression as a requirement of art. Because his version of the theory involves both self-expression and audience engagement, it presents us with the strengths and weaknesses of both approaches to expression.

In *What Is Art?*, Tolstoy (1996 [1898]) argues that art is distinguished from other human production by its aim of communicating emotion. Humans naturally express their emotions, externalizing their emotional states in ways that others can observe. Tears can express sorrow or joy. Raised eyebrows can express surprise. Art arises when people intentionally externalize their emotions in a more permanent or repeatable medium, such as by telling stories, drawing pictures, and composing songs. By manipulating the pattern or form of these externalizations, artists can transfer their emotions to people who experience their art. This last point reflects an important assumption about emotions. Tolstoy adopts the position that an emotion is only understood by actually experiencing it. Saying "I am sad because my mother died" cannot really convey one's sadness to another person. One can only communicate one's sadness by getting the other person to feel the same kind of emotion, in the same degree.

Tolstoy's definition of art is therefore different from his definition of artwork.

- Art is the activity of intentionally selecting combinations of movements, lines, colors, sounds, and other materials in order to transmit to others the same felt emotion that one has personally experienced.
- An artwork is an intentional combination of movements, lines, colors, sounds, and other materials selected in order to transmit to others the same felt emotion that one has personally experienced.

Tolstoy often uses the metaphor of "infection" to indicate that art is the activity of *transferring* an emotion from artist to audience. Mere recognition of an intention to communicate emotion is not sufficient for the status of art. In one of Tolstoy's examples, a boy is afraid of wolves and tells a story about the frightening wolves. Suppose the boy's audience merely recognizes that the boy is afraid, without actually feeling afraid too. This lack of "infection" indicates that the boy's story is not an artwork. Reversing the situation, suppose the boy was not actually afraid of wolves. The story might manipulate the audience into feeling something, but this situation would lack self-expression, and for this reason the story would fail to be an artwork.

Tolstoy's dual emphasis on self-expression and reception has undesirable implications. It appears to disqualify many cases of highly expressive art. For example, Muddy Waters (real name, McKinley Morganfield) is generally credited as the most important figure in the development of electrified blues music. He dominated the blues scene in Chicago, a key city in the development of the urban blues style. Many of his early songs, such as "Gypsy Woman" and "I Feel Like Going Home," draw on themes that he knew would appeal to other African-Americans who had recently migrated from the rural south to northern cities. Yet he also denied, in later interviews, that the songs are autobiographical. He did not believe in the rural superstitions that he sang about and he was never homesick for the life of the Mississippi sharecropper. If Tolstoy's account of the expression theory of art is accepted, then many of the great blues songs and performances of Muddy Waters do not count as art due to failure of the self-expression requirement. And this is despite the fact that Tolstoy wants to endorse "folk" art as our most important art! If we want to endorse one of the great figures of blues music as an artist, it appears that expression theory must give up the transmission model in favor of a weaker requirement.

A second objection to self-expression arises from works that effectively communicate a wide range of conflicting emotions. Is it plausible to expect *all* expression to be self-expression? Reading J. R. R. Tolkien's *Lord of the Rings* or watching Peter Jackson's film version, one cannot help but be impressed by the wide range of character types involved in its complex plot and many subplots. Is it plausible that Tolkien was always expressing his own emotional experiences in the emotions displayed by characters as diverse as Bilbo, Frodo, Sam, Gandalf, Aragorn, Sauron, Arwen, and dozens more? It is even less plausible to suppose that, years later, Jackson was engaged in self-expression concerning these same emotions when he put the same range of emotional expression into his film adaptation, and that he was able to find actors and actresses whose lives allowed them, in turn, to engage in self-expression in order to portray the emotions appropriate to their fictional characters. However, if we want to grant that anyone in this process was successfully communicating emotions without having personally lived through them, then we have no principled objection to expressive artworks that completely lack self-expression.

If you are tempted to brush off this argument because you doubt that either the book *Lord of the Rings* or the film version is an artwork, then the same point can be made with Shakespeare's play, *Hamlet*, and then with any stage or film production of it. Despite Tolstoy's denial that it is art, *Hamlet* is certainly an artwork, and so are its performances. Furthermore, it is unlikely that Laurence Olivier, Kenneth Branagh, and Mel Gibson were equally engaged in the self-expression of their own emotions when portraying Hamlet's emotions when each actor played that role. Because we are unlikely to want to deny art status to any of these performances simply because they lack sincere self-expression, the same allowance should be made for the author, Shakespeare, even if we suspect that Ophelia's madness (Act 4, Scene 5) is not sincere self-expression on his part. We might suppose that insincere art is less valuable than sincere art, but why deny that something is *art* on those grounds? Some great artists are keen observers of the emotions of other people. We can require art to be expressive without requiring self-expression.

Based on these considerations, the expression theory of art is often simplified to say this:

> Art is the activity of intentionally selecting combinations of movements, lines, colors, sounds, and other materials in order to generate a particular felt emotion in the audience.

Rejecting Tolstoy's requirement of infection – of emotional transfer from person to person – gives us the *arousal theory* of art.

Exercise: Do we give up anything important if we weaken the expression theory from transmission to arousal? Explain what, if anything, is sacrificed.

Tolstoy does not endorse this weaker account of expression. Instead, he defends the consequence that his stronger version of the theory disqualifies many candidates for art. He admits that his theory disqualifies plays by Shakespeare, most of Beethoven's music, most opera and ballet, and most modern poetry. However, he argues that art cannot be defined unless it has a unique function, and art is not worth the labor involved in producing it unless it has a socially valuable function. Consequently, he is quite willing to dismiss as "counterfeit" any candidate for art that does not transmit emotion from artist to audience, and so he endorses the conclusion that most famous art is not really art at all. Tolstoy's theory therefore faces the strong objection that it is too revisionist. That is, the theory does not actually define art as it exists. It attempts to tell us what *should* count as art, and on this basis it challenges prevailing linguistic practice. However,

Tolstoy's attempt at revising the definition is wrong-headed. "Art" is not a term of science describing a natural kind in nature, where large numbers of people might be very mistaken in their application of a term. (For example, many people routinely apply the nursery rhyme "Star light, star bright" to Venus, which is a planet and not a star.) Historically recognized art is just not the kind of thing that most people can be confused about. Any theory that tells us that *Hamlet* and its performances are not artworks is overly revisionist.

Tolstoy's theory also owes us a clarification concerning the audience. Is something an artwork if only one person (other than the artist) is capable of feeling the intended emotion? Tolstoy stipulates that artworks have universal accessibility. *Everyone* can (at least potentially) experience the emotion that an artwork transmits. This requirement reduces art to the lowest common denominator. Some artworks only transmit emotions to audience members who understand complex ideas or who grasp relatively unique cultural situations; these only succeed in communicating emotion to a small, elite audience. Tolstoy explicitly condemns, as counterfeit, any art that appeals only to intellectual or cultural elites. (Today, we might include most prose poems, installation art, and "independent" films.) Thus, he excludes the responses of elite audiences and their specialized tastes from counting in any determination of whether something is art. However, even if we allow that literary works can be translated and, for the sake of the illiterate, read aloud or otherwise communicated, there are certainly going to be some people who fail to be emotionally engaged. J. D. Salinger's *The Catcher in the Rye* (1951) is one of the most widely read and influential novels of the last century, steadily selling a quarter of a million copies each year. Yet many, many readers find nothing to relate to in the central character, Holden Caufield, a privileged white male who has run away from boarding school. Shakespeare's "What's Hecuba to him, or he to Hecuba?" becomes "What's Holden to me, or me to Holden?" Given the seeming impossibility of finding anything that emotionally moves everyone, does anything count as art in Tolstoy's theory?

The obvious response is that the arousal requirement should be modified so that an artwork only needs to arouse the desired emotion in an appropriately situated audience. Unfortunately, this move defeats the motivating idea of the theory, which is that art is valuable for communicating emotion. If works of art have no special power to communicate an emotion to people who would not otherwise encounter it, what is the purpose of expressive communication? For an answer, we turn to another version of the expression theory.

2.3 Collingwood's account of expressive art

Collingwood (1938) offers a philosophically rich and detailed analysis of art as expression. Like Tolstoy, Collingwood is primarily interested in expression as an activity, and so provides a definition of the activity of art as his basis for offering a definition of artworks.

- Art is the imaginative activity of shaping material until it expresses emotion, which consists in the artist's bringing a feeling into consciousness as a definite emotion.
- An artwork proper is an imaginative creation that expresses emotion by bringing it into the consciousness of its creator. More generally, an artwork is any material externalization that permits an audience to experience the same imaginative combination and to likewise express the same emotion.

Because imagination always draws on perceptual experiences, imagination draws from experiences that can be shared. Therefore the work of art proper is necessarily something that can be externalized and shared, even if this does not always happen in practice.

Collingwood often uses the example of a composer developing a melody in his head. The pitched tones that form the melody are the same pitched tones that others can both hear and imagine. What the composer supplies is an original shaping of this material. The tune is composed (and the work of art exists) once the artist finds that the composition gives a definite expression to an emotion that was previously only a vague, undefined feeling. Crudely paraphrased, the response to a work of art is a moment of discovery, something like, "Oh! So that is what I've been feeling." On this theory, many candidates for art status are merely so-called "art," for they fail to make anyone conscious of their emotions. For example, the Oscar-winning comedy film *Juno* (2007) is about an unwed pregnant teenager. The plot is designed to make the audience feel good about the girl's decision to offer the baby for adoption. Although it raises the issue briefly before getting it out of the way, the film is constructed so that the audience can avoid having to deal with feelings about the current epidemic of single mothers in poverty. Instead, it encourages us to repress our concerns. However, this design is contrary to the purpose of art. Art should explore feelings by bringing them into the open in a clear way. Like Tolstoy, Collingwood's account of artistic expression has the consequence of denying that a great deal of art is really art. Also like Tolstoy, Collingwood offers a revisionist proposal about the nature of art.

Despite some similarities, Collingwood's theory differs from Tolstoy's in two important ways. First, Collingwood has a self-recognition theory. He thinks that the audience already shares an emotion with the artist. An expressive artwork is one that leads the audience to have a parallel imaginative experience and, based on that, a parallel clarity of consciousness in which they recognize that it is their emotion, too. Tolstoy, in contrast, claims that the artwork arouses the emotion in the audience.

Second, Collingwood's account makes it implausible to expect universal access to an artwork. The choices made by the artist are unlikely to be understood by anyone whose cultural situation is too different. Artists select subject matter and make stylistic decisions in order to express the emotions that are significant in a particular place and time, perhaps only to a very limited audience. Cultural distance will limit the imaginative experience that can be obtained from an artwork produced in the past or in an unfamiliar culture.

For example, Emily Dickinson's poem "Essential Oils - Are Wrung" (c.1863) presents many obstacles to our recovery of its expressive element. It consists of sentence fragments that generate vague suggestions. What are we to imagine as we read it? What, to begin with, is the "it" of "It is the gift of screws?" The attar? But what's that? (It's an archaic term for an essential oil used to make perfume.) What is the general rose? Here is the complete poem as originally published:

> Essential oils are wrung:
> The attar from the rose
> Is not expressed by suns alone,
> It is the gift of screws.
>
> The general rose decays;
> But this, in Lady's Drawer,
> Makes summer when the Lady lies
> In ceaseless rosemary.

That is how "Essential Oils - Are Wrung" appeared in the late nineteenth century. One interesting thing about it is that it departs from what Dickinson wrote. Her early editors feared that readers could not cope with her use of dashes in place of standard punctuation, so they altered her writing to make it more accessible. Other changes included altering the endings of the verbs: her "decay" becomes "decays," her "lie" becomes "lies," and so on. By standardizing Dickinson's punctuation and grammar, her nineteenth-century editors simplified the imaginative process demanded by her poetry.

However, punctuation is not our only obstacle to imaginatively grasping what Dickinson is expressing here. Because few people in the twenty-first century have engaged in the process of making perfumes by pressing essential oils from flowers and herbs, few are likely to grasp the central image of using a screw press to extract the attar from the rose. This image is sometimes interpreted as a metaphor for the artistic process itself. Notice that the term "expressed" implies that force is needed to extract the oils, but of course it is also our common term for what the artist does! The final four lines direct the reader to a woman's experience, which is likely to present imaginative barriers for many male readers.

Generalizing from "Essential Oils - Are Wrung," artworks guide audiences by virtue of two intertwined elements: style and content. Beyond the problem of grasping the literal meaning and the intended metaphors, stylistic originality can be a barrier. Therefore Dickinson's editors, who hoped to publicize and popularize her work, replaced her unique punctuation system with standard English. For Collingwood, these concessions to accessibility are a serious error. Readers must replicate the imaginative process that Dickinson employed in coming to this particular arrangement of words. If Dickinson went to the trouble of using dashes, they must be there for a purpose. Simpler punctuation is likely to simplify and change the process of interpreting these short lines, changing the imaginative response. Accessibility will almost always reduce imaginative complexity, and with it the work's potential for expressing the precise emotion that the artist is exploring and revealing. For Collingwood, concessions to accessibility almost always produce bad art, which is art that fails in articulating an emotion shared by an artist and her community.

Collingwood's theory has the strength that it predicts that highly expressive art will fail to engage large numbers of people. It explains why you may not be to blame if you don't "get" the attraction of Emily Dickinson's poetry, Mark Rothko's abstract painting *Black on Maroon* (1959), or some of Arnold Schoenberg's atonal music. To express new emotions (and why bother to express old, familiar ones?), an artwork must be somewhat original, and this originality may be a barrier to engagement and comprehension. However, no artist creates in a cultural vacuum. All art is to some degree collaborative, because all communication is inherently a communal enterprise. The idea of the isolated but expressive genius is a dangerous myth. Artists cannot come to understand themselves, much less make themselves understood by others, unless they draw on communicative tools that they have culturally acquired. (We'll revisit this topic in section 3.4.)

For many, the most interesting element of Collingwood's account of artistic expression is his insistence on a sharp distinction between art and related activities, such as craft, entertainment, and mere representation. Craft involves imposing form on raw materials in order to bring about a preconceived result. For example, commercially produced kitchen cabinets are craft items. The manufacturer knows what people will use them for, and designs and makes them accordingly. In this case, designing and making are distinct activities: a cabinet manufacturer might hire a designer in Vermont and then send the design to Asia for manufacturing, where the preconceived plan is imposed on the materials. However, Collingwood argues that artistic discovery never proceeds in this way. Artists are engaged in self-discovery. The process of working with some kind of material leads to discovery of a form or design that is uniquely appropriate for expressing the emotion that is being expressed in that artwork. Genuine expression is always original, and achieved only through the process of shaping material. Although Stephen King might know in advance that the day's work will produce a chapter for his next horror novel, and never a painting or a string quartet, King is not making art if he knows, in advance of producing the chapter, just what the final product will be and what emotional effect it will have. That kind of writing is craft, not art.

A great deal of representation fails to be expressive as Collingwood defines "expression." In fact, he thinks that representations that arouse or incite emotions count as representations of emotion. If the death of Dumbledore shocks and saddens fans of the Harry Potter series, that is no evidence that J. K. Rowling has created expressive art. Arousing emotion is not the same as expressing it. What emotional self-discovery is made by readers as a result of this plot twist? According to Collingwood's theory, the Harry Potter books and films are provided for amusement, not for the serious business of art. They arouse emotions as part of a larger strategy of creating audience identification with the characters (particularly Harry, Ron, and Hermione), thereby encouraging the audience to feel good about themselves as a result of this identification. This is the very opposite of artistic expression. Genuine art is willing to explore and exhibit any emotion, pleasant or painful. Artworks facilitate self-discovery, not self-esteem.

Exercise: Explain the difference between "expression" as understood by Tolstoy and by Collingwood. Is it really the case that recognition of emotion is more valuable, and more properly the goal of art, than the communication of emotion by its transmission?

2.4 The expressive persona

A third position about emotion in art challenges both Tolstoy's infection model and Collingwood's self-understanding account. This third position tries to explain expression while eliminating the self-expression thesis. Art can express emotion without self-expression. In other words, the emotions communicated by an artwork do not have to be the emotions of the originating artist.

One of the most interesting – and debated – accounts of such expression is the *persona theory*:

> Something expresses emotion if and only if it provides evidence that someone is experiencing (or has experienced) a particular emotion.

On this view, there is no contradiction in saying that Mahler's *Kindertotenlieder* [Songs on the Death of Children] (1904) is the most expressively harrowing song cycle of German Romanticism, yet these five songs do not express Mahler's own feelings or fears for his children. The poems Mahler set to music supply characters whose emotions are expressed.

Jenefer Robinson (2005) argues that persona theory is the central insight of our major historical source for expression theory, the Romantic theory of expression. It is "Romantic" in the technical sense that it captures what many Romantic artists, such as the poets Shelley and Keats, thought that they were doing with their art. In this view, the artist intentionally constructs a perceptual object, such as a poem, a painting, or a symphony. This object has features that provide evidence that *someone* is feeling (or previously felt) a particular emotion. That person does not have to be the artist or even an actual person. Many artists create a fictional character or some other kind of human persona as the person expressing the emotion. For example, Keats' sonnet "Bright Star, would I were stedfast as thou art" is normally interpreted as an autobiographical expression of his feeling for Fanny Brawne. However, suppose that biographers come to believe both that Keats loved no one before he loved Fanny and that Keats wrote the poem before he met her. Suppose it was one of several poems that Keats wrote as a practice exercise in the construction of Shakespearean sonnets.

Because it would then lack genuine self-expression, Collingwood and Tolstoy would deny that "Bright Star" expresses love, from which it would also follow that it is not a work of art. The advantage of Robinson's view is that the poem would still count as expressing emotion upon discovery that Keats was creating a persona rather than voicing his own feelings. (In fact, it is reasonably clear that Keats was conscious of this strategy of constructing a persona. One of Keats' letters to Fanny Brawne explicitly talks of his plan to write a poem about a situation *based on* their relationship, and he cites a fictional person, Shakespeare's Hamlet, in order to characterize the emotional state he plans to express.)

One advantage of persona theory is that it calls attention to an important distinction between characters and narrative persona. Reading *Lord of the Rings*, a reader who understands fictional literature will attend to how various word choices in the narration express the emotional attitudes of the narrator toward the various characters. In other words, Tolkien does not leave it to the readers to decide for themselves whether Gollum is to be admired or pitied. The narrative voice is not neutral about who is admirable and who is not. It guides our emotional response. This narrative persona (which may differ in different books by the same writer) is the place to locate a book's expressive dimension. While this point is a useful reminder about the difference between expressive characters and the work's expressive tone, it is not entirely useful when we move from the written word to the performing and visual arts. Many are skeptical of the idea that each play and film invites us to imagine a controlling narrative persona who communicates expressively about the characters and events.

Furthermore, the objection is often made that instrumental music explores emotions without offering either self-expression or a persona. Because this music is art, neither self-expression nor Romantic expression is a requirement for art. For example, the "funeral march" of the third movement of Chopin's Piano Sonata No. 2 is expressively sad, yet it is merely a series of piano notes and chords. There is no character, like Hamlet, whose persona is sad. Thus, we might suppose that we have arrived at a simpler proposal: something is expressive if and only if its perceptual features convey emotion. We know which emotion is presented by Chopin's music, yet there is no need to imagine a person who is sad.

The persona theorist has a counter-argument. We are naturally disposed to interpret musical tones and structures by analogy to parallel aspects in the human voice. Chopin's music is expressively sad because it sounds like the voice of a sad person. Or it sounds sad because music conveys a sense of motion, and the motion of this music reminds us of the physical motions of a sad person. Composers exploit both these similarities. To listen to expressive music without imagining a persona is to misunderstand what the composer was doing, so the Romantic theory survives the objection.

But critics of persona theory are not persuaded. Perhaps it is true that some composers expect us to understand their music in terms of a constructed persona, but that does not show that all artists operate in this manner. Furthermore, we still lack a general theory of expression. If we find expressive phenomena that cannot be attributed to intentional human design, are we willing to postulate imaginative discovery of a persona there, as well? Nature frequently displays expressive features, and we often appreciate nature aesthetically by focusing on its expressive surfaces. A sky can look angry, an isolated tree can look lonely, a wide stretch of the Mississippi River can be (deceptively) serene, and the weeds that keep appearing in the garden can seem intentionally vindictive. Are we necessarily thinking of nature as person-like when we experience these expressive features? Moving beyond nature, we find expressive features in surprising places. The gyrations of the stock market can display nervousness, a building can be welcoming or imposing, and the tile pattern of a kitchen floor can be overly aggressive. Where is the persona in each of these cases? The persona theory may be a useful way to understand some art, but persona theory does not provide a general account of expressive features.

2.5 Expression as arousal

Let us backtrack and examine what remains of Tolstoy's account of art after we subtract his emphasis on sincere self-expression. What remains is an account of audience engagement that provides a general theory of how we recognize expressive features. According to this account, when we experience Chopin's funeral march as sad, the sky as angry, and the stock market as nervous, we are merely projecting our own emotional responses back onto the objects that arouse those emotions. Sad music is simply music that makes us feel sad. *Der Untergang* (*Downfall*) (2004) is a sympathetic cinematic treatment of Hitler's final days by virtue of the fact that it makes audiences feel some sympathy for him.

The psychological reasons for our responses are best explained by psychology, not philosophy. What philosophy contributes is the insight that our use of expressive language has a peculiar logic, and this use is the same whether we are identifying expressive features of nature or of art.

> As a thing that cannot literally possess emotions, a work of art x possesses the expressive feature e if x causes the emotion e in qualified respondents.

For example, in describing blues music or Mahler's *Kindertotenlieder* as "sad music," we mean either that the music makes us feel sad, or that it is the kind of music that typically has this effect on people. The same logic would apply to saying that *Titanic* (1997) is a sad movie, Tolkien's Mordor is a desolate place, and so on. (We must assume that the respondent understands this kind of art, a requirement that is captured by the restriction to qualified respondents. This requirement is sometimes rejected in order to make room for the claim that music is a universal language of emotion. Tolstoy, you'll recall, rejects this requirement.)

Known alternatively as emotivism and the arousal theory, this analysis faces two serious objections.

1. Works of art do not actually arouse emotions in this way.

2. If artworks did arouse emotions in this way, we would not like the art that we like.

The first objection is quite simple. Surprise is an emotion. Many works of art evoke surprise. For those who have never seen it before, this is generally the case with Picasso's *Les Demoiselles d'Avignon* (1907). Yet no one has ever claimed that this painting expresses surprise. Therefore it is not true that the emotions evoked in the audience account for the work's expressive content. Alternatively, Plato observes that some of the emotional displays encountered in narrative art evoke disgust. The arousal theory predicts that audiences interpret such scenes as expressing disgust, when in fact the audience directs disgust at the expressive content.

This first objection can be developed by recalling our earlier argument that expressive features can be present despite the absence of artistic self-expression. I offered the argument that self-expression seems unlikely to be present whenever a large range of emotions are in play at the same time. A parallel point holds for members of the audience. When multiple expressive features are attributed to a single scene in a fictional work, it is not likely that all of them will straightforwardly match the emotions felt in response to it. For example, consider some of the scenes set in Mordor late in the story of *Lord of the Rings*. Frodo experiences hopelessness, Gollum feels mixed emotions for Frodo, and Sam feels loyalty for Frodo and contempt for Gollum. Is it plausible to think that we grasp their various emotions by ourselves feeling the emotion of the one and then the other and then the third, then the one and then the other and then the third, and so on, switching back and forth between their distinct feelings, which we then attribute to the various characters? Yet remember that, if the arousal theory is taken seriously, it requires us to feel the feelings of each character as a precondition of identifying what is being expressed.

What typically happens is quite different. The emotionally engaged film viewer directs appropriate emotions toward the characters, and these emotions are not identical with the emotions that the characters display. When Frodo experiences hopelessness, we feel a mixture of fear and pity for him. Recognizing that Gollum struggles emotionally as he prepares to betray Frodo, we feel both pity and anger toward Gollum – and so on, with various characters and their emotional states. Responding to the scene as a whole, the audience experiences a growing apprehension about Frodo's fate. Yet the arousal of apprehension certainly does not encourage us to describe the scene as apprehensive.

The second objection to the arousal theory observes that if artworks arouse emotions as claimed, we would dislike most of the art that we like. Some people dislike tragic stories. They simply refuse to engage with stories and plays and films that lack happy endings. Why subject yourself to *Hamlet*, to Giacomo Puccini's opera *Madame Butterfly*, or to the film *Requiem for a Dream* (2000) when you know that the ending is going to cause you intense grief? As someone who admires the expressive dimension of these three works, I might criticize people who avoid tragic art as shallow entertainment seekers who do not grasp the power of art. But this objection cuts both ways. A great many people look at the lover of tragic art and see an abnormal, unhealthy desire to wallow in pain and suffering. Life gives us plenty of opportunities to observe the world's misery, but if someone spent their recreational time observing the suffering of real people in order to feel vicarious pain, we'd be concerned about that person's mental health. Why aren't we equally concerned about the mental health of opera lovers? This issue is nicely raised by Willa Cather in her story "Paul's Case" (1905), whose opera-loving protagonist is not so far removed from the character of Holden Caulfield in *Catcher in the Rye*. (Versions of this objection are often used in defense of censorship, particularly concerning materials directed at supposedly impressionable adolescents, like Paul in "Paul's Case.")

Furthermore, art is supposed to give us pleasure, and no normal person gets pleasure from the intense arousal of unpleasant, negative emotions like fear, sadness, and anger. If Chopin's funeral march is expressively sad because it generally causes sadness in listeners, then Chopin's music causes an unpleasant experience. To the extent that people experience art for the pleasure it provides, it is mysterious that people voluntarily listen to Chopin's Piano Sonata No. 2.

Exercise: Supplying your own example of expressive art, explain how the two objections undercut the arousal theory. Does this pair of objections decisively defeat that theory?

2.6 Revising the arousal theory

An important response to these arguments is to deflect them by identifying something unique about our felt responses to artworks. One strategy is to argue that we don't feel *emotions* when we respond to representations of characters and situations. This strategy does not require a denial that we typically *feel* something. It requires, instead, a distinction between feelings and fully fledged emotions. Someone can feel sad without literally being sad. This distinction explains why it is appropriate to engage with fictional misery and documentations of real misery when it would be wrong to adopt the same attitude toward events of the same type while they are actually taking place. The desirability of various emotional responses in real life should not be used to judge the desirability of the responses people have to representations of counterpart situations.

While variations on this response have been offered for centuries, let us consider a recent version by Kendall Walton (1978, 1997). Walton discusses a person, Charles, watching a horror film. Because Charles is aware that he is watching a movie, he does not form the proper beliefs required to fear the monster (e.g., beliefs that the monster is near, and that it will harm him). Walton grants that richly imagining that one has access to a situation can cause physiological responses of the sort that one would have if one were in the real situation. However, because the situation is only make-believe, so is the response. Since Charles is only *imagining* that various things are happening, any feelings that he has in response to the movie are "quasi emotions," not the real thing. The movie is frightening, which means that it provides Charles with an occasion to imagine being afraid. After all, real fear would cause Charles to flee the room. However, he continues to sit there, eating his popcorn. Because Charles understands the true situation, including awareness that he is not really afraid, it is completely appropriate for him to entertain himself with expressive art. Cut off from practical concerns, these feelings lack their usual unpleasantness. Walton proposes that our enjoyment is primarily a matter of appreciating how the work's design successfully engages us in the way that it does.

The obvious problem with this account, as noted by Alex Neill (1991), is that Walton makes too much of the proposal that Charles is aware that the fictional monster is make-believe. Why should this fact have any bearing on whether Charles feels real emotion? Walton's account requires the audience to understand what is fictional and what is not. Because Walton identifies "quasi fear" as something less than genuine fear, his account implies that Charles is aware that his response involves make-believe emotion. (Another common way to put this idea is that people understand that they are merely pretending to believe there is a monster and, within this pretend scenario, they also understand that they are pretending to feel emotions in response.) However, it is not at all obvious to people that their tears of joy or their heart-pounding fear is not a real emotion. Walton's explanation of arousal assigns overly sophisticated and highly doubtful beliefs to the audience. Neill agrees with Walton that horror films do not incite genuine fear. Neill proposes that they are constructed so as to produce genuine shock, startlement, and anxiety. These emotions are easily mistaken for fear by an audience that is concentrating on material that would produce fear if those events were real. Although ingenious, it is not clear whether this proposal helps us with other emotions, such as sadness.

Derek Matravers (1998) provides a different correction to arousal theory. Let us reconsider our first objection to the theory. In postulating a direct correlation between what an artwork expresses and what the audience normally feels in response to it, the standard theory is simplistic about how we apply our expressive vocabulary to people, situations, and artworks. Matravers asks us to consider why we use the term "sad" to describe the plight of refugees in wartime. This description is appropriate even if you recognize that the refugees do not feel sad. They feel bewildered and frightened, not sad. Their situation is sad because sadness is a normal response to their plight in observers who are not themselves trapped in that situation. We thus identify expressive content by responding *appropriately*. However, responding appropriately to someone does not require matching or mirroring their feelings. One person's anger can cause another's shame, or irritation, or fright. It will depend on the details of the situation. Feelings of jealousy or envy do not normally encourage us to attribute those same emotions to the people and situations that arouse them. What matters, Matravers argues, is that some emotive responses to a particular situation are more typical than others. Having learned what these are, you can second-guess your own response before you characterize something. You do this by asking whether your response is appropriate, given the circumstances, and so you can avoid the error of supposing that you are always a reliable judge of the emotions of others.

Matravers proposes that the situation is similar when we respond to expressive artworks.

> As a thing that cannot literally possess emotions, a work of art x possesses the expressive feature e if x arouses feelings that would be an aspect of an appropriate reaction to a person expressing e.

Notice the reoccurrence of our earlier distinction between feeling and emotion. Matravers endorses the view that emotions are grounded in beliefs. If we are aware that we are dealing with art, we withhold belief that the situation is as it is depicted or described in the work. Lacking the proper grounding in belief, the physiological response cannot be a genuine emotion. For example, the feelings evoked when I witness the death of two orphan refugees in the William Wellman film *Battleground* (1949) are not the fully fledged emotions of sadness and anger. I lack the appropriate belief that two such children really died in that way in Bastogne in December 1944. Nonetheless, I feel something in response. Distinguishing feeling from fully fledged emotion, Matravers proposes that normal people learn which feelings are typical aspects of which emotional responses. Experiencing certain distinctive feelings in response to the movie, feelings associated with sad situations prompt me to identify the content of that scene as sad.

Matravers argues that the standard arousal theory gets something right, namely that people can and should respond emotionally to appropriate aspects of artworks. However, the standard arousal theory goes very wrong in its simplistic assertion that the expressive character of an artwork is a case of projecting our own emotional responses back onto the objects that arouse those emotions. Matravers preserves the insight that expressive content involves more than a simple projection of feeling onto artwork. *Battleground* is expressively sad when it arouses feelings associated with sadness in a qualified member of the audience who responds in a normal and appropriate way. However, additional responses are equally relevant. The scene injects sadness into the film by portraying the consequences for civilians. It also causes feelings of anger toward the Germans. This angry feeling supports my assertion that Wellman is expressing sadness about the cruelty of war, for anger is an appropriate response to the indiscriminate bombing of civilians. In contrast, the standard arousal theory predicts the judgment that the scene is expressively angry. Yet I would not describe this sequence as expressively angry. The standard arousal theory fails to acknowledge the complexity of the process by which we draw upon our own typical emotional responses in order to identify the emotions of others and then, by extension, the expressive features of artworks. Although it is appropriate to react to emotionally charged human situations, the emotions felt by normal observers are not always the same ones that others are expressing.

Exercise: What should we think about people who do not respond emotionally to the fictional portrayal of emotionally charged situations?

2.7 Expression as cognitive recognition

Finally, let's consider the position that recognizing the expressive dimension of art does not require emotional engagement with it. When you observe a dog with its tail, hindquarters and head lowered, and its knees bent and back arched, that dog is afraid. You do not have to feel anything in response to the dog in order to interpret its posture as an expressive gesture. It is quite enough to see the combination of signals and to understand that they indicate fear. Your recognition of the expressive nature of the posture is cognitive, not affective. By extension, it should be possible to recognize the expressive dimension of various designs without feeling anything in response to those designs. Viewers see, rather than feel, a painting's mood. Listeners hear, rather than feel, music's sadness. The cognitive account of expression therefore consists of two proposals, one positive and one negative:

1. As a thing that cannot literally possess emotions, a work of art x is expressively e if x has the expressive appearance e.
2. Recognition that a work of art x has the expressive appearance e does not require x to arouse any feelings.

Peter Kivy (1989) has been influential in arguing that this account is the best analysis of the expressivity of instrumental music where there is no text to guide our interpretation. He proposes that music is happy, sad, or otherwise expressive when its design resembles expressive human behavior. For example, the sadness of the oboe part at the beginning of the second movement of Bach's Brandenburg Concerto No. 1 is due, in large part, to the drooping quality of the slow musical line. Its motion resembles that of a sad person, and we can hear its sadness without feeling anything in response to that expressive quality. Notice that there are two dimensions to Kivy's analysis. There is the cognitive theory itself, which limits expressivity to expressive appearance. But there is also an explanation of how it is that we recognize expressive features of music:

3. A musical work x possesses the expressive appearance e if x resembles the posture and/or behavior of a person expressing e.

That is not the complete theory, for Kivy also recognizes that arbitrary cultural conventions can play a role in expression. The sentence "Pat is sad" communicates Pat's emotional state through the conventional meaning of the word "sad." Similarly, the use of minor chords to convey sadness is a cultural convention. However, we will skip over this aspect of the position in order to focus on the central claim that resemblance plays an important explanatory role in an account of our consensus about the expressive character of a musical work.

This account may remind you of the persona theory discussed earlier. The narrator of a literary work can have a persona, as can the fictional characters. We locate expressive appearances in the activity of storytelling, as well as in the activities of the characters. In dance and theatre, dancers use human movement as their very medium, while actors mimic expressive movements, facial expressions, vocal tones, and other behaviors. It is natural to "read" their behaviors expressively. However, Kivy (2009) denies that recognition of a persona is necessary for recognition of expressivity. Instrumental music does not supply enough details to provide anything like a persona. As Eduard Hanslick (1986) asked in the middle of the nineteenth century, who, simply by listening to a Beethoven symphony, will arrive at the idea of an unmarried man, going deaf, with democratic political ideals? Instrumental music offers nothing of this kind, and looking for a persona in a musical design is a fool's errand.

Exercise: Distinguish the cognitive theory of emotion from the cognitive account of expression.

Distinguished from the persona theory, does the cognitive theory of expression provide a plausible account of musical expression, and does it help to explain expressiveness in other artforms? Its critics argue that the cognitive account fails on both counts, for in both cases it is quite easy to give counterexamples of expressive art that do not seem to have any resemblance to expressive human behavior. For example, Matravers (1998) quotes a concert guide that describes a passage in Beethoven's Fifth Symphony as creating "an uncanny, heavy mood . . . of scary suspense." But how does a human gesture have a mood of scary suspense? How is it uncanny? (Ask yourself how a mime could communicate an uncanny mood of scary suspense. Can it be done?) Moving beyond music, many paintings and sculptures are expressively rich. One way to achieve this effect is to paint and carve things that are already expressive, such as the posture of a grieving mother as she clutches her son's corpse, as in Michelangelo's sculpted *Pietà* (1499). But what about abstract paintings and sculptures? They pose much the same problem that Kivy observes about instrumental music. They don't give us the kinds of details that amount to a distinctive persona. Viewing the peaceful simplicity of Piet Mondrian's *Untitled (composition with blue)* (1935), I am at a loss to say what human posture or behavior is conveyed by its five black lines and one blue square. Recognition theory is difficult to endorse because we seem to have no good account of what we recognize to guide our assignment of basic expressive qualities.

Issues to think about

1. Tolstoy's theory of art requires art to both express and arouse emotion. What is the difference? Do some artworks accomplish one but not the other?

2. Does emotional engagement with the world of a video game support the view that the video game is art?
3. "Poetry is the spontaneous overflow of powerful feelings," says the poet William Wordsworth, "it takes its origin from emotion recollected in tranquillity." How plausible is this position?
4. Both Collingwood and Matravers make a distinction between feeling and emotion. Compare and contrast the implications for their analyses.
5. Given that video game players are aware that the game narrative is fictional, is there any reason to be concerned about someone who spends huge amounts of time playing violent, first-person shooter games? Is this behavior different from that of someone who spends a lot of time reading horror literature?

Further resources

As the length of this chapter indicates, the literature on this topic is huge. Those seeking a sample of recent thought on the topic might begin with the collection of essays assembled by Hjort and Laver (1997). For more about the cognitive theory of emotion, you could begin with its ancient source, Aristotle's *Rhetoric* (1991: Bk. II), or proceed directly to its most important recent exponent, Robert Solomon (2007). For a more detailed survey of the classic problems of looking to art for expression, see Dadlez (1997) and Yanal (1999); concerning the irrationality of responding emotionally to fictional characters, see the classic formulation of the problem in Radford (1975). The most important contemporary advocate of art as expression is Jenefer Robinson (2005). She defends modest versions of both the persona and the arousal theories. Robinson is opposed by Davies (1997) and Kivy (2009), both of whom support versions of the cognitive theory of expression (Davies 1994; Kivy 1989). Derek Matravers (1998) defends the modified arousal theory and offers many criticisms of the cognitive theory. I argued that both Tolstoy and Collingwood are too revisionist to be acceptable. Amie L. Thomasson (2006) provides strong reasons to avoid revisionist definitions.

Numerous films concentrate on artists and artistic processes, and most of them explore the theme that art requires self-expression. Two recent examples are *Bright Star* (2009), about the poet John Keats, and *Cadillac Records* (2008), about Muddy Waters and the Chicago blues scene. *Art School Confidential* (2006) offers a nice twist on the whole topic.

3 Meaning and Creativity

Americans for the Arts is a non-profit organization that promotes the arts. It does so indirectly, by raising awareness of the importance of arts education in schools, and it mobilizes arts supporters to generate political pressure for policies and resource allocations that will be more favorable to the arts. How does it do this? What message does the organization promote in order to redirect policies and funding in this manner? Crudely summarized, Americans for the Arts emphasizes two things: economic development and creativity. Economically, the arts provide millions of jobs and associated tax revenues. However, this is not really an argument in favor of the arts. Faced with the decision to expand the local art museum or build a new football stadium, a city might conclude that professional sports is a safer choice for economic development purposes. Americans for the Arts therefore emphasizes something more: the arts are our "creative industries." While they acknowledge that creativity is present in all industries, they emphasize that the arts encourage creativity, and we should therefore support the arts in education and in our communities generally. But why is this? How is creativity in the arts different from creativity in computer programming or engineering, and why is it so important that we would want to make it an essential part of every child's education? Digging into the various explanations found on the Americans for the Arts website, creativity is almost always equated with something else: innovation. Employers desire workers who display creativity and innovation, and therefore modern societies should promote the arts in order to foster this capacity in workers.

Although it is plausible to say that creativity involves innovation, does this defense of the arts really make any sense? Does training in the arts really promote *general* creativity? For example, is a bank manager likely to be more innovative on the job because she reads poetry in her leisure time? Will a soccer coach be more creative as a coach if he plays the mandolin in a bluegrass band at the weekend? To get our bearings on the plausibility of such views, let's look at some major figures in the history of philosophy to see what they've proposed on the topic of artistic creativity – what it is, and what psychological and social conditions encourage it.

3.1 Plato on creativity

You might suppose that all societies value the arts for displaying and promoting creativity, but this would be a serious error. Painting and poetry were highly prized in Chinese culture, yet over the course of nearly two millennia of critical discourse we find that creativity was valued far less than adherence to tradition. Written seventeen centuries ago, Lu Chi's *The Art of Writing* is one of the foundational documents explaining the principles of literature and its production in the Chinese Taoist and Confucian traditions. His advice is expressed in an elegant metaphor. Study the masters: "When cutting an axe handle with an axe, surely the model is at hand" (Lu 2000: 4). An informed renewal of the literary tradition is far more important than originality. Pursued for its own sake, creativity encourages departures from truth and sincerity that trivialize the resulting artwork. Or consider the sand "paintings" of the Navajo Nation, one of the principal artforms of Navajo culture. These elaborate and beautiful designs are made from sand and pulverized rock. However, the designs are specific to certain rituals, and for the sake of the ritual it is extraordinarily important to reproduce each design just as it was learned. In other words, creativity is not valued here.

The ancient Greeks, in contrast, were greatly impressed by artistic creativity, and their discussions of artistic processes are the source of many of our assumptions about this topic. One influential source is Plato's short and accessible dialogue, *Ion* (1996), which focuses on poetic composition and its dramatic performance. The philosopher Socrates argues that neither composition nor performance requires genuine knowledge of the subject matter portrayed. (If the dialogue were written today, Plato might use the example that Clint Eastwood has never killed anyone and yet many of his films have him portray a cold-blooded killer, which he does very effectively.) In fact, the best artists are generally inarticulate about artistic processes and media. Having identified a gap between what individual artists know and understand and what they successfully portray to an audience, Plato concludes that composition and performance cannot be genuine "arts" – they cannot be based on a learned skill, for that would involve acquiring levels of understanding that artists do not possess. Plato concludes that poets are literally "not in their right minds" when they create (Plato 1996: 13).

> Since, then, it is not by art that poets compose and say many beautiful things about their subjects, . . . they each can do well only that to which the Muse directs them . . . For they speak these things not by art but by divine power, since if they knew how to speak well by art about one thing, they could do it about all the rest. (Plato 1996: 14)

Artists are inspired by forces outside themselves, forces that they cannot control. For the ancient Greeks, this force was supernatural, and their doctrine of divine inspiration remains a powerful model of creativity. Since artists do not control their own work, we should not admire them for creating it.

Exercise: If artistic creativity requires inspiration rather than learned skills, what is the purpose of providing art instruction to all children – and of art programs at colleges and universities?

A modern twist on the doctrine of inspiration was popularized by Sigmund Freud, who locates creativity in the urges of the unconscious mind. The seat of creativity is therefore internal to the artist, who struggles to repress troubling impulses but then brings them to the light of consciousness in a coded, symbolic externalization. By learning to manipulate the form of these externalizations (e.g., a musician employs harmony), artists can shape these symbols into artworks that give pleasure to others (Freud 1922). Nonetheless, there is an important sense in which Freud agrees with Plato that artists are "not in their right minds," and therefore the basic art impulse is beyond teaching and conscious control. A great deal of interesting work has been done since Freud on the psychology of creativity. However, these explanations presuppose that we already have clear criteria for creativity. In contrast, philosophy challenges these assumptions and seeks clarification of the basic concept and its claim to value.

Although it has been an important influence on our tradition, Plato's *Ion* is not explicitly concerned with explaining creativity. Its primary philosophical point is that the creation of poetry requires less understanding of the world than does production in the practical arts, such as farming and engineering. Because the production of fine art involves a peculiar frame of mind, Plato wants us to agree that it cannot be a legitimate source of knowledge. So our culture has inherited two important themes from the *Ion*. First, the artistic mind works differently, in some special way. Second, art cannot be a path to knowledge, and so leads us away from – and so competes with – the teachings of science and philosophy. Where Plato draws the conclusion that art is therefore inferior to them (Plato 2004), modern philosophy of art has often answered him by insisting this difference does not imply inferiority. The most important text in ushering in this modern reappraisal is Immanuel Kant's "Critique of Aesthetic Judgment," the first part of his *Critique of Judgment*. Published in 1790, this book is generally credited with making philosophy of art into a distinct and credible field of philosophical inquiry (Kant 1987).

3.2 Kant on genius

Kant's "Critique of Aesthetic Judgment" can be read as a modernization of the Platonic thesis that artistic creativity involves a unique state of mind. However, Kant's discussion revises that idea in two important ways. First, he attempts to isolate the various features of an artwork that constitute "genius," as he likes to put it. Second, he offers an updated account of the psychological bases of these features, and he concludes that works of genius require the interplay of different mental abilities. Drawing on the work of others, most notably Johann Tetens and Alexander Gerard, Kant codifies the idea that imagination is the key to genius. It is easy to overlook the fact that this was once a highly controversial philosophical thesis. If it strikes you as common sense, that is because, as one historian of ideas observes, "imagination is now considered, without question, the supreme value of art and literature. Yet this supremacy was established [during] the eighteenth century" (Engell 1981: x). By moving creativity into the powers of the mind, eighteenth-century philosophy internalized the "divine inspiration" model and made it plausible to think that creativity might be shaped and encouraged by art education. In fact, Kant thinks that art education plays an essential role in correcting the excesses of genius. In the absence of trained knowledge of form and design, creative imagination will "produce nothing but nonsense" (Kant 1987: 188). Excessively original art is unintelligible. Kant arrives at a paradox: education cannot produce the level of creative imagination that constitutes genius, but genius without education cannot be expected to produce anything worth sharing with anyone else.

Kant's analysis of artistic creativity is driven by the assumption, common in his day, that fine art involves "the beautiful presentation of an object" (Kant 1987: 180). In other words, Kant is working squarely within the tradition of representational art discussed in chapter 1, with the added assumption that the artist must contribute a beautiful form or design. However, one cannot produce beauty by studying design rules and then applying them mechanically. A beautiful design stimulates the imagination, encouraging the audience to mentally "play" with various unifying concepts. Mental play is stifled when the audience readily understands the formal patterns that produce the design. So formulaic art is dull instead of beautiful. Genius, then, "is the talent (natural endowment) that gives the rule to art" (Kant 1987: 174), and "hence the foremost property of genius must be *originality*" (1987: 175). Lesser artists borrow designs and forms from works of genius. In effect, they identify and extract design principles from the artworks created by geniuses, and these acts of stylistic imitation organize artworks into distinct stylistic movements.

For example, much of Pablo Picasso's reputation as a genius rests on crediting him with the first Cubist painting, *Les Demoiselles d'Avignon* (1907). Its lack of pictorial depth and the geometric faces of three of the five women in the picture are characteristic of Cubism. However, the artist's own contemporaries felt that Cubism really began in 1908, when Georges Braque responded to Picasso's innovations by extending them to every aspect of a picture. Cubism is born when Picasso's limited experiment with perspective inspires the more radical stance of offering multiple perspectives on the primary object within a scene. (Braque's *Church at Carrieres Saint Denis* [1909] is a prime example.) Picasso and Braque became close friends and talked about painting on a regular basis as they worked out further implications of Braque's expansion of Picasso's stylistic experimentation. Within three years, French art critics were discussing a recognizable Cubist "school," now expanded to imitators such as Albert Gleizes and Fernand Léger (see Ganteführer-Trier 2004: 6). In this sequence of events, Picasso and Braque display genius, because their art is exemplary for others. By their example, works of genius furnish a model for others to follow – including, above all, other geniuses.

However, there is more to Kant's analysis than the idea that artistic genius is the source of stylistically original and exemplary artworks. Kant advances a third requirement: a work of genius imaginatively presents ideas. Originality of form is meaningless and trivial if it fails to generate a play of ideas. In this context, "idea" is a technical term that refers to a particular category of conceptual thought. Most of our language refers to empirical objects found around us in the material world. For example, if you don't understand the words "water" and "lorry," I can point to examples, and this ostensive definition should be sufficient to convey their basic meanings. However, some thoughts cannot be adequately exhibited in particular empirical examples. Due to their wide scope or level of abstraction, some concepts take us beyond our concrete experiences. We think about the world's moral and spiritual dimensions, about the mystery of death, about eternity, and so on. These are *ideas*. Their special status raises a problem. How can we communicate and develop them? Kant proposes that artistic genius is the talent for finding a suitable vehicle for ideas; genius "ventures to give sensible expression . . . in a way that goes beyond the limits of experience" (Kant 1987: 183). In other words, Kant proposes that art's primary function is to stimulate thinking about ideas, by producing *aesthetic ideas* or original images that promote imaginative associations with a variety of related concepts and which therefore communicate indirectly what we cannot say directly.

Based on the goal of generating and communicating aesthetic ideas, Kant ranks poetry as the most successful art. To see why, consider Matthew Arnold's poem "Dover Beach" (1867). Here are the opening lines:

> The sea is calm tonight.
> The tide is full, the moon lies fair
> Upon the straits; on the French coast the light
> Gleams and is gone; the cliffs of England stand,
> Glimmering and vast, out in the tranquil bay.
> Come to the window, sweet is the night air!

The narrator's literal meaning is simple. He is looking out of a window at the English Channel and he asks a companion to join him in admiring the view. But gallons of ink have been spilled explaining the deeper implications of this poem, revealed in the third verse: "The Sea of Faith / Was once, too, at the full." The poem is a meditation on the status of Christian faith in the modern world, on the value of love, and the likely fate of the world. However, these abstract musings are made concrete in images of the sea, the tide, of "confused alarms of struggle and flight / Where ignorant armies clash by night." Arnold's genius consists in finding images to convey his complex abstractions, and then in designing an equally complex, shifting rhyme scheme in which to present them. (This Kantian analysis should remind you of the discussion of R. G. Collingwood in section 2.3, with the important difference that Kant stresses abstract ideas and Collingwood stresses emotional expression.)

However, Kant's analysis of genius carries a high price, because genius cannot display itself in any artforms that do not promote an imaginative engagement with aesthetic ideas. Instrumental music, for example, is an entertaining play of form, but most instrumental music conveys no ideas at all. This emphasis on ideas leads to an unflattering assessment of one of the most important artistic developments to occur in Kant's lifetime, the blossoming of classical music. Kant's contemporary, Joseph Haydn, was highly influential in the development of musical form in the areas of symphonies and string quartets, setting the stage for Ludwig van Beethoven – not coincidentally, Haydn's pupil for a short time. For Kant, symphonies and string quartets do not engage us with ideas. Although they provide entertainment, they must be assigned "the lowest place among the fine arts" (Kant 1987: 199).

Kant's analysis of genius also implies that art education does not unlock artistic creativity. Genius is innate, not learned. The purpose of art education is to educate an artist's taste or capacity for critical evaluation – the ability to distinguish between what's structurally impressive but shallow and what's genuinely good. An educated taste equips an artistic genius to engage in self-criticism during the creative process, which involves refining and reworking an initial inspiration until its form strikes a balance between originality, communicative adequacy, and beauty (Kant 1987: 180).

Exercise: The films Titanic *(1997) and* Avatar *(2009) are amazing technical achievements. But are they works of genius according to Kant's analysis? In terms of Kant's analysis, can innovative video game designers be artistic geniuses? Can innovative chefs?*

3.3 Metaphorical exemplification

If you are among the many who object to placing a Beethoven symphony or a spectacular jazz improvisation in "the lowest place among the fine arts," one solution is to explain how non-linguistic, non-imagistic art communicates complex ideas. From there, it's a short step to extending a Kantian theory of genius to both instrumental music and abstract visual art. (Be careful not to confuse this with the challenge of explaining how art expresses emotions, which is the primary topic of chapter 2.) Looking carefully at Kant's explanation of aesthetic ideas, it turns out that he offers few examples, all of which are cases of poetic metaphor (Kant 1987: 183–5). So are aesthetic ideas simply metaphors? Can a piece of instrumental music function like a poetic metaphor? Nelson Goodman offers an account of metaphorical communication that might explain how this could be (Goodman 1976, 1978). Goodman calls attention to a special mode of creative invention that emerges when we combine two familiar communication techniques, metaphor and exemplification. He thus claims that *combinational creativity* in art can achieve *transformational creativity*, or the capacity to transform our existing conceptual tools for understanding the world. To make sense of this proposal, we'll examine the concepts of metaphor and exemplification singly, then bring them together.

As Goodman puts it, a metaphor is basically "a calculated category-mistake" when describing something (Goodman 1976: 73). William Shakespeare's plays are full of metaphors. Here's one, spoken by Hamlet as he is dying: "this fell sergeant, death, is strict in his arrest" (*Hamlet*, Act 5, Scene 2). Hamlet is saying that he will die very soon. He does this by treating death as a person who holds a particular job. In Shakespeare's time, a sergeant made arrests relating to the security of the monarch and the monarchy. This description is a metaphor because it knowingly assigns properties to the literal subject, death, which the speaker understands to belong to a different, secondary subject (i.e., the speaker is not simply making a mistake). The speaker expects the audience to understand both these points, too. On this basis, the audience is to understand that a relationship that holds in the secondary or "figurative" subject is to be carried back to the literal subject. The sergeant is fell (i.e., fierce) and strict. He "arrests" people, which carries the literal meaning of stopping their action and the more usual meaning of placing them in confinement. The metaphor conveys that Hamlet has very little time left to continue talking with Horatio.

What about exemplification? According to Goodman, exemplification is a kind of self-reference that arises in the social practice of providing a sample. A sample is an object that is being used to call attention to some of its own characteristics. Movie trailers and food samples are familiar cases of exemplification. Most movies on DVD are front-loaded with previews or trailers of other films from the same studio. Like the small bits of pizza given away in the grocery store in order to encourage you to buy that brand of pizza, a preview lets you get a "taste" of a movie in order to encourage you to watch it. However, samples only work if the audience grasps *which* of the sample's various properties are exemplified. Consider a sample of pizza that has mozzarella cheese and a tomato-based sauce. It is two inches square and cooked on Wednesday. Only two of these features are exemplified (i.e., are what it's a sample of). The small squares are not indicative of the size and shape of what's in the pizza boxes in the store's freezer, and the pizzas can be cooked on days besides Wednesday. Similarly, suppose the trailer for a particular film shows a particular actor (say, Nicolas Cage) and is edited in an exciting way, with no scene lasting more than four seconds. Only two other characters appear in the trailer. The viewer should understand that Cage is in the film and that it is exciting, but *not* that there are only three characters and that the editing is unusually frenetic. As Goodman summarizes the point, "a sample is a sample of – or *exemplifies* – only some of its properties, and . . . the properties to which it bears this relationship of exemplification vary with circumstances" (Goodman 1978: 64–5). So, given a sample, how do we know *which* among its many properties are exemplified? The basic answer is that it depends on the purposes served in offering the sample. Ask why someone is inviting you to engage in sampling by interacting with a particular object on a particular occasion and you'll begin to understand which properties are being highlighted and exemplified.

Although metaphor is generally linguistic and exemplification is generally non-linguistic, Goodman proposes that any object can serve as a sample of properties that it metaphorically possesses (Goodman 1978:

68). Through metaphor, an object can exemplify a property that it does not literally possess. For example, visual objects can metaphorically exemplify non-visual properties. Suppose that a friend says that her vacation was peaceful, but not serene, as she'd hoped, and you reply that you don't understand the difference. She points to the miniature Japanese karesansui garden on her desk (a "dry" garden containing sand and rocks). Three smooth rocks rest on white sand that has been raked into neat furrows. "That's peaceful," she says. Then she removes the three rocks and shakes the tray until the sand is completely smooth. "That's serene." Since peace and serenity are not literally present here, the exemplification of peace and serenity depend on thinking of the sand as something other than sand, so that the literal properties of the sand can serve as a metaphor for the exemplified properties of peace and serenity. When art critic Debra Mancoff describes Vincent Van Gogh's *Wheatfield with Crows* (1890) as ominous, dramatic, and turbulent (Mancoff 2008: 89), she does not mean that the painted canvas literally has these properties. According to Goodman, it metaphorically possesses properties corresponding to those three labels. Furthermore, it highlights and exemplifies them. Their metaphorical presence is the main reason to experience this painting.

As these examples suggest, Goodman treats emotional expression in art as a special case of metaphorical exemplification. However, artworks can also explore ideas. As such, Goodman praises art as a major force in human creativity. In *Ways of Worldmaking*, he links metaphorical exemplification to his philosophical commitment to "the Kantian theme of the vacuity of pure content" (Goodman 1978: 6). Humans interpret their world, and different symbol systems reveal different yet equally legitimate aspects of reality. Examining the same object or event, two people who employ different symbol systems will apply distinct conceptual frames of reference to it. As a result, they will engage with different realities. In sum, symbols make worlds. The relevant point, then, is that artistic metaphors extend our capacity for symbolic worldmaking. As Goodman explains it, metaphor arises when someone consciously extends a symbol into a realm where there are no established rules for its literal application. The predicate "red" only denotes red so long as it picks out salient features within the realm of color. When musician Robert Fripp gives the title "Red" (1974) to a piece of instrumental music, the predicate is extended to the sonic realm and the term is used metaphorically. The music's capacity to metaphorically exemplify redness can unlock new aspects of the world. Art is especially creative and potent, then, when artists exploit the technique of metaphorical exemplification to open up new realms of relationships. A painting by Van Gogh metaphorically depicts aspects of the world that a physicist can never show us (Goodman 1978: 3). Goodman's theory strongly recalls Kant's position that aesthetic ideas are characterized by their capacity to "quicken the mind by opening up for it a view into an immense realm of kindred presentations" (Kant 1987: 183–4).

You might object that the Japanese karesansui garden is not an artwork, and therefore Goodman's theory is not specific to artistic creativity.

Goodman recognizes this point. Metaphorical exemplification is neither necessary nor sufficient for artistic communication. Instead, he treats it as one of several symbolic strategies that are highly characteristic of artworks (Goodman 1978: 68–9). More importantly, you might object that the three examples – calling the smooth sand "serene," calling *Wheatfield with Crows* "turbulent," and calling the music "red" – suggest that the act of attaching a verbal label does the real work of generating metaphors. Just as Shakespeare's verbal allusion to "Sergeant Death" invites us to think metaphorically about death, the art critic's description of Van Gogh's painting invites us to think metaphorically about its literal properties. Fripp's title directs our interpretation of the music. So the "worldmaking" is accomplished linguistically. It is not fundamental to the processes of painting and composing. As with the last objection, Goodman meets this one halfway. Paintings and symphonies are non-verbal symbols, but their proper interpretation arises from guidance provided by "points of contact with language" (Goodman 1976: 58).

Due to Goodman's prominence as a philosopher, his theory of metaphorical exemplification has been closely scrutinized. Here are four objections that merit attention.

1. Goodman holds that a metaphor extends a symbol system into a new realm. Therefore existing symbol systems do all the heavy lifting in the "worldmaking" process. Goodman's theory does not assign significant levels of creativity to individual artists.
2. An indefinitely large number of labels might be attached to a particular artwork. Where critics disagree on how to understand a work, Goodman's minimization of the artist leaves us without any basis for deciding which properties are metaphorically exemplified by the artwork.
3. There is a widely held view (derived from the work of Donald Davidson) that metaphors are linguistic constructions, and whatever is said with a metaphor could be said literally. Therefore, whatever is metaphorically communicated by abstract paintings and instrumental music can be "said" in some other manner, and so artworks have no special capacity to communicate.
4. Because Goodman does not adequately explain how the artwork's own properties function metaphorically, there is little to recommend it as an alternative to standard accounts of the representative and expressive dimensions of artworks.

Exercise: Select an abstract painting and a short piece of instrumental music. Have several people look at the image and listen to the music. Have each person write a list of words that describe each piece. Then compare the lists, sorting the labels into literal and non-literal ones. Locate agreement among the lists. Does the resulting descriptive consensus suggest that Goodman's theory can avoid the criticism that it is overly open-ended?

In Goodman's defense, the primary criticisms arise from his insistence that individual symbols have a determinate meaning only through interpretation within an established symbol system. His theory of metaphorical exemplification attempts to explain how new meanings can arise while still satisfying the most basic requirement of communication, which is to be understood by an audience. Goodman therefore rejects another common way to make artistic communication more intelligible, which is to put more weight on artists' intentions. Known as *intentionalism*, this position holds that Van Gogh's *Wheatfield with Crows* exemplifies whichever properties (literal or otherwise) the artist intended to exemplify. Unfortunately, intentionalism limits the number of people who understand the work to those who correctly grasp the underlying intentions. However, we identify intentions by examining what is said, not vice versa. Any attempt to understand an artist's intentions requires a shared, preexisting symbol system. Thus, an appeal to intentions does not really solve anything, and it has the disadvantage of complicating the communicative process. A sample of pizza can exemplify blandness even if that is not intended in offering you the sample. Similarly, Van Gogh's *Wheatfield with Crows* can exemplify properties he never consciously intended for it.

3.4 Hegel and Marx

Goodman pursues one direction for developing Kantian themes into a richer account of creativity and communication in art. Art's communicative function also drew the attention of two of the nineteenth century's most influential philosophers, G. W. F. Hegel and Karl Marx, philosophizing in the immediate wake of Kant. Like Goodman, they downplay Kant's strong emphasis on personal genius. They downplay the idea that art is the achievement of particular individuals who make communicative breakthroughs. However, Hegel and Marx part company with Goodman in their very strong emphasis on the *historical* dimensions of artistic processes. Goodman focuses on the *synchronic* conditions for exemplification within a symbol system on a particular occasion of "worldmaking." Hegel and Marx recommend a *diachronic* approach, which assumes that cultural systems evolve over time. This perspective undercuts the standard idea that individual artists should be assigned credit for the creativity displayed by their art. The level of creativity displayed by a particular artwork is a byproduct of its historical position within a particular society at a particular stage of its development. Artistic success is a matter of *cultural* significance. Bruno Nettl, a prominent musicologist, summarizes this emphasis on culture when he says that the organization of art displays "the relevant central values of culture in abstracted form" (Nettl 1983: 159). Supplement this insight with the further idea that these values are not static – not set in stone – and you have a good start on understanding how Hegel and Marx account for creativity. As Sir Isaac Newton famously said about his great scientific breakthroughs, "If I have seen further [than my predecessors], it is by standing on the shoulders of Giants" (Newton 1959: 416). Hegel and Marx invite us to extend this metaphor further. Cultural work requires standing on the shoulders of other workers. If Beethoven and Virginia Woolf moved music and literature forward in any significant way, they did it by standing on the cultural and economic scaffolding assembled by countless people, not all of them "artists." Individual artists belong to art movements, and art movements are aspects of larger historical processes. (For a longer discussion of culture, see especially section 5.4.)

It is important to recognize that Hegel and Marx treat philosophy of art as an application of their philosophies of history. While this is not the place to discuss competing philosophies of history, it is important to observe that there are different ways to make sense of the past. Broadly summarized, we can distinguish between historical chronologies and narratives. A chronology tells us the order of important events: this event follows that one. A historical narrative contains a chronology, but chooses event within it in order to show how later events arise out of the earlier ones. World War II didn't just *follow* World War I. The bungled resolution of the first war all but ensured the outbreak of the second. Furthermore, most narrative histories are teleological, which means that they focus on how a particular *goal* has been realized. (Before World War II broke out, many Americans viewed their intervention in World War I, "the war to end all wars," as a major step toward the goal of world peace.) On the narrative model, an event is historically important for either of two reasons. A particular event moves people toward the goal or it poses an obstacle to progress and must be overcome before the goal can be realized.

Understood from this perspective, artistic creativity has little to do with what any particular artist intends to accomplish. Every artist has a complex relationship to a historically situated culture. Creativity should be understood as a cultural step forward, rather than a breakthrough fueled by an individual's innate genius. Although many orthodox Marxists hold that art reflects economic and social change, Marx's writings imply that art is more than a mere reflection of existing forces. Artists and art movements play an important role in reshaping society. Some writers influenced by Marx, such as Theodor Adorno, conclude that most music and literature is not art. Art status is limited to works which stimulate revolutionary progress. (See section 5.6.)

In sum, Hegel and Marx are far more interested in whatever is communicated *through* an artwork than in the content intentionally communicated *in* it (Novitz 1995). Historical hindsight allows us to scrutinize artworks for the presence of ideas and social commitments that individual artists do not consciously intend to communicate. One influential extension of Marxist aesthetics advances a *pseudo-individualization thesis*: audiences admire superficial differences between "artworks" that disguise their numbing similarity and their message to surrender individuality in favor of conformity (Witkin 1993: 103–6). Fans of jazz music and fans of country music will insist that these are very different kinds of music, but the pseudo-individualization thesis says that there is no real difference. Despite their obvious surface differences, the sociohistorical perspective of "Dover

Beach" is likely to be roughly equivalent to that of *Wheatfield with Crows*, and neither will express the underlying worldview of Lu Chi's *The Art of Writing*.

Marx's emphasis on social class and economic struggle makes the Marxist position more accessible than the Hegelian. Consider the Marxist insight that artworks display social conflicts. Consider what we can learn though a comparison of Leonardo da Vinci's *Last Supper* (*c.*1498), which is a fresco, painted on a wall, with his *Lady with Ermine* (1493), which is painted on a board. The former was commissioned by a religious order and the fresco mode of painting reflects their commitment to communal living. The artwork is literally merged with the communal property. In contrast, *Lady with Ermine* reflects the economic model of the emerging merchant society of Renaissance Italy. Its status as an independent object allows it to function as a commodity that moves easily from owner to owner. Furthermore, we should look beyond the implications of these material differences to the conceptual "superstructure" that was emerging in new ways of talking about art and artists. Da Vinci's contemporaries collected and preserved stories about his innate talent as an artist (Vasari 1991). Biographies are cultural products, just like paintings. Therefore the sociohistorical perspective encourages us to read these biographical anecdotes as yet another symptom of that particular period of European history. Biographers assembled anecdotes about innate talent in order to confirm society's emerging respect for individual skill and individual creativity. As such, these biographies are both a symptom and a cause of a cultural shift away from medieval expectations about ranks and occupations fixed by birth and kinship. Without explicitly saying so, they endorse independence and mobility for educated, skilled artisans. Praise for the innate creativity of da Vinci and his contemporaries reflects a shift in ideology that supports economic trends, prejudicing the collection of "facts" in the construction of their biographies. From this perspective, the organization Americans for the Arts is interesting for so blatantly celebrating capitalism by describing the arts as "creative industries."

In sum, Hegel and Marx invite us to think about art, artists, and artistic value within a broad teleological narrative. From this perspective, artistic creativity is an artistic achievement that moves people toward a historically significant goal. If we cannot specify such a goal, it makes no sense to talk about *progress* in art. (Notice that this teleological emphasis on moving forward distinguishes this position from the Taoist and Confucian traditions mentioned at the beginning of this chapter, for they do not recognize the possibility of artistic progress.) Once we build the ideal of social progress into our analysis of creativity, genuine artistic creativity has relatively little to do with any particular artist's power to give us pleasure, and it may be independent of the art's power to emotionally engage us.

The overarching issue, then, is how we are to identify the goals that give coherence to the history of art, for these goals provide our standard for artistic creativity. Here, Hegel and Marx part company.

- According to Hegel, art history displays broad stages of progress in human consciousness. Overall, art moves through three broad historical stages that gradually reveal the human mind or "spirit" to itself. According to Hegel, art has stopped making progress, for art's reliance on material media deprives it of relevance in our final stage of development (Hegel 1975).
- According to Marx and his sometime co-author, Friedrich Engels, changes in art generally display changes in social patterns, which in turn reflect underlying material, behavioral, and economic changes. Overall, history displays progress toward human freedom. However, humans cannot achieve their full potential within capitalism, our current stage of social organization. Therefore art will continue to evolve. Genuinely creative art will call attention to the inadequacies of our system, which will help move us forward. In the hands of exceptional artists it can even be a tool of social revolution.

As a result, the Hegelian and Marxist positions disagree on the amount of creativity that we can expect to find in contemporary art, because they disagree on art's usefulness in moving us toward the relevant goals.

- According to Hegel, art has stopped making progress, because the literary arts have already reached the stage of maximum self-consciousness permitted by the embodiment of ideas. Following this line of thought, Arthur Danto argues that visual art reached this "end" stage about five decades ago (Danto 1986). Art has nothing more to accomplish, and all future art will lack creativity when measured against past accomplishments.
- According to Marx and his followers, art will not reach its final stage of development until capitalism collapses and economic conditions permit genuine individuality. Under the current restraints of multinational, "late" capitalism, the most significant art media have been film and, now, video (Jameson 1991: 76).

Exercise: Theodor Adorno is one of the most important philosophers of art to be influenced by Marx. Adorno is famous for his position that popular art lacks genuine artistic value, because it cannot be popular if it genuinely disrupts dominant modes of thought. Can you propose any examples of popular art that have genuinely radicalized a large audience?

3.5 Material bases of creativity

For Plato, Freud, Kant, and Goodman, creativity is primarily a matter of an artist's ability to think in a non-standard yet valuable way. Goodman stresses the artist's dependence on an enveloping symbol system, yet this does little to counteract the fact that these analyses do not pay much attention to material, non-mental conditions for creativity. Like Hegel, Goodman's emphasis falls on the symbolic structures that shape human thought. Despite his general interest in the material conditions of culture, even Marx admitted that some highpoints of artistic "flowering," particularly those of ancient Greece and Shakespeare, are only very loosely connected to the artist's material and economic circumstances (Marx 1998: 342). Nonetheless, Marx proposes that material circumstances cannot be ignored, because they encourage the development of some artistic forms and the abandonment of others: "is Achilles possible with powder and lead? Or the *Iliad* with the printing press, not to mention the printing machine? Do not the song and the saga and the muse necessarily come to an end . . . hence do not the necessary conditions of epic poetry vanish?" (Marx 1998: 343) In other words, Homer's *Iliad* could not have been written in the nineteenth century. The virtues exemplified by Homeric warriors lose their value when armies trade spears for guns, and a society that communicates with mass-produced newspapers and magazines produces short stories and serialized novels, not epic poems. This perspective invites us to assign creativity to artists who are developing new media – to Charles Dickens, whose serialized novels exploited the new possibilities that were created by high-volume printing machines, rather than his contemporary, Robert Browning, whose epic poem *The Ring and the Book* (1868–9) is a revival of an archaic artform.

One need not endorse Marxism in order to credit Marx with an important insight. But how far can we push this idea? Do material developments *necessitate* subsequent artistic developments, or do they merely furnish general conditions that happen to evolve one way rather than another? Art historians debate the importance of the 1841 English invention of the collapsible paint tube, which permitted the mass production of mechanically produced, ready-to-use oil paints that did not harden as they were used over a period of weeks or months. It has been claimed that the commercial spread of paint in tubes was a direct encouragement to paint outdoors, on site (rather than the established practice of sketching on site and then painting in the studio, where color was mixed with oil in small batches as needed). Although the commercial production of paint tubes made it much easier to paint outdoors, does this non-artistic breakthrough *explain* the subsequent exploration of the medium of oil painting in the second half of the nineteenth century? Pushing back another step, linseed oil dries quickly and it contributes a degree of yellowing. Poppy oil does not yellow and dries more slowly. Once poppy oil was commercially available, it became the base for most oil paint, especially tube paint. So does poppy oil explain the freer paint handling of Impressionism? Finally, consider the fact that Claude Monet and Pierre-Auguste Renoir bought their paints from the same dealer. That dealer sold chrome yellow paint that tended to fade. Monet therefore eliminated chrome yellow from his palette, but Renoir kept using it (Callen 2000: 105). The material properties of that color in that brand of paint explain a difference in their palettes, so it seems that their creative differences are partially explained by the material basis of their shared medium.

How far should we push this explanatory model, and what does it contribute to our evaluation of art? The general issue has been explored at length by Noël Carroll (1996), a philosopher who has written extensively about film as art. He is extremely skeptical of what he calls the *medium specificity thesis*, the proposal that the artistic developments of each artform are inherent in its tools and materials. Carroll criticizes the frequent appeals to medium specificity by artists and critics who were defending the emerging arts of photography and then cinema. For example, Rudolf Arnheim argues that the visual appearance of a photograph necessarily differs from the look of whatever is photographed. Early filmmakers succeeded, therefore, by *exploring* and *exploiting* these unavoidable differences for expressive effect. Subsequent attempts to make film more realistic – first with sound, then with color – were creative steps backwards, not forward. Most movies fail as art, according to Arnheim, because their expressivity is primarily due to plot and dialogue, instead of "rich silent action" (Arnheim 1957: 230). Most movies fail to exploit the inherent essence of cinema.

Carroll observes that the specificity thesis takes two different forms, depending on whether its advocates intend to *explain* creative developments or to *justify* criteria for evaluating art. Explanation and justification are frequently confused, but the distinction is readily grasped if you see that explaining a car crash by reference to the recklessness of a drunk driver does not justify harm done in the accident.

- The *descriptive*, explanatory version of the specificity thesis says that each art medium has unique characteristics that direct artistic developments in that medium. Marx appears to have been advocating medium specificity as a descriptive, explanatory thesis.
- The *prescriptive* version says that each medium has design or style implications "about what should and should not be made in it" (Carroll 1996: 1).

The descriptive version says that each medium will encourage some choices while discouraging or even prohibiting others. At best, it offers a partial explanation of why a particular artform develops in one way rather than another. In contrast, the prescriptive version attempts to prioritize choices or identify success and failure by reference to the unique features of the medium. This version implies that creativity is not valuable for its own sake, because success requires concentrated exploration of a medium's unique implications. Arnheim's criticism of standard Hollywood films offers a paradigm case of the prescriptive version of the specificity thesis.

Both the descriptive and prescriptive versions face serious objections. As Carroll emphasizes, there is no point in spelling out the implications of the prescriptive principle if the descriptive principle is true (Carroll 1988: 82–3). After all, there is no point in praising a dance choreographer who explores bodily movement if that is what dance essentially involves. If the medium of dance already directs dancers to explore bodily movement, they can't do otherwise, and nothing is accomplished by invoking the prescriptive principle. So is the descriptive principle true? Not if it is intended to mean that distinct material bases always translate into *unique* ways of structuring art. Narratives and characters can appear in distinct media;

Achilles and the fall of Troy are artistically developed in Greek epic poetry, but this does not prevent their cinematic depiction in *Troy* (2004). A single artistic medium can be developed using several distinct material bases. Sculptures, for example, are made with bronze, marble, wood, and so on. Films are made using film stock, video, and digital code. So it is not always the case that the material basis of an artistic medium explains its allegedly unique capacities. However, if there is no underlying material explanation of a medium's distinctive possibilities, it is hard to see why different media will imply specific opportunities for creative exploration. And we will have given up any claim to a general theory if we tighten the connection between material and medium by maintaining that paints made with poppy oil are a completely different art medium from paints made with linseed oil, or that movie dialogue is a different medium than theatrical dialogue.

A final problem arises from arguments that treat the prescriptive principle as advocating that a medium should be restricted to whatever it does *best*. On this interpretation, film can be used in a parallel manner to theatre, but "filming" is essentially a recording of physical reality (Kracauer 1997). Therefore film, hand-drawn animation, and computer-generated visuals are different artforms. Film should be confined to documentary or non-fiction filmmaking. Although this criterion does not exclude creativity, it limits film's creative potential to the exploration of real events (Carroll 1996: 193–4). However, it seems a mistake to sacrifice the pursuit of "excellence" in other kinds of filmmaking on the altar of what is uniquely cinematic. There is no reason to suppose we'll discover the full potential of an artform by directing artists to limit their uses of it; our interest in an artform is frequently an interest "in how artists learn or discover new ways of using their medium" (Carroll 1996: 32). In other words, the specificity thesis places unjustified limitations on the creative exploration of art media.

Exercise: Are traditional filmmaking and digital moviemaking different arts? Is creativity enhanced or diminished when they are combined?

3.6 Feminism and creativity

Rejection of the medium specificity thesis does not imply that an artist's choice of medium is irrelevant. As part of a larger process of limiting access to high-status social roles, societies limit access to various artistic media. These limitations are frequently aligned with gender and social class. Reflecting the general feminist commitment to end women's subordination in all spheres of life, feminist analyses of art have explored the multiple social mechanisms by which women have been denied access to knowledge, social institutions, and attendant opportunities. At the level of theory, some highly influential philosophers have insisted that women are by their very natures incapable of creating great art (summarized by Korsmeyer 2004: 66–7). At the level of practice, entire media are excluded from the realm of art because they are primarily "feminine" (e.g., fiber arts such as knitting and quilting, and the "decorative arts" generally).

Feminist analyses are not limited to identifying patterns of gender stereotyping and discrimination. Identification of systematic gender discrimination in the arts frequently prompts a call for positive action that will remove these barriers. However, another argument asks whether this response reinforces another, more subtle sexist stereotype. Perhaps the appeal to women's equal capacity for genius and creativity is itself part of the problem. Linda Nochlin provoked considerable controversy with her argument that recent attempts to define and explain genius are pointless and perhaps harmful, for the project can only reinforce prevailing stereotypes about art making (1988). Like Goodman, Nochlin emphasizes that artistic creativity must be measured by an artist's relationship to existing symbol systems. However, she combines this point with a Marxist insight: "The language of art is, more materially, embodied in paint and line on canvas or paper, in stone or clay or plastic or metal" (Nochlin 1988: 149). Artistic creativity requires access to, and training with, art materials. Ironically, Kant's brief discussion of art education might be his most important insight, but it has been historically overshadowed by his belief in innate genius and the low status of craft.

Stated directly, Nochlin proposes that a gendered society affirms gendered standards of artistic success. We cannot seriously suppose, then, that our own culture has ever advanced a gender-neutral concept of artistic creativity. By way of illustration, consider a short but revealing passage from Henry James' novel *Roderick Hudson* (1875). On the surface, it explores personal and social conflicts that arise when a young man with innate talent receives art training in a foreign country.

> Once, when they were standing before that noblest of sculptured portraits, the so-called Demosthenes, in the Braccio Nuovo, [Mary Garland] made the only spontaneous allusion to her projected marriage, direct or indirect, that had yet fallen from her lips. "I am so glad," she said, "that Roderick is a sculptor and not a painter. . . . It is more manly." (James 1983: 392)

Mary Garland has travelled to Rome to visit her fiancé, Roderick Hudson, who has become a promising young sculptor. Hudson's education is due to the benevolence and support of his friend, Rowland Mallet. The novel makes it clear that Hudson would not have progressed if he had remained with Garland in rural Massachusetts. Without Mallet's funding, Hudson would never have seen great sculpture and he would not have had the freedom to experiment with the medium, much less buy the materials for making sculptures. The novel asks whether the process of unleashing Hudson's genius is worth the emotional toll on everyone around him.

James' novel unintentionally illustrates numerous points made by Nochlin and many other recent feminists. They are, in turn, expanding on points originally articulated by Virginia Woolf in 1929. Suppose Shakespeare had an equally talented sister. Sexism among the Elizabethans ensured that she could never have a written a play as good as one of his (Woolf 1998: 60–8). Woolf then argues that little progress has been made between the sixteenth century and the 1920s. Although James' *Roderick Hudson* is not considered a feminist novel, it illustrates the gender and class barriers that interest Woolf, who was born not long after its publication. Suppose Mary Garland had displayed the same degree of raw talent as Roderick Hudson. She faces a double obstacle: Garland's internalized understanding of appropriate masculine and feminine roles would have led her to self-censor development of "manly" sculptural talent, while external social expectations would have prevented Mallett from taking her to Rome for an education. (One of the novel's major themes is the stifling effect of social roles on Christina Light, a young American brought to Rome to secure a rich husband.) As Hudson and Mallett cut a path through the Roman art scene, they encounter only one female artist in the "artistic fraternity," Augusta Blanchard (James 1983: 238). Conforming to Garland's stereotype about painting and sculpture, Blanchard paints, and her subjects are flowers and sentimental religious scenes. Although the novels of Jane Austen might be taken as evidence that a female genius can flourish, Nochlin argues that Austen had access to her medium in a way that an Augusta Blanchard could not. Blanchard would have been denied the level and kind of art instruction available to men. For example, she would never have learned to draw and paint figures properly, because she would have been denied access to nude models and therefore to professional life-drawing instruction (Nochlin 1988: 159-63). *Roderick Hudson* confirms Nochlin's point. Blanchard does not paint human figures well, so she paints them with their backs turned to the viewer (James 1983: 238-9). Once we give up our inherited myth of "magical abilities" in a few male geniuses, we will begin to understand that creativity is a dynamic activity – one that arises from interaction with appropriate environmental triggers – and we may begin to reformulate the basic terms of the debate (Nochlin 1988: 153, 157).

Exercise: The production of oil paints in tubes is frequently credited with freeing nineteenth-century painters to pursue plein-air painting (i.e., painting in the "open air" rather than in a studio). However, the scarcity of Impressionist landscapes painted by women suggests that social rules limiting travel for unaccompanied women canceled out this "freedom" for them. How would you rate the relative importance of technical breakthroughs and gender expectations in supporting or hindering creativity?

Issues to think about

1. William Shakespeare's *A Midsummer Night's Dream* (1595) contains these lines:

> The poet's eye, in fine frenzy rolling,
> Doth glance from heaven to earth, from earth to heaven;
> And as imagination bodies forth
> The forms of things unknown, the poet's pen
> Turns them to shapes and gives to airy nothing
> A local habitation and a name. (Act 5, Scene 1)

Which one of the analyses of creativity reviewed in this chapter is most compatible with this description?

2. What is the significance of Kant's observation that untrained genius will "produce nothing but nonsense?"

3. Explain the difference between combinational creativity and transformational creativity.

4. Should we credit particular individuals with artistic creativity?

5. Why do men but not women dominate the fields of graphic novels and video games? Why didn't a woman win an Oscar for Best Director until Kathryn Bigelow received it for *The Hurt Locker* (2009)? Is it significant that Bigelow made a war film and not a "chick flick?"

Further resources

The best one-volume overview of recent philosophical work on artistic creativity is Gaut and Livingston (2003). A valuable historical overview of the topic is Nahm (1956), who stresses the tendency to treat creativity as either literally or figuratively divine. Sigmund Freud's general influence should not be underestimated (Freud 1997), but there is an unfortunate tendency to ignore his late-career thoughts about the importance of artistic technique (Freud 1922). However, his influence on psychology of art has withered, and Margaret Boden's *The Creative Mind: Myths and Mechanisms* (2004) is a better resource for exploring recent psychological theorizing about creativity. It also contains a useful account of the distinction between combinational and transformational creativity. The details of Nelson Goodman's theory of metaphorical exemplification are provided in *Languages of Art* (1976). For critical replies to Goodman, see Davies (1994: 137–50), Young (1999), and Jensen (1973). Hegel's theory of the "end of art" has been developed by Arthur C. Danto, most notably in *The Philosophical Disenfranchisement of Art* (1986). Theodor Adorno is probably the most important philosopher of art in the Marxist tradition. Given his notorious difficulty, a good starting point is Robert Witkin's *Adorno on Popular Culture* (1993). To get a sense of the continuing influence of Marx and Engels, see Berger (1977), Eagleton (1990, 2002) and Jameson (1991). Excellent overviews of feminist philosophy of art are available from Korsmeyer (2004) and Eaton (2008).

The movie *Muse* (1999) asks what Hollywood would be like if artistic inspiration was literally as the Greeks claimed. *My Kid Could Paint That* (2007) is a documentary exploration of the possibility of artistic genius revealing itself in early childhood. *Amadeus* (1984) powerfully explores creativity as either innate talent or divine inspiration (and Peter Shaffer's adaptation of the screenplay from his own play makes it an interesting test of the medium specificity thesis). *Lust for Life* (1956) is one of many artist "biopics" reinforcing the theme of madness as the source of inspiration, while *An Angel at My Table* (1990) reinterprets this perennial theme from a feminist perspective. For confirmation of the feminist critique of a sexist artworld, count the number of women artists and gallery owners featured in *The Cool School* (2008), a documentary about the struggle of modern art in Los Angeles. *Art School Confidential* (2006) playfully examines the topics of talent, madness, and creativity in symbolic systems in the contemporary art school.

4 Fakes, Originals, and Ontology

4.1 Multiple and singular

Visiting an art museum, you are delighted to find two artworks that you read about in previous chapters of this book. There is Katsushika Hokusai's "Ejiri in Suruga Province" (*c.*1830) (known as "A Sudden Gust of Wind"), a woodblock print from the series *Thirty-Six Views of Mt. Fuji*. In another room you find one of Andy Warhol's Brillo boxes (1964).

You may have noticed that I did not name the museum. That is because you can go to many different places to see these works. They belong to the category of *the multiply instantiated work of art* or, more simply, of *the multiple work.* A multiple artwork has multiple legitimate instances or embodiments. For the audience, the obvious advantage is that different embodiments of the same work are simultaneously available in different places. Suppose you are a Christopher Nolan fan and stand in line for hours in order to get a good seat at the very first showing of Nolan's new Batman film, the follow-up to *Batman Begins* (2005) and *The Dark Knight* (2008). Suppose your best friend does the same. It does not follow that you stood in the same line. Your friend could attend the opening screening at a different theatre, one of many hundreds showing the film. For an artist, the obvious advantage of multiple works is the ability to sell the same artwork again and again, or to sell admission to showings at many different places at the same time. (For the related topic of mass art, see section 8.1.)

In contrast, there are also singular works of art. Interaction with a singular work requires interaction with a particular physical object or with a unique performance event, such as a dance or music improvisation. Rembrandt van Rijn's *Night Watch* (1642) is a good example. You have not seen *Night Watch* unless you have stood before the actual piece of canvas that Rembrandt covered with paint in the seventeenth century. In contrast, interaction with a multiple artwork requires interaction with any one of its many legitimate instances. An important consequence of the distinction is that *Night Watch* will cease to exist if the canvas is destroyed. However, a film or a woodblock print continues to exist if at least one instance survives. A piece of music will continue to exist so long as people know how to perform it.

Exercise: Give examples of artworks in three different performing arts. Better yet, think of four different performing arts. Based on these examples, how do the performing arts align with the distinction between multiple works and singular works?

We have now entered the realm of ontology, the philosophical subdiscipline that explores the fundamental categories of existence. Different sorts of objects do not necessarily exist in the same way. If two things have different conditions for existing, then we say that they belong to distinct ontological categories. Ontology attempts to identify the range of such categories and the differences among them. Ontology of art explores the possibility that different kinds of objects are created by different kinds of artists. To take an obvious example, musicians frequently perform music composed by someone else, so the performing art of music distinguishes between the creative activities of performing and composing. If you have ever watched *American Idol, Pop Idol,* or any of the other *Idol* franchises, you will be aware that very few contestants ever perform their own compositions. *Idol* is a performance competition, not a composition competition. Much of the fun of watching *Idol* is hearing what contestants will do with familiar material, which is to say that we pay attention to the distinction between musical works (songs) and their instantiation in particular performances. But this distinction only makes sense if we are making an ontological distinction between two kinds of objects in the same artform.

The two creative activities of performing and composing can be also be distinguished in cases where composers perform their own compositions, be it George Gershwin playing piano at the 1924 premiere of his own *Rhapsody in Blue* or Lady Gaga singing her song "Poker Face" (2008) on *American Idol.* The activity of composing generates a musical work, one kind of thing, and the activity of performing generates a different kind of thing, a performance. For simplicity's sake, we will first discuss performances without considering the complications that arise from the fact that most people know *Rhapsody in Blue* and "Poker Face" by means of yet another kind of entity, a recording. (This topic receives more attention in chapter 8.)

We can distinguish a performance from the work that is performed because each has distinctive *identity conditions.*

- Gershwin premiered *Rhapsody in Blue* on February 12, 1924, and Lady Gaga gave her *American Idol* performance of "Poker Face" on April 1, 2009. Yet *Rhapsody in Blue* and "Poker Face" existed before those two dates, and both continue to exist after those dates.
- Performances are events that last for some duration of time. The premiere performance of *Rhapsody* lasted 14 minutes. Lady Gaga's *American Idol* performance lasted about 3½ minutes. However, neither *Rhapsody in Blue* nor "Poker Face" has a fixed time length. There can be shorter and longer performances of both musical works.
- Gershwin's premiere performance of *Rhapsody in Blue* took place in New York City. Lady Gaga's *American Idol* performance took place in Los Angeles. However, performances of *Rhapsody in Blue* and "Poker Face" are not restricted to those cities.

In sum, each performance of a musical work is a spatiotemporally specific event, which is just to say that it occurs at a specific place and for a fixed length of time. However, the work that is performed cannot be identical to a spatiotemporally specific event. (At least, not if there are to be multiple performances of it.) Like the plays that Shakespeare wrote and the elaborate choreography of the "stair dance" associated with Bill "Bojangles" Robinson, musical works are generally thought to be objects that can continue to exist during periods of time when there is no event in space and time that counts as an instance of that work. What kind of entity behaves in this way?

4.2 Abstract objects

Suppose you were asked to explain the idea that *Rhapsody in Blue* was composed in 1924. You might propose that this music did not exist until 1924, when Gershwin somehow created it. But if it did not exist until 1924, then how does it exist now? Where is the music during moments of time when no one is playing it? At this point, you should understand enough to realize that the latter question is bogus. It involves a *category mistake* (Ryle 2000), for it mistakenly supposes that we should think about *Rhapsody in Blue* as if it is belongs to the category of physical things. Particular physical things are always in some location or other during every moment of their existence. However, musical works are not like that. Musical works are more like water. Water is H_2O. But there could be moments when no hydrogen and oxygen has bonded in the right ratio to be water. Does water go out of existence at those moments? What about goodness? If no one is really good, has goodness ceased to exist? Almost everyone will answer that these things do not cease to exist. Yet the mode of their existence calls for an explanation.

For 24 centuries, this issue has been known as Plato's problem of the relationship between the one and the many (Plato 1997). For Plato, the problem arises each time we recognize sameness in a collection of objects. If we say that Jane's Chihuahua and John's iguana are both pets, we postulate a shared identity. This identity ("the one") should be exactly the same in "the many" things that we label as "pets." Because it is shared, whatever establishes the identity cannot be a property that also distinguishes particular instances from one another. Since any two pets share a common identity, that shared identity is somehow independent of the various spatiotemporal identities of the many instances. To make sense of this situation, Plato looks to the way that various spatial relationships provide imperfect instances of well-known formulae of geometry. A drawing can serve as an instance of the Pythagorean Theorem. Yet they are not identical, for there is still a distinction to be made between the drawing and the theorem (Plato 1989). Generalizing, Plato suggests that when two spatiotemporal objects share an identity, they do so by reference to the same invariable abstract object. The Pythagorean Theorem is an eternal truth, one of many that is subject to human discovery and application. Two squares constructed on the short sides of a right-angled triangle have always equaled the area of a square built on the third side, the hypotenuse. Our *discovery* of this relationship did not *create* the relationship. Generalizing, ontological Platonism holds there is an eternal truth about each "universal" or shared nature that unifies a collection of particular instances. Platonism claims that this proposal holds for every classification of objects. There is also a true nature or essence of pets, and it preexists and informs Jane's relationship to her Chihuahua, Joe's relationship to his iguana, and the relationship of future generations to species of animals that are not yet domesticated.

While you might be skeptical of Plato's proposal that there is an invariable essence that allows us to distinguish pets from triangles, many mathematicians and scientists think that Plato's distinction between abstract objects and spatiotemporal particulars is a good way to think about things. Mathematicians and scientists study invariable abstract relationships. If you can grasp how a square and a rectangle are both parallelograms, or how the orbit of the earth around the sun and an accelerating object in free fall are two instantiations of the law of gravitational attraction, then you have a good start on understanding Platonism in art. We are asking what each performance of *Rhapsody in Blue* has in common with every other. Platonism points to a complex, abstract relationship that is embodied in the particular sequences of sounds. (Rhythms are time relationships and musical notes are manifestations of relationships within musical scales.) To the extent that musicians play the right themes in the right order, they produce an instance of *Rhapsody in Blue*. A note-perfect performance will be one that gets *all* the musical relationships right. Yet no performance will ever *be* the musical work, any more than the most precise diagram will *be* the Pythagorean Theorem.

Platonism is attractive because it account for our intuitions that the performing arts display relationships between two kinds of objects. On the one hand, we have patterns or abstract structures. On the other hand, we have spatiotemporal realizations of those structures. The artworks in the art of dance are the choreographed sequences of movements. (You may not know the standard 1895 choreography for the Swan Queen in *Swan Lake*, with some acts by Lev Ivanov and some by Marius Petipa. There's a good chance, however, that you know how to do the Hokey Cokey (or Hokey Pokey) or the Macarena, and so you already understand the basic difference between "the" dance and your own instantiations of it.) Similarly, works of literature are word sequences. Works of literature are not identical with their printed copies. Plays are sequences of dialogue and action. Plays can be distinguished from both their printed copies and their staged performances. My copy of Shakespeare's *King Lear* is not *King Lear*, nor is any particular performance of it.

Literature demonstrates that Platonism about multiple works and their instances has application beyond the performing arts. However, thinking a bit more about the case of literature generates some interesting puzzles. The next section presents four of them.

4.3 Problems and implications

Allen Ginsberg's poem "Howl" (1956) opens with the words "I saw the best minds of my generation destroyed by madness." This word sequence is an invariable abstract structure. Although the words consist of 48 letters in written English, the experience of the poem does not require its instantiation in written English. The 48 letters are only fixed in a particular order because we employ a particular alphabet and we have a tradition of publishing poems. Poems are assigned greater flexibility in oral traditions, where preservation and transmission relies on memorizing and reciting them. Given the existence of oral traditions, it appears that publication of the written poem is not a necessary condition for the existence of "Howl." For example, Allen Ginsberg has been known to recite the poem. But if sounds can replace printed letters in generating some instances, then letters are not essential to the poem. Once you understand why the 48-letter sequence is not essential to "Howl," you will recognize that many of the most notable features of multiple artworks are accidents of instantiation. According to Platonism, abstract structures are invariable. However, we have observed that spatiotemporal objects display variation within a kind. One person can recite "Howl" with a Norwegian accent. Another can recite it with a lisp. Because every multiple artwork differs from each of its spatiotemporal instantiations, each instantiation will always have some properties that cannot be attributed to the artwork itself. The problem, then, is to draw the line between the properties of the work – the essential properties of "Howl" or of the standard choreography for *Swan Lake* – and those of its embodiments or instances.

Exercise: Is Rhapsody in Blue *a musical work? Does that imply that it is a sound sequence? The composer Johannes Brahms famously refused to hear Gustav Mahler conduct a performance of Mozart's opera* Don Giovanni *on the grounds: "If I wish to enjoy it I lie down on the sofa and read the score." It is implausible to think that Brahms could construct all of the sounds of the opera in his imagination. Should we interpret Brahms to mean that* Don Giovanni *is an abstract structure and therefore essentially silent?*

In order to understand the problems that arise for Platonism, we will focus on a very simple example of an invariable abstract structure. The two-word sequence "poker face" was instantiated six times in this chapter prior to its incorporation into the sentence that you are now reading. These six instances – now made seven by the last sentence – must stand to some common object in the same ontological relationship that holds between *Rhapsody in Blue* and its many performances. These objects are abstract patterns, which philosophers call *types* or, sometimes, archetypes. Because an abstract pattern or archetype is not itself a spatiotemporal object, it is tempting to say that its existence cannot *depend* on any spatiotemporal particulars (Dodd 2007). Therefore, the word-sequence-pattern of "poker face" does not depend on the historical development of the modern English language from a medieval intermingling of Germanic and Romance languages, nor on the historically accidental combination of American slang and Latin that gives us "poker" and "face," respectively. It is clear, therefore, that the word-sequence-archetype for each instance of "poker face" is historically rather than essentially linked to the meaning that it has in the American context, where it refers to a face that betrays no emotion. Modern instances *could* have meant something very different. This result generates two serious problems.

The first problem is that Platonism denies that any multiple artwork has an essential meaning. There are cases where this might be an acceptable view, as when Peter Kivy contends that a number of works of instrumental music do not possess meaning (Kivy 1993). However, it is hardly plausible that the poem "Howl" is an eternally invariable object that lacks meaning, for that would be to contend that the *poem* is not subject to interpretation. But what is a poem if it is not a piece of communication? You might be tempted to go to the other extreme and claim that the phrase "poker face" means what it means eternally. However, that solution requires an eternal, invariable relationship between the card game (i.e., the game as an abstract structure) and the word sequence. That claim is implausible, because it is a historical accident that the game of poker is called "poker." It is not a conceptual contradiction to suppose that the game might have been called something else and that the phrase "canasta face" would then mean what we mean by "poker face." Given this possibility, there is no reason to grant that "Howl," the eternally existing abstract pattern, has any determinate meaning at all.

Suppose that we attack this idea by insisting that each sequence of words has an eternally fixed meaning, so the meaning of "poker face" is independent of the accidents of history. We still do not get the desired result that poems have the determinate meanings that we read into them. Ordinarily, we would say that the word sequence "my generation" in Ginsberg's opening line refers to a different generation from the same word sequence when it occurs in the Who's song "My Generation" (1965). That is because "my" is an indexical term, a term that assigns reference according to the context of its use. "Howl" is a composition by Allen Ginsberg and "My Generation" is a song by Pete Townshend. Since Ginsberg and Townshend are from different generations, their *uses* of "my" refer to different generations. As Jerrold Levinson expresses the general point, "literary meaning cannot be equated simply with untethered word sequence (or sentence) meaning" (Levinson 1996: 177). Because literary works are communicative acts, and instantiations of the same word sequence can have different meanings in different communicative acts, it just makes no sense to suppose that the literary meaning of "Howl" is completely independent of the fact that Ginsberg composed the poem. (This result squares with contextualism, which is explained in section 5.1.)

The Platonist's response to the first problem sets up the second problem. Platonism denies that Ginsberg's work is *Ginsberg's* work in any important sense. In section 4.1 above, I motivated the distinction between musical works and performance instances by observing that the activity of composing generates a musical work. However, if multiple artworks are abstract structures, then artists discover works. Platonism denies that Gershwin composed *Rhapsody in Blue* and Ginsberg composed "Howl," if by "composed" we mean that their activities brought those two patterns into existence. Recall the earlier point that the discovery of the Pythagorean Theorem did not *create* the theorem. If musical works are patterns of sounds and literary works are patterns of words, then the works are identical with eternally invariable patterns. Eternally invariant objects are discovered, not created. It now appears that artistic creativity is not what we normally think it is.

You might be tempted to respond to this strange result by saying that it is easily refuted. Suppose that Ginsberg had selected the following word sequence as the first line of his poem: "I saw the brightest minds of my generation destroyed by madness." Had Ginsberg decided to do that, then *that* would be the first line of "Howl." Since he actually chose "best" instead of "brightest" for the fourth word, and so on for all the other words, we know that he did something more than discover something. Unfortunately, the Platonist has a ready answer to this argument. In offering my alternative first line, I have simply identified a pattern that is very, very similar to the one that Ginsberg discovered. This closely related pattern is a different eternally invariable object. Identifying a pattern is not the same as creating it. So what we call composition is really an activity of selection among close rivals. Writers and composers *select* works for presentation to audiences. Gershwin's *Rhapsody in Blue* might have featured a flattened note in a melodic phrase that has no flattened notes in the work as we know it. Perhaps his rough sketches reveal that he toyed with that possibility and then rejected it. Had he selected the version with the flattened note, the work that we know as *Rhapsody in Blue* would be that one, rather than the one he actually selected in 1924. However, that point should not be confused with a capacity to create eternal objects. Humans cannot do that.

A third problem is that there is no clear reason why we would apply Platonism to multiple works but not to single works, such as *Night Watch*. We started this chapter with the assumption that there is an ontological distinction between multiple artworks and singular artworks. However, there is no *philosophical* reason to maintain this distinction. Gregory Currie raises this issue when he asks us to imagine a machine that makes perfect replicas of objects down to the molecular level (1989). The machine can produce a duplicate of *Night Watch* that is identical to the object that currently hangs in the Rijksmuseum in Amsterdam. Why should we deny that this copy is another instance of *Night Watch*? Presumably, people go the Rijksmuseum and stand in front of *Night Watch* to view its specific visual structure. Given the existence of a second object with an identical visual structure, what good reason is there to suppose that the second object is not an instantiation of the same visual archetype? The answer cannot be that visual artworks do not have multiple instances. After all, Hokusai's *Thirty-Six Views of Mt. Fuji* is a multiple artwork. The mere absence of a technology that mechanically reproduces oil paintings is no reason to deny the possibility that oil painting is an artform which is singular *in practice* but multiple *in principle*. The historical fact that something has always been one way in practice does not exclude changing that practice in the future.

This line of thought says that it is a mere accident of history that we do not recognize that all artworks are multiple artworks. Unfortunately, many newcomers to ontological questions will react to it with suspicion because it rests on a bizarre thought experiment. However, we can look to practices that show it is not so bizarre. Photographs and other visual copies of famous paintings offer support for the idea that our singular arts are merely singular in practice. It would be irrational to reproduce small photographs of paintings in art history textbooks if we thought that the precise *size* and *look* of a painting are essential to it. David Davies argues that, because we attend to objects and events in order to attend to the artist's creative activity, the real work of art is the action informing the object or embodying event (Davies 2003). Gregory Currie says that works of art are the patterns of creative discovery that inform the instances. (Davies identifies the work with a particular action, while Currie identifies it with an action-type. However, this technical difference is not essential to the present argument.) If either is correct and we attend to objects and performances in order to acquaint ourselves with artistic creativity, then any reasonably good copy that provides access to the artist's creative activity should be regarded as a legitimate instance of the work. Our willingness to look at reproductions when we cannot see an original work is evidence that all art is multiple, at least in principle.

Furthermore, the history of Western art presents real cases of painters who produce multiple artworks (Gracyk 2001a). For example, Hans Holbein the Younger completed a number of portraits of Henry VIII. However, the king could not find the time to sit for every painting made of him. Holbein compensated by sketching King Henry on large sheets of paper, known as cartoons. After the king approved the cartoon, small holes were poked along the lines Holbein drew. The holes provided a stencil for transferring the drawing to a piece of board, or to canvas, or on a wall. This process was employed for Holbein's 1537 mural in the Palace of Whitehall, for which the cartoon but not the mural survives. Using another cartoon, Holbein created two copies of the painting *Henry VIII and the Barber Surgeons*. For many years it was assumed that one painting was the original and the other was a copy. In truth, neither painting is a copy derived from the other. Both are the original work of Holbein, independently executed from the same cartoon in the last year of his life, 1543 (B. Cohen 1982). Here is a clear case of a painting as a multiple artwork. There are others, such as Diego Velázquez' two copies of the same painting of Philip IV of Spain in 1623.

Exercise: Great works of architecture are treated as singular artworks. However, if a building is designed by an architect and then realized by following the architect's plans, is it merely an accident of architectural practice that it produces a singular artwork? For example, the Guggenheim Museum Bilbao is a celebrated building designed by Frank Gehry. Is the building in Bilbao, Spain, merely the lone copy made of a multiple artwork? Then consider the two towers of the World Trade Center, famously destroyed on September 11, 2001. Did the Center consist of two instances of a multiple artwork?

A fourth problem now comes into focus. There can be no such thing as a highly accurate fake or forgery if we identify artworks with abstract patterns and structures. There can only be better and worse instances of the abstract archetypes. If forgeries are good enough to fool experts, then they aren't forgeries. They are genuine instances of the abstract pattern or structure. Given this result, we ought to reject this ontology as too revisionist to provide us with the identity conditions for artworks, for it implausibly tells us that we are horribly confused about the nature of art (Thomasson 2006). As we said about Leo Tolstoy's theory of expression in section 2.2, the theory does not actually discuss art as it exists. Since art as it exists is subject to forgery, that topic is a useful entry point into further exploration of the ontology of art as we actually practice it.

4.4 Fakes and originals

In 1997, the director of the Museum of Modern Art in Stockholm, Sweden, announced that the 6 Brillo boxes in its collection were fakes. The boxes were constructed three years after Warhol's death as part of a set of 106 replicas fabricated in Sweden for a Russian art show. An unknown number of these replicas are now in art museums, exhibited as artworks made by Warhol in the 1960s. Similarly, Hokusai's prints were so highly valued both in Japan and in Europe that a number of Japanese printers/publishers carved new woodblocks to replicate Hokusai's work. Placed side by side, some of these replicas cannot be distinguished from the real thing. Unless, that is, one flips them over and discovers that some replicas are revealed by the presence of the publisher's identifying seal. However, not every replica is marked as such, so it is likely that many collections of nineteenth-century Japanese prints contain "Hokusai prints" that were made in the decades following his death in 1849.

Having stood before an object identified as a "Warhol Brillo box" and a "Hokusai print," it remains possible that you did not actually see artworks corresponding to those labels. However, if the counterfeits are so well executed that virtually no one can see the difference, then why does it matter if you have only seen replicas of Warhol Brillo boxes and Hokusai's prints? Since the debate surrounding this question turns on an understanding of the distinction between an original and a fake, we will turn to that distinction.

Suppose that you have a bit of money to spend on art, and an art dealer with a shady reputation tells you that two of Rembrandt's paintings are currently available on the black market. They are *The Storm on the Sea of Galilee* (1633) and *Night Watch*. You might wonder if these paintings are really available for sale, especially given that the size of the latter – 363 by 437 centimeters (about 143 by 172 inches) – would make it hard to steal. A quick Internet search will reveal that someone stole *The Storm on the Sea of Galilee* from a Boston museum in 1990. However, there are no reports of anyone ever having stolen *Night Watch* from the Rijksmuseum in Amsterdam. So if someone is selling you *Night Watch*, you will not be buying a Rembrandt. You will be buying a forgery. However, if you have the money for *The Storm on the Sea of Galilee* and have no scruples about buying stolen goods, you have a chance of buying it.

It is very tempting to think that this difference in calculating the odds of buying a Rembrandt follows from the physical object hypothesis, "the hypothesis that works of art are physical objects" (Wollheim 1980: 4). According to this hypothesis, *Night Watch* is a physical object, and because a particular physical object cannot be in two places at once, its presence in the Rijksmuseum conclusively demonstrates that it is not presently in the hands of a black market art dealer. In contrast, the whereabouts of *The Storm on the Sea of Galilee* are unknown, so it might be available.

The physical object hypothesis is attractive because it justifies our belief that some artforms are singular in principle as well as in practice. It also justifies our belief that some paintings are forgeries. Each artwork is a particular physical object, so where there are multiple copies, there are forgeries. It should be immediately obvious to you that this thesis does not work for every artform. It does not make sense for the performing arts, at least not if we characterize performances as spatiotemporal instantiations of abstract structures. At best, the hypothesis holds for the range of practices known as the "plastic" arts, those that involve making an object. If we adopt it with that restriction, it follows that artworks – as opposed to performances and the abstract structures they instantiate – are unique particular things. Unfortunately, limiting the physical object hypothesis to some artforms does not immediately reveal the extent of its proper application. What about multiple artworks that do not involve performance? This chapter opened with the observation that some artforms produce multiple physical objects. It makes no more sense to say, "Hokusai's 'Ejiri in Suruga Province' is identical with that framed piece of paper," than to say, "Shakespeare's *King Lear* is identical with this printed book." It might be the case that a print or a book is the sole remaining copy of something, but that is a different claim. We want to understand why "Ejiri in Suruga Province" is a multiple artwork and yet its copies divide into genuine instances and forgeries. As it stands, the physical object hypothesis does not help us with this problem.

For now, let us suppose that the physical object hypothesis is appropriate for *Night Watch* and all other paintings. Painters produce unique physical objects for presentation. Where there is more than one copy of a painting, only one of them counts as "original." When a copy is passed off as the original, the copy is a forgery. However, some multiple works have copies such that some of them are "originals" and some of them are forgeries. For these works, being an accurate copy does not settle whether the copy is a legitimate instantiation. Consequently, there must be more than one way to be a forgery. Another complication is that we seem to have a third category of art, multiple works whose accurate copies are never forgeries. What would it mean to claim that some performances of *Rhapsody in Blue* are forgeries? It should now be clear why philosophers take such an interest in forged Brillo boxes and fake Hokusai prints. They demonstrate that we are not going to generate a general account of the distinction between originals and forgeries by dividing artworks into the two camps of physical objects and abstract patterns. The physical object hypothesis does not do much work for us.

Exercise: Before proceeding, stop and think about the processes by which sculptors, printmakers, and filmmakers distribute multiple works for presentation at multiple locations. Is there an important difference between filmmaking and the other two processes – and between filmmaking and literature?

Taking stock, we seem to have good reasons for dividing artworks into three kinds:

- some works are unique physical objects and are subject to forgery (e.g., *Night Watch*);
- some works are multiple works and are subject to forgery (e.g., Hokusai);
- some works are multiple works that are not subject to forgery (e.g., Gershwin's *Rhapsody in Blue*).

If we can explain what the first two categories have in common, then we will have a general account of forgery and a coherent ontology of art.

Nelson Goodman proposes that there is a basic distinction that gets us the result we are seeking. Artforms that are subject to forgery are *autographic* arts. Artforms that are not subject to forgery are *allographic* arts. As you might guess from our previous discussion of Goodman (see section 1.2), the difference hinges on regarding artworks as objects for interpretation and then considering how our interpretations are directed by our symbol systems. The meaningful structure of any particular artwork is either specifiable in notation, or it is not. If it is, then the work is allographic and any object that conforms to the notational specification will authentically instantiate all of its essential features. These features will be the symbolically important aspects of the instances. Literature, theatre, dance, and music are the primary examples of the allographic arts. In contrast, if what is meaningful is not specifiable in a notational system, then the work is autographic and the identity of the object presented to the public depends on its actual history of production. (Notice the link between the words "autographic" and "autobiographic," and you should get the sense that we are expected to connect autographic works to particular authors or creators.) *Night Watch* is not an instance of something specifiable in notation, but rather an object made by Rembrandt in the seventeenth century. *All* of its perceptible properties can be relevant to its meaning.

The next step in understanding Goodman's theory is to understand why Hokusai's prints are autographic artworks. As with singular physical works, we look to a particular object's history of production. There is no notational specification of the work. In the world of autographic multiple artforms, genuine copies are restricted to physical objects with the right causal link to an original physical template or model. Hokusai and his assistants carved a set of woodblocks, inked each one with a different color of ink, and printed copies of "Ejiri in Suruga Province." Hokusai almost certainly made a drawing to guide the carving process, but that drawing is not the artwork. The legitimate copies of the work are the physical things that derive their image from a specific set of carved blocks of wood. Copies made by any other process are not "real" Hokusai prints, because they lack the correct history of production. In the last section we considered Holbein's two copies of the painting *Henry VIII and the Barber Surgeons*. The parallels between his process and Hokusai's process are sufficiently strong to justify the conclusion that neither painting counts as a copy or a fake.

At first, you might suppose that Goodman is saying that allographic artworks are Platonic universals and autographic artworks are physical objects. However, that is not quite right. Goodman defends nominalism, the position that abstract objects are not real things. When I ask you if you have ever heard *Rhapsody in Blue*, nominalists say that my question does not refer you to embodiments of an abstract thing. Instead, the question refers you to the class of sonic events that conform to the score. If you have heard one such sonic event, you have encountered the work in question. There is no *thing* that counts as *Rhapsody in Blue* over and above the spatiotemporal particulars that constitute this set.

Goodman's formulation of the autographic/allographic distinction does not align with the distinction between single works and multiple works. Nor does it align with a distinction between physical objects and the performing arts. Printed copies of the poem "Howl" are physical objects. Yet literary works are allographic. Theatre performances and poetry readings are events, not physical objects. So literature turns out be an odd duck. It is an allographic art in which the same artwork can be instantiated in either of two ways: in physical objects providing notation and in events that conform to that notation. When "Howl" is printed in a book without any errors, the ink on the page is an authentic instantiation. But recall that literary works do not *require* printed copies. Consequently, Goodman's chief criterion for allographic art is that it must be *specifiable* in notation, not that it must be *specified*. And this point can be extended to an entire artform. Dance is an allographic art, yet it remains highly problematic. There is disagreement about the adequacy of the existing notational systems. Furthermore, notations are often treated more like an outline than as definitively dictating everything that is notated. Ivanov's choreography for Act IV of *Swan Lake* was eventually recorded in a form of notation that *only* indicates foot placement. Asked whether you have seen Ivanov's choreography, Goodman says that this lack of detailed notation does not matter. It does not deprive the choreography of identity conditions. You have seen Ivanov's Act IV if and only if you have seen a ballet performance that *would* conform to an adequate notation of his choreography, including his expectations about body and arm movements. Like folk songs passed from generation to generation in an oral tradition, choreographed dances can remain in circulation independently of their actual specification in notation. Unlike a folk song with collective authorship, Ivanov's Act IV of *Swan Lake* must conform to *his* choreography. Unfortunately, agreement with this point does not settle the question of what we should choreograph – how relevant, for example, are small variations in arm movements? These issues are not unique to Western art. They also arise for *nihon buyo* (traditional Japanese dance), where dances developed in the seventeenth century have been handed down from generation to generation. As in the West, the accompanying music was generally notated with greater care than was the dance choreography. In some cases, conformity to the traditional choreography was reinforced with sketchy written notation that refreshed the memories of teachers and dancers (Hahn 2007: 135–6).

If adopted, Goodman's analysis provides a coherent theory of art forgery. Autographic artworks have identity conditions involving time and place of creation, whereas allographic artworks have no such conditions. So autographic artworks are subject to forgery, for which Goodman offers the following definition: "A forgery of a work of art is an object falsely purporting to have the history of production requisite for the (or an) original of the work" (Goodman 1976: 122). (Against those who take his wording too literally, Goodman means that some person intends that others take the object to be something that it's not. If the Brillo boxes at the Museum of Modern Art in Stockholm had been labeled as copies, they would not have fallen into the category of forgery.) Since Goodman defines allographic artworks as ones for which history of production is irrelevant to their status, allographic art is not subject to forgery. Music is an allographic art, and "in music, unlike painting, there is no such thing as a forgery of a known work" (Goodman 1976: 112).

Exercise: When film director Ridley Scott delivered Blade Runner *to Warner Bros. studio in 1982, Scott's version fared poorly in test screenings. When the studio re-edited the film, they added footage shot by another director for another film. The studio allowed Scott to produce a director's cut of* Blade Runner *in 1992. He removed this footage. Was the film that audiences saw from 1982 until 1992 a forgery?*

Goodman's primary point is that forgery can only take place in an artform where an object's history of production determines its artistic identity. An extraordinarily important insight follows from this claim. If we ever succeed in making a molecule-by-molecule copy of *Night Watch*, it will not posses the history of production of *Night Watch*. As a result, the original and the copy will differ in aesthetic value. Awareness that an object has the wrong history of production can influence our responses to it, including the way that we see it and what we see in it (Goodman 1976: 105–6). For example, the painting that we know as *Night Watch* has suffered violence. It was cut down in size after Rembrandt completed it. A manufactured copy will not have the historical property of having been cut and having lost two portraits from the left side of the canvas. Looking at *Night Watch*, we can experience it as having been violated. However, it would be a mistake to view the molecule-by-molecule reproduction in that way. For Goodman, criteria of identity are aesthetically important. We have a reason to care that a copy is a fake. (For more on aesthetic value, see chapter 9.)

4.5 Objections and alternatives

Many responses have been directed at Goodman's account of forgery. Four challenges are worth considering:

1. Goodman is wrong to claim that allographic artworks are not subject to forgery.
2. Goodman's theory of allographic art misrepresents what is valuable in performances.
3. Goodman's identity conditions for allographic artworks exclude too many performances from the set of instances of the work. This problem is illustrated by the wrong-note paradox.
4. Goodman is wrong to think that history of production is irrelevant to the identity conditions of some artworks.

The first objection emerges from Peter Kivy's argument that known musical works can be forged (Kivy 2001). Although Kivy thinks that a musical work is an eternal abstract pattern and Goodman thinks that the work is the set of genuine instances, they otherwise agree that there is an important difference between a musical work and its variations. A variation takes a known work as its starting point and then rearranges some features of the work. Some musical variations are quite radical, such as the improvisation on "Body and Soul" recorded by Coleman Hawkins in 1939 in which the original melody is nowhere evident. Kivy's example of musical forgery involves starting with a known work and then introducing variation while forging an autograph manuscript of it. An autograph manuscript is a score written by the composer, such as the scores that Ludwig van Beethoven sent to his publishers. Autograph manuscripts of works by major composers can fetch millions of dollars at auction. Furthermore, they often reveal that published scores are actually variations of the composer's original work. A musically trained forger might identify a composition by a major composer for which there is no known autograph manuscript, copy the composer's handwriting by studying known autograph manuscripts, and then produce a forged autograph manuscript that deviates from the correct version by a few notes. The forged variation will be a variation on the genuine work. If accepted as genuine by the musical community, the forged *manuscript* will alter the status of what was accepted as the work. The genuine composition will be reclassified as a *variation* on the work notated in the forged manuscript. In reclassifying the real work as a variation, the forger will have forged a work by a major composer. Kivy's example shows that it is a mistake to think that allographic artworks are not subject to forgery, and therefore Goodman's theory fails to restrict forgery to autographic artforms.

The second objection is directed against Goodman's point that forgery has aesthetic implications. His account of the performing arts misrepresents the aesthetic value of performances. Goodman treats notation as the source of the identity conditions for the performing arts. However, it is often remarked that many important dimensions of musical performance are left unspecified by notation. Tempo, or the speed at which a work is performed, cannot be notated. On Goodman's theory, what cannot be notated is irrelevant to the musical work, and so a performance of Frédéric Chopin's *Minute Waltz* (Op. 64, No. 1) that lasts three hours is no less authentic on that account. However, that performance would be an aesthetic disaster, not to mention historically inaccurate. Therefore Goodman is wrong to link performance identity so tightly to what can be fixed in notation. Even the best notation severely under-specifies or underdetermines what performers are to do with the notation. The general lesson, Stan Godlovitch maintains, is that notation is best understood as necessarily incomplete and therefore "as an open invitation to discretionary collaboration" (Godlovitch 1998: 87). Two copies of a Hokusai print should differ hardly at all, but that is not true of two musical performances of the same work. James Booker plays *Minute Waltz* with a New Orleans jazz sensibility, and it sounds very different from Evgeny Kissin's "straight" take on the same piece of music. Yet Booker's interpretation is no less legitimate than Kissin's, much less Chopin's, if only Chopin had lived long enough to leave us a recording.

Exercise: Think of the story of Beauty and the Beast. *Does it involve singing teapots and furniture? If so, you are thinking of the Disney studio animated interpretation. The 1946 French film version,* La Belle et La Bête, *has no singing furniture or teapots. The two versions tell a common story, and stories can be notated. Should we look to notation to determine whether one version of the story is less authentic than the other? To determine whether either one is a fake? Or should we agree with Godlovitch (1998) that a story is a loose framework for elaboration in performance – and that musical works are, too?*

The third objection is closely related to the second. It calls attention to the fact that performers almost always make mistakes when performing. Beethoven premiered his Eighth Symphony in 1814. The performance required the services of 36 violinists. Suppose that one of the violinists got distracted at one point and failed to play one of the notes specified in the score. As a result, the premiere performance did not actually comply with the available notation. For Goodman, the so-called "premiere" of the Eighth Symphony would then not actually feature a performance of that work. Only a performance that complies with the score can be a performance of it – that is, a genuine instance. Getting one note wrong appears to have the audience admiring a highly successful instantiation of a different work (though similar) from the one that the performers are trying to perform. In other words, we have another case of having a variation instead of the promised work. In fact, it is quite possible that the Eighth Symphony has never had a performance, for there has never been a performance that complied with everything in the score.

One way to deal with the wrong-note paradox is to say that an allographic work is a *norm kind*. According to Nicholas Wolterstorff, the activity of composing is the activity of deciding which eternal abstract pattern will be normative for performances of a specific work (Wolterstorff 1980). This abstract pattern or kind is the thing that performers aim to embody. Sometimes our aim is true, and sometimes it is less so. A performance is an instance of whatever the performers aim to realize, where the properties of the norm kind serve as a guide to the level of accuracy in the performance. Despite its obvious attractions, this solution has the problem that it returns us to the idea that allographic artworks are discovered, while autographic artworks are created in a more robust sense. An alternative method of dealing with the paradox is to introduce a technical distinction between instances and performances (Levinson 1990). A musician gives a performance of *Rhapsody in Blue* if the performance is guided by Gershwin's score, but only a note-perfect performance is an instance of that work. However, this way of saving music's allographic status has the consequence that it is possible that superior performances of a musical work can still fail to be an instance of it. But what is gained by saying that the greatest performances of Beethoven may not be genuine instances of his music? These attempts to preserve the spirit of Goodman's identity conditions for music are simply too far out of line with ordinary ways of understanding musical practice and musical evaluation to count as an acceptable analysis.

Ironically, the best way to preserve some measure of common sense in the face of the wrong-note paradox is to make a detour into another strange thought experiment. This one will have a familiar ring, because it employs the notion of indiscernible counterparts. (See section 1.4). A melody is generally understood to count as a very simple musical work, so that anyone who can hum the melody to "Greensleeves" can produce an instance of that work. Adapting an example offered by Jerrold Levinson (1990: 85), suppose that two composers come up with the same simple melody. One composer does so in the middle of the nineteenth century and the other does so in the late twentieth century. Let's designate their melodies as works *A* and *B*. Although *A* and *B* will have identical note patterns, they are different musical works. They will differ because they will differ by virtue of some additional property. For example, they are likely to differ in their expressive character. *A* will have a contemporary feel relative to other music composed at that time, while *B* will have a nostalgic feel, because it will be stylistically old-fashioned. Differing in their historically emergent properties, *A* and *B* must be different works. Next, suppose that Megan hears the tune but knows nothing about the conditions of its composition. She plays it by ear on the piano. Although we know that Megan is either performing tune *A* or tune *B*, we cannot say *which* of the two works is being performed, for that will depend on which of the two composers was the source of the melody that she heard and reproduced. Generalizing, the example shows that when music is performed, the identity of what is performed cannot be reduced to compliance with a pattern of sounds that is subject to notation. A musical work is more than a mere sound structure. Minimally, it is a sound structure as indicated or specified by a particular person.

Exercise: Some improvisations are improvisations on an established work. Basically, they are variations. In contrast, some improvisations are not variations of an established work. However, a jazz or dance improvisation of the latter type remains subject to notation. Is being subject to notation a sufficient reason to regard them as allographic artworks? Or is this sort of improvisation valuable because it is a unique, once-only performance that is composed in real time? If the latter is the case, are jazz and dance improvisations autographic artworks?

Notice the dilemma that has emerged. Goodman's account of allographic art is attractive because it explains how the identity conditions of artworks can be used to explain the nature of artistic forgery. The account squares neatly with standard ontological assumptions about other abstract objects. However, the account also generates some highly counterintuitive results. Is it better to accept what the theory dictates, however counterintuitive, or is it better to seek greater ontological complexity in order to preserve some core intuitions about the nature of artistic creativity? Or should we sidestep the whole issue by denying that there is an important difference between originals and fakes?

Examining cases of indiscernible counterparts in music, Stephen Davies (2001) proposes that the identity of any musical performance depends on its actual history of production. Therefore the identity conditions of a musical work are surprisingly similar to those for a painting or a print. Looking just like Hokusai's "Ejiri in Suruga Province" is not sufficient to be an authentic instance. A print that looks like Hokusai's "Ejiri in Suruga Province" is not authentic unless it traces back to Hokusai in the right way. A parallel result holds when different composers create compositions A and B with identical sound structures.

- A performance of that sound structure is a performance of A only if the score or other directions for the performance are the result of the activity of composing A.
- A performance of that sound structure is a performance of B only if the performers base their performing decisions on the activities that produced B.

In short, the identity of a musical performance depends on a causal sequence that links the sounds made by the performer(s) with the compositional decisions of a particular composer. Although attractive, this proposal does not imply that we can always tell who composed what. The fact that Alfred's carelessly tossed cigarette resulted in a forest fire does not imply that fire investigators will be able to determine that Alfred's cigarette caused the fire. In our example, the pianist plays *A* if the nineteenth-century composer's activities caused the pianist to play the melody. The pianist plays B if the twentieth-century composer's activities caused the pianist to play the melody. It does not follow that musicologists will be able to figure out that it was *A* rather than *B*.

If Davies is correct and the identity of a musical performance is determined by tracing a causal chain back to the compositional activity that explains it, then we have arrived at a curious conclusion. Goodman defines an autographic work as one for which the identity of the object presented to the public depends on its actual history of production. *Night Watch* is our paradigm of a singular work of art. Hokusai's "Ejiri in Suruga Province" is our paradigm of a multiple work of art that has physical objects as its authentic instances. Davies proposes that the identity of a musical performance depends on its history of production. So *Rhapsody in Blue*, our paradigm of a multiple work in the performing arts, is an autographic work. If this result can be generalized across the performing arts, then the distinction between autographic art and allographic art appears to be an empty distinction that will not help us to make sense of the topic of forgery.

Issues to think about

1. Select a literary work and a musical work. Explain the basic distinction between the works and their instances, and then explain whether there is an important ontological difference between literary works and musical works.

2. In 1990, singers Fab Morvan and Rob Pilatus received the Grammy Award for Best New Artist for their pop group, Milli Vanilli. However, the National Academy of Recording Arts and Sciences took back the award when it was revealed that Morvan and Pilatus did not sing on the award-winning album, *Girl You Know It's True*. Afterwards, a class action lawsuit in the United States awarded refunds to 10 million consumers who purchased Milli Vanilli recordings or concert tickets. Was *Girl You Know It's True* a forgery? Did the concerts featuring Morvan and Pilatus feature a fake Milli Vanilli? If you are tempted to say that fakery was involved in both cases, then what original was faked in each case?

3. Which is more useful, the distinction between autographic and allographic artworks or the distinction between multiple and singular artworks? Explain why we might have to abandon one of these distinctions.

4. Select an autographic artwork that is very familiar to you. Explain Goodman's account of why it matters whether you view an original or a forgery of that work.

5. Here is the complete poem "In a Station of the Metro" (1916 version), by Ezra Pound:

> The apparition of these faces in the crowd;
> Petals on a wet, black bough.

Kivy (2006) proposes that readings of literary works are performances of them. When you read "In a Station of the Metro" to yourself just now, you gave a performance of the poem to yourself. If we agree with Kivy that printed literary works provide notation to guide a performance, and that only performances are instantiations, then it follows that printed books are not instantiations of literary works. Is this a plausible distinction between notation and instantiation, and does it demonstrate that literature is a performing art? If so, where did your performance of "In a Station of the Metro" take place, and who was its audience?

6. What is the wrong-note paradox? How would the paradox arise for literary works? For theatre? How does Wolterstorff's notion of norm kinds for performance avoid the paradox? Compare and contrast Wolterstorff's solution with Stephen Davies' solution.

Further resources

Radnóti's *The Fake: Forgery and Its Place in Art* (1999) is a fine overview of the history and implications of art forgery; it opens with the accusation that Michelangelo stole artworks by borrowing them, copying them, and then returning the forgeries to the owners. Dutton (1983) collects a number of essays that respond to the theory of art forgery developed in Nelson Goodman's *Languages of Art* (1976). Stecker (2003) and Lamarque (2010) offer extended explorations of the relationship between ontology and interpretation. Their arguments are highly critical of Krausz (1993). Wolterstorff (1980) focuses on the distinction between physical objects and norm kinds; Wollheim (1980) responds with a distinction between physical objects and types. Currie (1989) shifts the focus to action types. Focusing on music, Kivy (1993) and Dodd (2007) are the most important contemporary supporters of Platonism. It is useful to compare Kivy's example of a forged musical work (2001) with examples discussed in Gracyk (1996) and Janaway (1999). Between them, Godlovitch's *Musical Performance* (1998) and Hamilton's *The Art of Theatre* (2007) emphasize the performance aspects of the performing arts in a way that treats performances as the central works. Selma Jeanne Cohen (1982) makes similar points in her extended discussion of the choreography of *Swan Lake*. Davies (2001) is a comprehensive treatment of the full range of ontological issues that arise for music, while Goehr (2007) and Ridley (2003) offer important challenges to the whole enterprise of devising an ontology for music.

Fahrenheit 451 (1966) explores the survival of literature in a future where there are no books. *The Fake* (1953) and the 1999 version of *The Thomas Crown Affair* are decent heist films that highlight the role of art forgery in hiding the theft of paintings by Leonardo da Vinci and Claude Monet, respectively. Documenting the culture clash between aesthetic response and scientific forensics, *Who the #$&% Is Jackson Pollock?* (2006) explores implications of the hypothesis that history of production is the key to a painting's identity. Be on guard; the forensic evidence may have been faked. *Be Kind Rewind* (2008) is a comedy that raises the question of whether remakes of films are new films. (Pay particular attention to the plot twist that shuts down their business.) Then compare the different "cuts" of *Blade Runner* collected in the box set *Blade Runner (Ultimate Collector's Edition)* (2007).

5 Authenticity and Cultural Origins

Consider three films. The film comedy *Clueless* (1995) focuses on a wealthy spoiled high-school student. Adopting the role of matchmaker, she interferes with the romantic lives of everyone around her. Misunderstanding herself, she misunderstands everyone else, too, and these mistakes – paired with some sharp social commentary – are the source of the movie's laughs. *Bride and Prejudice* (2005) is another romantic comedy infused with social satire. The plot opens in India and follows the fortunes of a young woman who becomes involved with an American man. Like *Clueless* and many other comedies, the plot depends on misreading situations, intentions, character, and cultural differences. However, it is somewhat unusual in the category of recent British films in being a musical. The story pauses periodically to give screen time to elaborate song and dance productions. Contrast these two films with a more serious romance, Ang Lee's *Sense and Sensibility* (1995), in which two sisters with opposite sensibilities seek husbands within the socially oppressive context of rural England in the early nineteenth century. There is a small amount of social satire, highlighted by the presence of actors Hugh Grant and Hugh Laurie.

It is not an accident that this trio of films explores the impact of social roles and customs on the fortunes of young women. You may have recognized that one was adapted for film from the Jane Austen novel *Sense and Sensibility* (1811). The other two films are looser adaptations of other Austen novels. *Clueless* is *Emma* (1815) and *Bride and Prejudice* is *Pride and Prejudice* (1813). From the vantage point of ontology, these films have an interesting status. Each one is both a version of an existing artwork and an artwork in its own right. For our purposes, the important point is that this dependency relationship is an objective fact about each film. The relationship is not an observable or manifest property, in the way that Kate Winslet's hair color is observable and manifest to viewers of *Sense and Sensibility*. Given that far more people watch movies than read novels, the financial success of *Clueless* and *Bride and Prejudice* suggests that the majority of their viewers are not Jane Austen fans, and so a great many of them remain clueless about the relationship to eighteenth-century novels. Yet the objectivity of the dependency relationship is a central assumption of this chapter, for it is the basis for evaluating the films as more or less authentic adaptations of Austen. Because *Sense and Sensibility* employs nineteenth-century clothing and British settings, it seems more authentic than *Clueless* and *Bride and Prejudice*, which introduce modern fashions, non-English locations, and non-English customs. However, there is more to authenticity than imitation of a novel's time and place. A 2007 film adaptation of Austen's *Mansfield Park* (1814) uses authentic costumes and locations. Yet it is generally despised for misrepresenting Austen by casting Billie Piper in the central role of Fanny Price. There is, quite literally, more to authenticity than meets the eye.

5.1 Two kinds of contextualism

The last chapter discussed Nelson Goodman's proposal that knowledge of the origins and history of an artwork can influence audience response. (See section 4.4.) Consider the *Rokeby Venus* (1644–8), a painting by Diego Velázquez. Our interpretation of the nude woman in the painting as Venus depends on its relationship to an established tradition of clues, such as the legend that Venus often gazed on her face in a mirror, as does the woman in the painting. However, those details are not decisive. If a similar mirror and pose was pictured in Korean art of the seventeenth century, we would not interpret it as a portrait of Venus. Goodman claims that knowledge of origins can influence more than interpretation. It can also influence the more direct act of seeing the painting. Velázquez' painting was vandalized in 1914 in protest at the arrest of a suffragette leader. The day after the arrest, Mary Richardson walked into London's National Gallery, stood before the painting for several minutes, and then slashed it repeatedly with a meat cleaver. Because the *Rokeby Venus* is a large painting of a naked woman, knowledge that a flesh-and-blood woman assaulted the canvas can change the activity of looking at it. Standing before the restored painting, those who know of the vandalism will look for signs of it in the repaired canvas, an act of inspection that interferes with the erotic charge that the painter intended to produce.

Many philosophers think that there is an important distinction to be made between the facts that the painting portrays Venus, that it is erotically charged, and that it was vandalized. The first two properties are *essential* features of this artwork. The third property is a *contingent* feature. A *property* is a distinguishable feature that is common to several objects. Yet when two objects possess the same property, one can possess it essentially while the other possesses it contingently. The essential properties give a particular object its unique identity. The contingent ones are "accidents" of time and place that are not part of that identity. If Velázquez' painting had been kept in Waplington Hall instead of Rokeby Hall, it would be known as the *Waplington Venus*. So the name is a contingent property. Philosophers generally distinguish between contingent and essential properties by asking if we can imagine the same object existing without the property in question. If so, then that property is contingent or accidental for that particular object. For example, being a painting is essential to the *Rokeby Venus*. It is also true that I have seen this painting. Would anyone say that the *Rokeby Venus* would not exist if I had never been born and so had never seen it? Certainly not! Because it has no bearing on the work's identity, my having seen it is a contingent or accidental property. (Important implications of identity preservation and alteration are explored below, in section 5.2.) While this test is usually accepted as a way to distinguish between the two types of properties, it does not resolve all debate. Among those who would say that it is essential to the *Rokeby Venus* that it is a painting, some disagree on whether its having been painted by Velázquez is among its essential properties. Stephen Davies (2001) argues that the identity of the artist is not essential, while Jerrold Levinson (1990) maintains that it is.

Exercise: Here are four facts about the 1995 film version of Sense and Sensibility. *First, Emma Thompson wrote the screenplay. Second, Emma Thompson appears in the film. Third, Ang Lee directed the film. Fourth, the film won an Academy Award (an "Oscar"). Which of these facts identifies an essential property of this film? Which are contingent properties of it? Why?*

The obvious point of the distinction between essential and contingent properties is that the essential properties are more relevant to audience interpretation and response. However, there are competing criteria for articulating the distinction. The difference is sometimes described as a contrast between what is "internal" and what is "external." In an extremely influential essay, "The Intentional Fallacy," William K. Wimsatt and Monroe C. Beardsley (1946) argue that an author's intentions and personal biography are not relevant when interpreting a poem. The author's intentions and biography are external to the literary work. Only internal evidence is relevant. In the case of Emily Dickinson's poem "Essential Oils – Are Wrung" (*c.*1863), the placement of "oils" as the second word of the poem seems essential and internal. Dickinson's lifelong residence in New England appears to be contingent and external. Residence in many other English-speaking locations would still get us the same meaning and expression for the word structure that Dickinson created. (The poem's expressive dimension is discussed in section 2.3.) On this approach, it seems that relationships to other objects are not to be counted among any artwork's essential properties.

The Wimsatt–Beardsley analysis of the distinction faces two serious problems.

- Some properties of an artwork can depend on its style. However, style is essentially relational.
- Some interpretations of some artworks are misinterpretations. However, some standards for correct interpretation are inherently relational.

Examples will clarify the two problems.

The first problem is illustrated by Sergei Prokofiev's First Symphony, his "Classical" symphony (1917). Many listeners who are familiar with classical music recognize its stylistic similarities to the symphonies of Joseph Haydn, whose final symphony premiered in 1795. Although the details of Prokofiev's symphony are unconventional for the "classical" style of the late eighteenth century, its second movement could be swapped with the slow movement of one of Haydn's lesser-known symphonies without arousing the suspicions of many listeners. Yet where Prokofiev's music would be avant-garde for the eighteenth century, its Haydnesque quality is positively quaint for the early twentieth century. Since being Haydnesque is one of its essential features, and being Haydnesque depends on a historical relationship to Haydn's style, it follows that some artworks have essential properties that depend on things "external" to themselves.

For the second objection, imagine that someone reads Dickinson's "Essential Oils – Are Wrung" and contends that Dickinson wrote an extended metaphor about Barack Obama's economic policies. We would certainly want to reply that, while the poem might be read in that way, the poem itself is not a metaphor about President Obama. Unless one holds that Dickinson was a gifted psychic, she could not write a poem about Obama, who was born 85 years after she died. The example shows that some interpretations are constrained by historical facts. Therefore, interpretation is not confined to what is "internal" to an artwork. Note that the argument is not saying that a poem about fragrances cannot comment on Obama's economic policy. The argument says that this poem does not do so, on the grounds that a poem's meaning is limited by what a poet could have meant by it. No nineteenth-century poet could have meant *that*.

Both objections call attention to the social and historical context in which the artwork was created. Who created it? When? In what culture? Also known as *provenance*, this art-historical context is a relational framework. (The term "provenance" is also used to mean an artifact's history of ownership, but that meaning is not central to the term's use in this chapter.) The relevance of an object's art-historical provenance demonstrates the error of thinking that an artwork's essential properties are independent of its relationships to other things. Drawing on such examples, a number of philosophers support ontological contextualism. This position is distinct from constructivism (also called "imputationalism"), which draws a different lesson from the importance of art-historical context.

- According to *ontological contextualism*, some aspects of an artwork's identity depend on the art-historical context of its time of creation (e.g., Carroll 1988; Davies 2001).
- According to *constructivism*, there are no good reasons to "freeze" identity at the time of creation (e.g., Silvers 1991; Krausz 1993; Bacharach 2005). Artworks gain and lose properties after their creation, reflecting the art-historical context of audience appreciation and interpretation.

As with contextualism, constructivism is actually a group of related positions. However, we do not have the space to sort out the various versions here. (See Stecker 2003: 95–152.)

Constructivism is defended by extending the two arguments just offered against restricting essential properties to non-relational properties.

1. Later artworks can reorder the importance of properties of artworks that were created earlier. The development of Cubist painting in the twentieth century assigns new significance to cubist elements of Paul

Cézanne's paintings. (Recall our brief discussion of Cubism in section 3.2.) Therefore, later artworks influenced by a particular work are as stylistically relevant as earlier ones that influenced it.

2. The meanings of words can change. Gareth Evans (1982) points out that "Madagascar" currently refers to an island east of Africa. It used to refer to an area of the mainland. Its reference changed. Therefore the reference of any communication is subject to change. What would have been a misinterpretation of a work in its own art-historical context is not necessarily a misinterpretation of it at a later time. (See Stecker 2003: 111–12.)

Exercise: Before you read further, think of a familiar story, film, song, or painting that had one meaning for you at one time and a different meaning for you at a later time. Did your reinterpretation change the object of interpretation? Or was one of the interpretations actually a misinterpretation? What are some implications of the difference?

Ontological contextualists owe constructivists a clear account of why earlier art-historical contingencies are relevant to artwork identity, yet later ones are always irrelevant. Against the Cubism example, ontological contextualists say that Paul Cézanne's paintings were *always* proto-Cubist. It simply took the emergence of full-blown Cubism to reveal this aspect of Cézanne's style. In the same way that the telescope allowed Galileo Galilei to observe Jupiter's moons, the work of Pablo Picasso and Georges Braque opened our eyes to what is already present in Cézanne. The paintings themselves remain unchanged. Against the "Madagascar" argument, it is important to note that it generalizes from the fact that most words have multiple meanings. However, a string of words is a different matter. The meaning of a word sequence is relative to time and place of use, as a socially and historically located act of communication.

Suppose you are with friends in a restaurant and you are the second person to order food. You place your order by saying, "The same." Suppose the waiter responds by repeating the same two words back to you, but with a raised inflection at the end. You placed an order, and what you ordered depends on what the first person ordered. The waiter did not place an order. The waiter confirmed your order. The point is that two uses of the word sequence "the same" are to be interpreted in light of who said it, when they said it, how they said it, and what social roles were occupied by the speakers in that time and place. However, later uses of the same phrase in different social circumstances will not change the meaning of what you said on the earlier occasion. Likewise, George Orwell condemned totalitarian government in the novel *1984* (1949), but later events will never change *his* condemnation to praise, where *his* point of view is one of the reasons to read the novel. (See Stecker 2003: 111–15; Lamarque 2010: 167–80).

In addition to criticizing arguments offered by constructivists, contextualists issue a direct challenge to the rival theory. Constructivism is only plausible so long as we regard every artwork as an abstract structure that lacks determinate meaning. We discussed this point earlier, with Nelson

Goodman's argument that the shape of a line in a print by Katsushika Hokusai refers to Mount Fujiyama because a specific symbol system is exploited. In a different context, an identical line indicates something about the electrical activity of a patient's heart. (See section 1.2.) In response, constructivism denies the priority of applying one symbol system rather than another. Switching symbol systems allows a single artwork to change its essential properties over time. Against that supposition, it can be granted that the word sequence of a poem would mean something else if composed in a different art-historical context, but the identity of two *texts* or word sequences is no reason to conclude that the same *artwork* is involved in both cases. As Peter Lamarque observes, "The text/work distinction is an instance of a broader distinction running across all the arts and indeed other cultural objects, between that which possesses only physical (or 'natural') properties and that which is 'practice-dependent' [and] cultural" (Lamarque 2010: 167). In section 5.2 we will pursue Lamarque's point about culture by exploring an implication of adopting ontological contextualism rather than its more radical rival.

5.2 Four kinds of appropriation

When Aristophanes wrote *Clouds* (419 BCE), he portrayed Socrates as literally lost in the clouds. He captured the common view that philosophers trivialize life with their weird thought experiments. Many people who love the arts have a similar view of philosophy of art, as when philosophers draw conclusions from the shared shape of a line in a woodblock print and an EKG. Here, it is clear that the philosophical conclusions are drawn from coincidental similarities. However, there is an important field of examples where correspondences are not coincidental and where the practical stakes are high. Forgeries are one example. (See chapter 4.) There is also cultural appropriation, which may prove to be a more widespread and significant practice.

Cultural appropriation is a cultural exchange in which a society adopts (or adapts) cultural elements that originate in a different society. The idea is best understood by distinguishing different kinds of appropriation (Young 2008).

- *Object appropriation* occurs when a physical object is removed from its cultural provenance and then displayed to people in a different culture. For example, Picasso's *Guernica* (1937) was commissioned by the exiled Spanish Republican government, was exhibited in Paris, and eventually wound up at New York's Museum of Modern Art. For many years after Picasso's death, the museum refused to acknowledge Spain's ownership of the painting. The museum appropriated a Spanish national treasure.
- *Content appropriation* occurs when ideas, stories, and other content originate in one culture and are then used in a different cultural context, as when the film *Clueless* adapts content from Jane Austen and the Disney film *Beauty and the Beast* (1991) adapts a traditional French fairy tale.

- *Design appropriation* occurs when either a particular design or a distinctive style originates in one culture and is then used by people of another culture, as when designers of government buildings in the United States adopted many features of Greek and Roman classical architecture into their designs. Design appropriation is frequently a vehicle of content appropriation; American use of ancient design was intended to communicate allegiance to classical principles of liberty.
- *Voice appropriation* occurs when representations made in one culture portray thoughts and behaviors – the "voice" – of members of a different culture. For example, *The Searchers* (1956) is regarded as one of the best western films ever made. Many Native Americans appear in minor roles in the film, yet a German-American actor portrays "Scar," the central Comanche character. (See Colonnese 2004.) Ironically, some voice appropriation is problematic for the *absence* of any exploration of the thoughts and perspective of the characters, as with the one-dimensional portrayal of Vietnamese soldiers in *We Were Soldiers* (2002).

Exercise: Give your own examples of object, content, design, and voice appropriation.

You might wonder how object appropriation differs from ordinary theft. The distinction lies in the assumption that the harm of theft is restricted to specific individuals. In contrast, appropriation takes something that belongs to the whole society or the general culture. For example, when the musicians in Led Zeppelin recorded the song "Babe, I'm Gonna Leave You" (1969) and failed to credit its composer, Anne Bredon, they deprived Bredon of her royalty payments and thus stole from her. It was unintentional theft. (They corrected their error when they learned of it.) But when they recorded "Hats Off to (Roy) Harper" (1970) and claimed it as their own intellectual property, they misrepresented its stylistic debt to several Mississippi blues recordings (including Booker White's words for "Shake 'Em on Down" (1937)). In obscuring their debt to African-American music and musicians, the members of Led Zeppelin misled a generation of listeners about the collective source of the music. Their borrowing is appropriation and not mere theft. Looting of art treasures during wartime is another example where appropriation compounds the wrongfulness of theft. There might be identifiable owners who are wronged, but the transfer of art to another country deprives a society of access to their cultural heritage.

Although it is common to think of cultural exchange as a positive thing, appropriation is often criticized as inherently wrong. Appropriation deprives a society of a cultural treasure or resource. In fact, the use of the term "appropriation" instead of "exchange" is usually intended to call attention to the presence of additional factors that invite criticism. First, there is a significant difference in political power. The "receiving" culture is more powerful than the "sending" culture. Second, the weaker, originating culture does not control the exchange. Spain was in no position to force the United States to return *Guernica*, and the Comanche Nation was not consulted on the accuracy of the voice appropriation at the heart of *The Searchers*. From this perspective, some critics of the practice see appropriation as a byproduct of a European colonial mentality.

Exercise: Ang Lee was born and raised in Taiwan before attending college in the United States. Contemporary Taiwan is culturally very different from the Regency Period in nineteenth-century England. Setting aside questions about power relationships, is Ang Lee's film Sense and Sensibility *a content appropriation? Is it voice appropriation? If you agree that it is voice appropriation, what follows from the fact that Lee is directing a film written by Emma Thompson, an English woman?*

Ontological contextualism implies several important points about cultural appropriation. In object appropriation, the essential properties of an object are exactly the same before and after its appropriation. *Guernica* is the same object in Spain or the United States. Its identity is not changed, so philosophers say that its appropriation is an identity-preserving behavior. Given its art-historical provenance, *Guernica* is essentially Spanish in origin, and its relationship to Spanish history is a significant reason to regard it as a Spanish national treasure. (There is also the fact that Picasso left it to Spain in his will, but that is not itself the point; England asserts the right to purchase *all* English national treasures at market value whenever a foreign buyer attempts to purchase one.) These claims rest on recognition that the identity of the work is fixed by its origins. Spain can object that Americans have stolen *Guernica* and thus have stolen a Spanish national treasure and harmed the Spanish people. In contrast, it is not clear that the Walt Disney Company has stolen something in its appropriation of *Beauty and the Beast*, or that Ang Lee has stolen from Jane Austen or the English people. It is unclear how a society can *own* content. Furthermore, it is difficult to give a precise explanation of why a case of content, design, or voice appropriations harms anyone (Gracyk 2001a; Young 2008).

A related problem is that content, design, and voice appropriation render a cultural product inauthentic. Content, design, and voice appropriation seem to involve identity-altering behaviors, for they involve copying. Because the copyist is a member of a different culture, the copy is a new object that belongs to a distinct art-historical context. Therefore appropriation alters the *meaning* of what is transferred. Superficially, appropriations have the manifest properties of whatever is appropriated. However, the lesson of ontological contextualism is that the copy has essential, non-manifest properties that differ from those of the source object or design. Because theft requires an identity-preserving exchange while appropriations are identity-altering, it appears to be a serious error to say that these appropriations involve theft. These appropriations may be objectionable, but there is no defensible notion of "property" that would make these things the property of their originating cultures. As we will see in the next section, their transformation in appropriation is generally the basis for the claim that such appropriation is wrong. This identity-alteration undercuts the claim of theft, which is identity-preserving. (For more on the idea of identity-alteration, see Parfit 1984, chs. 16–17.)

Saying that some appropriations are identity-altering follows from the earlier point that cultural provenance informs correct interpretation. Consider the way that *Clueless* appropriates content (but not voice) from Austen's *Emma*. Because this relationship is an essential element of *Clueless*, viewers who know the novel will find *Clueless* more complex than will those who cannot make the connection. Is Amy Heckerling, the writer-director of *Clueless*, suggesting that the young ladies in Austen's novel are romanticized by the distance of time, and that modern audiences fail to grasp their utter frivolity until we experience their contemporary equivalents? Or is there a deeper point – that because the two sets of characters are equivalent, we ought to understand that Austen was documenting universal truths about young women of a certain age and status? Similar questions arise from the way that *Bride and Prejudice* recasts Austen's romance as an encounter between a Hindu woman and an American businessman. Does the film say that cultural differences are trivial and can be overcome with a small effort at understanding? Does it imply that romantic love is superior to arranged marriages? Comedy is often regarded as less "serious" and thus less important than tragedy or drama. (See chapter 8.) However, where appropriation informs the observable structure of a work, as it does with *Clueless* and *Bride and Prejudice*, a light-weight entertainment turns out be a surprisingly serious exploration of larger issues. Appropriation can be a valuable practice.

5.3 Moral concerns

Each species of appropriation generates situations that invite moral disapproval. The theft of objects does wrong to the rightful owners. Other kinds of appropriation involve more subtle issues, but they tend to involve the idea that the appropriation is either disrespectful or does harm. For example, Westminster Abbey is a major tourist attraction in London. At the same time, it is the Collegiate Church of St. Peter, a functioning church. Tourists will enter during church services, and some of them disrupt the services by talking and by taking photographs. When this happens, they are immediately escorted out of the building. I have witnessed such incidences, and have been embarrassed by members of my own culture who rudely disrupted religious services and who then disrupted them again by protesting that they had a "right" to behave in this manner! This situation is by no means specific to Christian churches. Every culture has beliefs about sacred and spiritual places and rituals, and trivializations and misunderstandings easily arise when what is sacred to one group is treated as an entertainment by members of a different culture.

Like the concept of property ownership, the concept of *art* may be part of the problem. When Westerners encounter objects and practices that parallel art as understood in the West, common assumptions about viewing art encourage Westerners to think that the parallel case in the other culture is intended for sharing with an audience and that therefore there can be no offense in viewing and admiring it. Unfortunately, a failure to respect what is sacred or spiritual in another culture can be a matter of very serious disrespect, and this disrespect is not excused by the assumption that whatever looks like art is art. Context matters. However, constructivism undercuts the argument just offered. Blurring the distinction between stable, essential properties that depend on provenance and properties that vary with audience perspective, it implies that "outsider" responses to the artifacts and artworks of unfamiliar cultures cannot be dismissed as misinterpretations. If properties are *imposed* rather than *discovered* during the process of interpretation, then we must accept the validity of the interpretation of viewers who think that the Comanche tribe is treated respectfully by *The Searchers*. Constructivism is no friend to the moral criticism of content, design, and voice appropriation.

Navajo sand "paintings" are an interesting example of this issue. (See also section 3.1.) Because they are aesthetically complex and pleasing, it is tempting to regard them as a species of Navajo art, with all that "art" normally implies. However, embodiments of these designs are not intended for human eyes, and it is a serious violation of Navajo spiritual practice to allow them to be viewed. Because they are fragile and because they are destroyed following their ceremonial use, stable versions are sometimes produced for exhibition and commercial sale – never, however, using an authentic design in all its details. To avoid religious sacrilege, exhibited designs must deviate from those used in actual rituals. Commercial sand paintings are merely similar to the authentic artifacts, and the identity-alteration makes them acceptable to most members of the Navajo tribe (Parezo 1991). The important complication arises whenever non-Navajo artisans produce sand paintings. Depending on the particular case, this activity falls into various categories of appropriation. The common thread is that the creation of an imitation is an identity-altering activity. The object looks like a sacred object, but its ritual significance is stripped away. The public circulation of the appropriations encourages a misunderstanding of, and disregard for, the important properties that give them such high value for the Navajo tribe. Appropriation cheapens the culture from which it borrows. Widespread appropriation can erase the original cultural significance, erasing the culture.

The difficulty is that someone from another culture can agree to everything just said about appropriation without receiving a satisfactory explanation of why these appropriations are so wrong. After all, they are not theft. In response, a series of moral concerns should be distinguished.

- Many cultural appropriations are highly offensive to members of a non-dominant culture, as when both an Arizona winery and a Vermont brewery use a representation of Kokopelli to sell alcohol. (Kokopelli is a flute-playing fertility deity known from Hopi rock art.) How would devout Roman Catholics feel about beer cans that feature images of the crucified Christ? Respect for others implies a respectful treatment of their most significant beliefs and cultural signifiers.

- Even when it is not offensive, appropriation trivializes the non-dominant culture, confusing its own members about the significance of its cultural indicators and cultural heritage. In the United States, the National Congress of American Indians and other Native organizations have denounced appropriation of their cultures as a form of cultural genocide, a racist eradication of genuine Native culture (Johnston 1993).

- Many cultures protect particular designs. They do not allow them to be shared within their own society, so it is wrongful for *anyone* to copy or imitate them. Appropriation of such designs is a violation of the intellectual property rights of those who control them.

- Commercial sale of appropriated designs seldom profits the people who originated the design or style. The widespread commercialization of Kokopelli images is not controlled by the Hopi Nation. Any parallel commercialization of corporate emblems is licensed and regulated, but these safeguards are not enforced when the image is regarded as "traditional."

Our general respect for the domain of the sacred is usually enough to trigger disapproval for Kokopelli images on beer and wine bottles. However, ethical disapproval is much less intense when the appropriation is unrelated to sacred material. It can be difficult to generate support for limitations on other cultural appropriations, even when subordinated cultures regard them as offensive or inappropriate. This lack of psychological motivation might be the result of conceptual confusions about the ethics of appropriation. For philosophers, the central issue is to determine criteria for assigning merit or disapproval.

Another dimension of the problem is that cultural appropriation highlights conflicts among our moral principles. At the risk of oversimplifying the issues, most ethicists recognize a fundamental conflict between respecting people and benefitting people. For example, many people agree that a starving person does nothing wrong in stealing food when there is no other way to get food. Some people justify the theft by emphasizing consequences, focusing on the relative levels of benefit and harm that take place. If the theft is small and a life is saved, the good of saving a life justifies the theft. Against this reasoning, others deny that the ends justify the means. Respecting others requires respect for their property, and from this perspective the theft cannot be justified. This chapter cannot address this long-standing debate. For our purposes, what matters is the point that the ends of promoting artistic and aesthetic value can conflict with the principle of respecting other people, for their wishes are relevant to the criteria for respectful interaction. The non-Navajo who fantasizes that appropriation of a Navajo design preserves and respects Navajo spirituality is engaged in wishful thinking. Within the Navajo Nation, only a small number of medicine men are allowed to work with these designs. If Navajo healers do not want their spiritual practices to be admired as art, then out-siders who reduce their sand paintings to mere designs are disrespectful. It is inherently disrespectful for anyone outside the tribe to suppose that they may engage in behaviors that are of such serious concern to that society. By appropriating the design, a cultural outsider creates an essentially disre-spectful, exploitative object.

The general problems that emerge here are not unique to appropriation across cultural boundaries. It also arises within societies. In *What is Art?*, Leo Tolstoy (1996) discusses an opera production and criticizes it on three counts. It is a voice appropriation that misrepresents the foreign culture it portrays, it relies on a system of art training that exploits large numbers of hopeful young performers, and it provides limited value for the cultural elite without advancing the interests of the majority of society. (Setting aside Tolstoy's point about voice appropriation, his concerns are currently echoed in criticisms of athletic programs that inflict physical injuries, sacrifice of serious academic training, and other personal costs on young women and men who prepare themselves for a sports career that only 1 in 1,000 will achieve.) Although a criticism based on wasted lives is easily understood, it is difficult to quantify the harm of the voice appropriation that Tolstoy identifies.

On the flip side, how do we go about measuring the benefits of appro-priation? James Young (2008) argues that commercial motivations never justify disrespectful cultural appropriation. Only artistic value, such as self-expression, is relevant to counterbalancing any disrespect or harms that result from appropriation. However, this principle can be rejected as arbitrary. Navajo sand painting does not arise from self-expression. So why is the recent Western preoccupation with self-expression relevant when deciding whether Navajo designs should be incorporated into the drapery patterns of a tourist hotel in New Mexico? If self-expression is a justifica-tion, why is Western capitalism any less relevant than self-expression? And if the drapery in tourist hotels seems too trivial to justify design appropria-tion, is that because we should presume appropriation is allowable except in the most offensive cases? Or should we presume that it is forbidden except in the most trivial of cases? The answers to such questions are not clear, yet they arise with increasing frequency. What is clear is that onto-logical contextualism recognizes that artwork identity is a matter of cultural provenance, and therefore borrowings across cultural boundaries give rise to serious political and ethical conflicts.

5.4 Culture

Up to this point, cultural location has been treated as a stable contextual framework for interpretation. We have mentioned appropriation of the Kokopelli figure from *Hopi* culture and a *Taiwanese* director's cinematic treatment of Jane Austen, an *English* writer. These familiar categories become less stable when the idea of culture is examined, for these clas-sifications assume that we can draw clear boundaries around cultures and that we can assign cultural identities to individual artists. Operating with those assumptions, we assign cultural provenance to artworks in order to identify their essential properties. This process seems relatively straightforward when culture is associated with geography, allowing us to say that Austen's *Sense and Sensibility* is an English novel and therefore Ang Lee, raised in Taiwan, must be imposing a non-English sensibility in his film version.

Identification of cultural provenance is complicated by the core idea of culture. Roughly, a culture exists when a social group's belief structure and values are intergenerationally transmitted: one generation transmits them to the next. Language acquisition is a central mechanism for intergenerational transmission, for language is our central tool for sharing beliefs and values. At the same time, language is not the whole of culture. Food, music, rituals, and visual design are other conspicuous embodiments of culture. Because these cultural expressions have an aesthetic dimension that rewards consumption even in the absence of a full cultural understanding, they often appeal to people from other cultures, making them targets for superficial appropriation.

Three important dimensions of cultural instability arise from the insight that each group's belief and value system survives by being transmitted and thus *learned.*

- Apart from cultural exchange, cultures evolve during the process of transmission. Younger generations can (and often do) change what is taught to them. Artistic creativity is an especially potent force for transforming a culture while preserving it.
- All but the simplest of societies recognize subgroups within themselves, and group distinctions are marked and preserved through cultural differences. Few societies are culturally homogeneous and most people already know how to identify and navigate cultural differences.
- Because culture is not innate, the continuation of a culture depends on its being shared. Whatever is shared intergenerationally can also be shared with another society or subculture, and intercultural exchanges between two groups will normally transform both cultures in the exchange.

In light of these points, what is "English" about Austen's novels? The novels display considerable disrespect for inherited power as it operated in English society of her time. Because her novels were widely read, the novels themselves contributed to an evolution in English values. Furthermore, every society permits and restricts selected behaviors as part of its cultural construction of gender identity. In Austen's time, serious literature was a male pursuit. Middle class women were not supposed to write for publication and so Austen published *Sense and Sensibility* anonymously. Critical respect for her writing permitted her to identify herself. As a result, her literary success was an important step in redefining gender roles in English culture. Finally, direct access to Austen's culturally saturated sensibility requires reading her novels. Yet there are bilingual readers, such as Ang

Lee. For those who cannot read English, Austen is translated. For those who cannot read (or, increasingly, prefer not to read), there are film adaptations. Because people in one society have easy access to films, novels, music, and other cultural products of different societies, they have direct access to a slice of "foreign" culture. Consequently, Austen's novels have the power to enter and transform other cultures, just as their integration into her own culture transformed it by that very process.

Modern life offers increased access to multiple cultures. As a result, the implications of cultural transmission and appropriation are not simple. We sell artists short when we try to restrict each artist to a narrow cultural category. Is Lee *merely* a Taiwanese filmmaker? Lee received both a bachelor's and a master's degree in the United States and one of his first experiences with filmmaking was working for Spike Lee, an African-American director. Rather than situate him culturally as Taiwanese, it may be more appropriate to classify him as cosmopolitan citizen – that is, as someone whose cultural position arises from the possibility of meaningful conversation across cultural boundaries and who respectfully integrates aspects of distinct cultures (Appiah 2006). The plot of *Sense and Sensibility* begins with a wrongdoing that is inflicted on the Dashwood women by other members of their own family. Their mistreatment is not merely wrong from the vantage point of English culture. The wrongfulness of depriving your own family of a home and other support when you have wealth is widely understood as morally wrong. The cosmopolitan perspective assumes that cultural perspectives are learned and that they are therefore accessible to anyone who is willing to learn them. If Austen has done her job, then her plot and dialogue will reveal that wrongdoing to any intelligent reader. While there can be difficulties in grasping background assumptions, that difficulty is equally present for 21st-century readers of *Sense and Sensibility*. So there is no unique problem about Lee's ability to grasp Austen's moral perspective on the mistreatment of the Dashwood family. His access is not all that different from that of a 21st-century reader in the south of England, the geographic location of Austen's novels.

Cosmopolitanism is neither modern nor rare. It has existed wherever and whenever distinct cultures have come into prolonged contact. Because cultural familiarity is acquired, the "foreign" and exotic associations of appropriated culture soon evaporate. Hybrid cultural expressions are appreciated and preserved and gain cultural legitimacy. Today, George Frideric Handel is best known for *Messiah* (1741), a large-scale choral work that sets Bible texts to music. Handel had emigrated from Germany to England, so the text is English. Yet Handel had previously lived in Italy and so the music of *Messiah* draws freely on English, German, and Italian musical styles. To audiences of his day, the effect must have been similar to the effect of Sergio Leone's "spaghetti" Western trilogy starring Clint Eastwood, in which an Italian film score accompanies an American actor in Spanish landscapes that marginally resemble the American southwest. Yet Handel's music is as English as the ritual of afternoon tea. Like Handel, "English" tea is imported from elsewhere.

The central points are that a single culture can embrace considerable diversity and that traditions are subject to constant revision. A simplistic conclusion would be that cases of successful appropriation and hybridization show that culture is too fluid and unbounded to allow meaningful application of labels such as "English" and "American." However, a different conclusion is also warranted. Cultural objects and artworks have cultural identities through their provenance. Different works are informed by distinct traditions of values and ideas. Unreflective references to "English values" and "American values" are best treated as broad general categories that encourage greater specification whenever they are used.

Exercise: Japan did not invent the technology of moving pictures. Does it follow that cinema is an inauthentic intrusion into Japanese culture?

5.5 Cultural authenticity

These introductory ideas about culture indicate that cultural authenticity or inauthenticity is a complex, contextual property of an artwork or other cultural product. Before we pursue that point, it is important to distinguish cultural authenticity from two other species of authenticity. In the last chapter we examined forgery. An artifact is a forgery when claims made about its provenance are not true because its actual history of production diverges from the time and place claimed for it. An artifact is genuine when claims about its provenance are accurate. A different species of authenticity is expressive authenticity. It arises in the relationship between an object's expressive properties and the emotions of its maker. Expressive authenticity presupposes an artist-centered theory of expression and directs us away from cultural expression, so we will not consider it here. (See chapter 2.) Cultural authenticity involves a third relationship between truth and provenance. It starts by locating time and place of origin and then looks to the broader social and historical context. Viewed as a cultural (rather than personal) expression, an object is culturally authentic if it reflects the beliefs and values of the culture that informs it.

A simplistic approach aligns cultural authenticity with static, "pure" culture. Any deviation from tradition renders art inauthentic. However, that approach tells us that the Impressionist movement in painting produced inauthentic art. The major Impressionist painters adopted a radically new approach to their art. Their techniques and their choice of content were so contrary to established French standards that their work was not accepted for exhibit in Paris' annual art show, the Salon de Paris. In 1863, the Salon rejected Édouard Manet's great painting *Le déjeuner sur l'herbe* [*Luncheon on the Grass*]. Impressionist painters responded by organizing their own exhibition, the Salon des Refusés (Gallery of the Rejected). By purist standards, the Impressionists broke from French tradition. Yet, looking back, art history regards Impressionism as among the most distinctively *French* of all French art movements! Impressionism demonstrates that a purist analysis of authenticity as adherence to established tradition will result in critical rejection of innovation and therefore of much that is expressively valuable in cultural innovation. Authenticity should not be defined in any way that privileges a routine continuation of established style and content.

You might respond that Impressionism was authentic because it was a *local* art movement and it would only have lacked authenticity if it arose from cultural appropriation. Cultural appropriations are necessarily inauthentic. So are hybrid designs, such as Handel's *Messiah*. Creativity that arises from these sources deprives art of authenticity. Since Impressionism was not inspired by cultural appropriation, the argument continues, it is authentically French culture. In response, arguments of this sort are generally uninformed by historical fact. Manet and many other Impressionists were directly influenced by the style and content of Japanese prints that were imported into France in the middle of the nineteenth century. Stylistically, these foreign influences encouraged French artists to revise their use of color and to reduce pictorial depth. With respect to content, there is a shift away from mythological subjects and toward portraying everyday reality. Again, if cultural appropriation is sufficient to destroy authenticity, then Impressionism lacks authenticity. And again, our sense that Impressionism is *not* lacking in cultural authenticity in relation to French life and values shows that this notion of authenticity should be rejected.

Another spin on the argument says that nineteenth-century France was cosmopolitan enough to absorb Japanese influences without loss of authenticity. However, a more homogeneous culture would become culturally inauthentic through a similar level of appropriation.

This general claim about homogeneous cultures is also implausible. Think of the three films mentioned at the beginning of this chapter, and then consider the fact that the art of telling stories with film is just over a hundred years old. The details do not require attention here. It is enough to recognize that filmmaking was initially a French, German, and American pursuit. Despite this fact, no one concludes that the strong film tradition of Japan is therefore inauthentic due to the relative homogeneity of Japanese culture. Technologies are subject to appropriation, and the fact that early films lacked soundtracks allowed "silent" movies to circulate globally with relatively few obstacles. (See the discussion of mass art in section 8.1.) Once we recognize that it is easier for a member of the next generation to become a competent film watcher than it is to become an equally competent reader of their "home" literary tradition, we have a good reason to allow that the Japanese film tradition arose as an authentic adaptation of a new technology by a new generation. Yet the widespread adoption of new technologies hastens the pace of cultural change.

If innovation through appropriation does not generate cultural inauthenticity, then a failure of authenticity must follow from details that are specific to a particular case. The real issue will be *how* the new content, style, or technology is adapted to local needs. Impressionism can be authentic, but some individual painters and paintings will be inauthentic. Japanese cinema can be authentic, but some filmmakers and films will be inauthentic. Here are two candidates. Akira Kurosawa's film *Ran* (1985) is a Japanese samurai movie. What's more Japanese than that? However, it is culturally inauthentic because its basic content is William Shakespeare's *King Lear* (*c*.1605). (Kurosawa had previously made other samurai movies based on other Shakespeare plays.) Another Kurosawa film, *One Wonderful Sunday* (1947), follows the interactions of a young couple on a single Sunday in postwar Tokyo. However, the music of nineteenth-century Viennese composer Franz Schubert plays an important role in the film's plot. For cultural purists, Kurosawa's cultural appropriations seem to be insurmountable obstacles to authenticity.

As before, we need only acknowledge that Japan has interacted with many Western societies since the nineteenth century. Educated Japanese of Kurosawa's generation were more likely to know about Shakespeare and Western classical music than educated Westerners were likely to know a similar amount about Japanese literary and music traditions. In making a film about his own time and place, *One Wonderful Sunday* accurately portrays a level of existing Japanese cosmopolitanism. The importance of Schubert's music reflects the infusion of Western high culture into the cultural life of Japan. Given the film's historical backdrop, the presence of this music strengthens Kurosawa's exploration of Japanese identity in the wake of his country's surrender to Western forces at the conclusion of the Second World War. With respect to *Ran*, it is worth noting that Shakespeare was no cultural purist, either. Shakespeare's content was drawn from many sources, including Roman history and Mediterranean culture. Although they are among his most famous films, Kurosawa's samurai films are also historically distant from his own place and time. His cultural appropriations appear to be a case of adopting Shakespeare's *methods* and not just his content. Furthermore, Kurosawa mixes the Shakespearean content with parallel Japanese myths. Several of the central characters of *Ran* display manifest influences of the Japanese tradition of Noh theatre. If Kurosawa's methods result in cultural inauthenticity, then Shakespeare's plays must be criticized as equally inauthentic. A better conclusion is that neither is inauthentic in any interesting way. It is both hypocritical and ethnocentric to praise creativity in one culture while criticizing parallel developments in another.

If we hesitate to say that Impressionist painting and Kurosawa's films are culturally inauthentic, it is tempting to say that authenticity is more than a simple *fact* about a work's cultural location. Authenticity is a *normative category* for evaluating art. In calling something "normative," philosophers mean that application of the concept requires a value judgment. "Evil" and "beautiful" are rather obviously normative. Saying that something is evil indicates that it is undesirable, and saying that something is beautiful praises and recommends it. Is authenticity meritorious? In other words, is it a term of recommendation, like "beautiful?"

It is not at all clear that "authenticity" is a term of recommendation. Because the presence or absence of authenticity is relative to the standards of the originating culture, the proposal that "authenticity" conveys a positive evaluation is undermined by a criticism that many philosophers direct at ethical relativism. Consider a society that excludes women from many meaningful social roles and that enforces rigid class distinctions that consign some people to a hereditary underclass. Some authentic art of this society will uphold these values. In this context, authenticity will function as a tool of discrimination and subordination. Art that violates problematic social norms will lack a degree of authenticity. Recall the earlier observation that Austen's fiction shows considerable disrespect for the customs and the titled nobility of her time. In *Pride and Prejudice*, the English inheritance system is challenged as a source of unjustified harm and Lady Catherine's prejudices and behavior are unfavorably contrasted with poor Elizabeth Bennet. Can we praise art for its inauthentic recommendation of respect for social outsiders and praise it for subverting prevailing values? We certainly can. However, to do so, we must reject the blanket assumption that authentic, tradition-affirming art is good art. Furthermore, the authentic art can be artistically shoddy and aesthetically boring compared to inauthentic art that affirms the worth of subordinated groups. Although we should interpret and evaluate art in relation to its social and historical context, inauthentic art can be both socially and artistically better than authentic art. (See also Gracyk 2007: 167–75.)

Exercise: Early jazz was the music of a geographically localized African-American subculture. The same was true of early hip-hop or rap. If the early stages of these two musical movements express values contrary to those of the dominant culture, do they count as authentic expressions of American life? Explain. Does the answer to that question have any relevance to their value as music?

5.6 Modernity and authenticity

A number of philosophers, artists, critics, and other intellectuals are drawn to a radical notion of authenticity advanced by Theodor Adorno (2004 [1970]). Influenced by the theories of G. W. F. Hegel and Karl Marx (see section 3.4), Adorno explores the issue of how modernity has redefined the conditions for authenticity. "Modern" does not simply mean "recent" or "contemporary." It refers to intellectual and social tendencies that developed in response to the rise of industry, capitalism, and urbanization in the mid to late nineteenth century (Ayers 2004). (Industry, capitalism, and urbanization predate the nineteenth century. However, their spread and synergistic integration accelerated in the nineteenth century.) Modernity gave greater legitimacy to individualism, secularism, and self-exploration, and it had an enormous influence on a great deal of twentieth-century art. Impressionism is arguably the first "modern" art.

Adorno emphasizes that capitalism has radically transformed life, and not for the better. Almost every aspect of modern life is structured by unseen economic forces. Although Adorno did not live to see the technology that provides texting from mobile telephones, it is a nice example of his point. Instead of dealing with other people directly, many people "text" their basic exchanges of information to one another, permitting telecommunication companies to transform routine interactions into a profitable commodity. Corporations increasingly re-engineer our lives for their profit. Art has also become a commodity. Major artworld institutions are capitalist enterprises. What does it matter, then, if art is "traditional" in its content and design? "Art for art's sake" was the great art slogan of the nineteenth century, and it indicated that artists should be free to make art that defies traditional expectations and conventional morality. When the same idea is put to work in the context of modern capitalism, art *seems* to be free of social constraints, but the truth about art is that it is just another element of industrial, corporate life. The Clash, a socially conscious punk band, captures Adorno's critique in "White Man in Hammersmith Palais" (1978). In lyrics set to appropriated reggae music, the song complains that commercialized punk rock is just another pop movement, "turning rebellion into money" by selling it to kids who are only "looking for fun." (For more on Adorno on popular culture, see sections 8.2 and 8.3.)

This brief summary of Adorno sets the stage for understanding his proposal that very little modern art qualifies as authentic. Art is a small part of our larger culture. It is the vital segment of culture that is not expected to perform any immediately useful social function. However, the minor amounts of creativity we see in most art are insufficient to distinguish it from mainstream entertainment. Relative to the art-historical context of modernity, Ang Lee's *Sense and Sensibility* is neither more nor less authentic than Amy Heckerling's *Clueless*. Both films are a commercial product that celebrates the personal growth and eventual success of the central characters. Both films are pleasing distractions for their intended audiences. If anything, the seeming "authenticity" of *Sense and Sensibility* opens it up to the charge that it promotes a greater lie. Both films are appealing because they distract us from social facts that we would rather not face. However, *Sense and Sensibility* romanticizes the past and so it is guilty of the additional sin of falsely suggesting that people are still in touch with pre-modern values. Artists should face the fact that modernity has separated authenticity from tradition. Today, the preservation of familiar, traditional design principles and content is inauthentic. There is no going back.

Exercise: List several distinct practices that you regard as traditional practices of your own culture. Does any of this "tradition" come to you without commodification? (Do not overlook the fact that digital access requires the purchase of electricity and access.) Then discuss whether "your" culture is unified in its traditions. Can you expect everyone in it to endorse these same traditional practices?

Adorno (1973 [1964]) adopts several binary oppositions in the construction of his argument. Tradition is opposed to the present, part is opposed to whole, and purpose is opposed to structure. He proposes that modern life has forever changed our relationship to traditional culture. The historical disruptions of the twentieth century have gutted our traditions. They have become empty structures. (In this respect, Adorno endorses constructivism, as discussed above in section 5.1.) Authenticity must be sought in contemporary relevance, rather than artistic tradition and cultural origins. *economic, industrial relevance* Endorsing the idea that art requires creative freedom, he proposes that authenticity derives from an artwork's structure rather than its representational purpose. Structural innovation must be radical, fragmented, and without formal closure so that it will resist commodification. Although Adorno tends to explain this point by discussing music, his idea has general applicability. Prokofiev's First Symphony imitates Haydn, but Adorno attacks all such neo-classicism and neo-traditionalism as inauthentic. At the same time, we hide the emptiness of such gestures from ourselves with our misleading appeals to "authenticity." Within modernity, only the most avant-garde music can be truthful and thus authentic. Finally, the various parts of a work are not important. A true artwork is the sum of the whole work. (Liking a movie or song because you like an actress or singer is a typical audience failure to understand art, and it is exploited by capitalism to "sell" commercial products.) By structurally resisting audience expectations, avant-garde music can function as a genuine social protest and so it can encourage audience members to confront their shallow expectations and thus their own social conformity.

Let us conclude by applying Adorno's idea to film. The narrative closure of the happy endings of *Clueless* and *Bride and Prejudice* is essential to their commodity status. However, no viewer becomes aware of her real social position by watching such films. So-called "independent" films are no better. Today, authenticity requires a fragmentation of narrative structure and resistance to all audience expectations. In short, an authentic film will not find its way to megaplex movie theatres. It is difficult to provide an example of a movie that satisfies this standard of authenticity. There are some strange and disturbing films that come close to satisfying this standard, such as David Lynch's *Eraserhead* (1976) and Guy Madden's *Archangel* (1990), but these were shown in theatres and they are available for purchase. They exist as commercial products in what Adorno calls the "culture industry," so they are not radical enough to count as authentic. If Adorno is correct, it is likely that you have never experienced authenticity in art.

Issues to think about

1. Explain the distinction between contingent and essential properties. Next, select two objects that you can see at this moment. (Do not select artworks.) Distinguish between some of the essential and contingent properties of each object. Finally, identify perceptible and imperceptible relationships that each object has to other objects. Are any of these relationships essential to the identity of either of the objects you selected?

2. Explain the difference between ontological contextualism and constructivism. Which position do you regard as more plausible when

assigning a meaning to Ogden Nash's line, "Candy is dandy, but liquor is quicker?" Which is more plausible in assigning a meaning to Mary Richardson's action of attacking the *Rokeby Venus* with a meat cleaver?

3. Crazy Horse was a leader of the Oglala Lakota tribe who inspired his people to resist the encroachment of the United States into Indian Territory. A century later, Native Americans sued a corporation for naming a product "Crazy Horse Malt Liquor." The Lakota people are also known as the Sioux, and many of them objected to the use of "The Fighting Sioux" as the nickname of a college athletics program. Many members of the dominant culture do not understand their objections and defended these appropriations. Do you think that the appropriations are acceptable? Why or why not?

4. American film director Kevin Smith was raised as a Roman Catholic. *Dogma* (1999), Smith's fourth film, deals with the topic of organized religion. It gives serious offense to many Roman Catholics. Are the offensive elements of *Dogma* excusable on the grounds that Smith is an "insider" who criticizes his own culture? Would the film be more objectionable if the only difference was that it was written and directed by a Jewish or Hindu filmmaker?

Further resources

There is a large literature on authenticity, some of which avoids talk of "authenticity" in favor of talk of what is "historically informed," among other euphemisms. Focusing on music, Peter Kivy's *Authenticities* (1995) surveys major types of musical authenticity. An alternative tradition on authenticity stems from Heidegger (1971) and it is the primary target of Adorno (1973). Stecker (2003) provides an excellent overview of contextualism. Varieties of contextualism are defended by Silvers (1991), Krausz (1993), Margolis (1995), Carroll (2001), Davies (2001), Bacharach (2005), and Lamarque (2010). Interesting philosophical discussions of appropriation are Gracyk (2001b), Brown (2004), Young (2008), and Rudinow (2010). Coleman (2005) discusses the topic from the vantage point of anthropology. Shiner (2003b) discusses the cross-cultural applicability of the concept of appropriation. Young and Brunk (2009) is a collection of essays that offers multiple perspectives on the moral issues.

The Gods Must Be Crazy (1980) is a slapstick comedy that explores problems that arise when a lone Western artifact finds its way into a tribal society. Chronicling the fortunes of gay prostitutes, *My Own Private Idaho* (1991) is a striking case of voice appropriation: parts of the script come directly from William Shakespeare's "Prince Hal" plays. Akira Kurosawa's *Throne of Blood* (1957) and *Ran* (1985) appropriate Shakespeare's content rather than his language. Tolstoy's criticisms of the exploitation involved in the production of opera are an important element of *Black Swan* (2010), a tragedy about the physical and psychological price of ballet. Sexual exploitation is added to Tolstoy's list.

6 Defining Art

Leonardo da Vinci's mural *The Last Supper* (*c.*1495–8), is a famous work of art. It is also a major tourist attraction in Milan, Italy. However, it was not commissioned in order to be a tourist attraction, and da Vinci did not paint it with that purpose in mind. Its status as a tourist attraction was acquired later, after the fact. In contrast to *The Last Supper*, some things are essentially tourist attractions, such as Disneyland, the London Eye (a massive Ferris wheel in central London), and the gambling casinos of Las Vegas. Perhaps, like *The Last Supper*, these are works of art, too. But that would take some argument. To make that argument we need a definition of art.

6.1 Philosophical definition

You might suppose we can simply look up "art" in a dictionary and settle it. Not so. Dictionaries are linguistic tools that explain the standard spellings and uses of words. However, we are seeking guidance in classifying objects, which normally requires identifying the features that distinguish artworks from other, similar kinds of things. Most dictionary definitions succeed by listing roughly synonymous terms, which is seldom of use in deciding whether a particular object is properly described by a particular word.

Exercise: Look up "justice" in a dictionary. Does it help you to resolve the question of whether it is just or unjust to tax married couples at a different tax rate from unmarried cohabiting couples? Next, look up "art" and produce a counterexample to that definition by naming a famous artwork that does not fit the primary definition given there.

In contrast to dictionary definitions, one purpose in constructing philosophical definitions is to resolve debates about the classification of difficult cases. The standard philosophical approach to definition is to locate the *necessary and jointly sufficient conditions* for being a particular sort of thing. We must locate the relevant set of features, each of which is individually required (necessary) for being that particular sort of thing and which, taken as a group, are unique to that sort of thing (jointly sufficient). It can be surprisingly difficult to locate the right grouping of properties. Suppose that someone argues that the London Eye cannot be an artwork because it was designed to be a tourist attraction. That argument misfires. To be successful, the argument must demonstrate that the object lacks at least one of the necessary properties for being an artwork. This argument proceeds differently, by pointing to a property the object possesses. Works of art possess a wide array of incidental properties, such as being made in 1830 or celebrating a revolutionary uprising. (See section 5.1.) Yet the presence of these two properties does not demonstrate that Eugene Delacroix's *Liberty Leading the People* – painted in 1830 to celebrate the Paris uprising of earlier that year – is not art. Likewise, being designed to be a tourist attraction does not demonstrate that the London Eye is not art. We must specify what it lacks.

Part of the problem is that a *property* is a distinguishable feature that is common to several objects. Therefore each of the individual requirements in a philosophical definition is likely to be a property of other kinds of things, too. The good news is that there is very strong consensus about the first necessary property for being an artwork. There is near-universal agreement that a definition of art must include the basic requirement that the thing in question is an artifact, that is, the product of human activity. (In this context, *artifact* is to be understood broadly. It is not restricted to material objects. As I am using the term, the song "Happy Birthday to You" is an artifact, as is each performance of it.) So far, the London Eye qualifies, and therefore we must consider other necessary properties. Unfortunately, there is very little agreement about which properties must be combined with the artifactuality requirement.

Newcomers to philosophy will often seize on the sufficiency of a set of conditions as a definition. However, this overlooks the importance of finding properties that are present in *all* objects of this sort. It sometimes happens that a loosely related set of properties will prove sufficient to indicate that a particular artifact is art. For example, being a Parisian tourist attraction that was painted by da Vinci is sufficient for being an artwork. (There aren't that many paintings by da Vinci in Paris, they're all tourist attractions, and they are all works of art.) Consider da Vinci's *La Joconde* or *Mona Lisa* (*c*.1503–7), one of Paris' preeminent tourist attractions. We can imagine removing it from Paris, or leaving it there but depriving access to tourists. Would it cease to be art? Certainly not. Being located in Paris and being a tourist attraction are contingent or accidental properties of art, because artworks will remain artworks even if they lose either of these properties. Admittedly, no one is tempted to *equate* art with tourist attractions painted by da Vinci. This example is merely an indication of how difficult it is to define art, since many other properties that you might regard as important for art status will turn out to be equally contingent. For example, *The Last Supper* was created by applying egg-tempera paint to a stucco wall. These properties are decisive in classifying it as a painting, and *that* property might be a reason to regard it as an artwork. Suppose that da Vinci made the mural by embedding small bits of colored stone into the wet stucco. Then it would be a mosaic rather than a painting. Furthermore, some of its related properties would be different – perhaps for the better, since the tempera paint faded quickly and a mosaic would have retained da Vinci's intended coloring. However, we are likely to agree that da Vinci could have created an artwork using either medium. Like its status as a tourist attraction, the actual material instantiation of *The Last Supper* seems to be incidental to its being art. (See the discussion of ontology in chapter 4.)

6.2 Historical background

Although debating the proper definition of art is a major topic in contemporary philosophy of art, this debate arose relatively recently. Plato and Aristotle debated about the *value* of art in the fourth century BCE, but they did not debate about the proper definition of "art." They had no such word in their vocabulary, nor any other word or phrase that neatly translates into our modern word. They discussed *technē*, which embraces all skilled making. Aristotle treats it as equivalent to rationally principled activity, which includes architecture, logic, and medicine (Aristotle 1997: 66). Plato and Aristotle concentrate on mimetic or imitative representation as a sub-category of *technē*. However, we have already seen (in chapter 1) that many representations are not art. Because we today recognize a great deal of non-representational art, such as abstract paintings, it is clear that our classification does not align neatly with the conceptual categories discussed in early philosophy of art.

It is also doubtful that da Vinci operated with our modern concept. Some of our oldest source material on da Vinci and his working methods was assembled by Giorgio Vasari (1511–74), the author, painter, and architect who first labeled his historical period as the "Renaissance," a rebirth. Although Vasari's collection of biographies is often translated as *The Lives of the Artists* (Vasari 1991), a more accurate translation is *The Lives of the Most Excellent Painters, Sculptors, and Architects*. In sixteenth-century Italian, the nearest equivalents for our terms "art" and "artist" were wider categories, closer to "craft" and "artisan" than to our modern concepts. A sixteenth-century book about "artists" would miss the mark, reducing art to mere craft. Resisting cultural consensus, da Vinci argued that painting is a significant activity. It is a science (da Vinci 1989: 13–20). He saw himself as an intellectual who advanced the liberal arts by exploring the structures of nature, rather than a mere skilled artisan.

Vasari died in 1574, shortly before the birth of what we now recognize as modern philosophy. The first explicit definition of art in something like our current sense, as fine art, appears in 1746, when Charles Batteux offers a definition of "les beaux arts" that combines the requirements of beauty, imitative representation, and exploration of nature (including expressive human behavior). Batteux employs the standard approach to philosophical definition, where several properties are proposed as individually necessary and then, in combination, sufficient. More importantly, Batteux wants to distinguish between the fine arts and the older meaning of "art" that embraces all of the technical or "mechanical" arts. He restricts the fine arts to music, dance, poetry, painting, and sculpture. From Batteux's perspective, Vasari made a mistake in grouping architects with painters and sculptors. Architecture is an impure or mixed art that must balance practical use against visual appearance. Recognizing that the fine arts are historically dependent on the patronage of a leisure class, he proposes that fine art has an essential *function*: fine art need not instruct us, but it must provide pleasurable diversion. To Batteux, da Vinci's claim that painting is a science amounts to a denial of the true nature of *The Last Supper*.

Exercise: Is it plausible that a great artist could misunderstand the purpose of art?

Batteux's definition was widely endorsed by European intellectuals. It was also widely amended. Many authors wanted to classify architecture as a fully fledged fine art. Others looked for ways to extend the definition to instrumental music, very little of which can be plausibly regarded as featuring imitative representation. However, the rising demand for such music – both for home performance and for the concert hall – led to a reconsideration of the mimetic or imitative requirement. Traditionalists stuck to their guns and adopted Batteux's suggestion that all music naturally imitates human expressive qualities. A more radical strain of post-Kantian philosophers proposed that music has a natural power to exhibit or represent the deeper, hidden structures of reality (Kivy 1997: 4–27). For them, music was the direct expression of the spiritual, which suggests that *all* fine art has a deeper spiritual purpose. Nineteenth-century intellectuals explored many variations on this idea, and then at the dawn of the twentieth century it spilled from music to painting in Wassily Kandinsky's highly influential book, *Concerning the Spiritual in Art*. When music is produced by a creative genius, such as Ludwig van Beethoven, it has a unique capacity to advance our spiritual progress. The best modern painting and literature can do the same (Kandinsky 1977). Taking instrumental music as the paradigm of spiritually advanced art, Kandinsky put theory into practice by becoming a pioneer in the field of abstract painting, confirming critic Walter Pater's famous observation, "All art constantly aspires towards the condition of music" (Pater 2010 [1877]: 124).

Although Batteux and Kandinsky sharply disagree on art's essential purpose, they are philosophically not so very far apart. Their overall strategy is the same. Both recommend a functional definition of fine art, identifying a distinctive purpose as a necessary condition. Given how many different functional definitions have been proposed, our next task is to take a step back and consider whether this general strategy makes sense. At the same time, there is an old saying that you should be careful what you wish for. If we are seeking a functional definition of *fine art*, it is possible that the recent historical recognition of the category is a symptom that the function in question was not valued until recently. Or perhaps this function was not distinctively present in a broad class of objects until shortly before Batteux constructed his definition. Either way, a successful definition might endorse a narrow, Eurocentric category. You might assume that Australian Aboriginal bark paintings are art, or that the architecture of the twelfth-century Hindu temple of Angkor Wat is an artistic achievement. However, you should not assume that they will turn out to be art according to a definition that successfully groups together Delacroix's *Liberty Leading the People* and Beethoven's piano sonatas while excluding the casinos of Las Vegas.

6.3 Functional definitions

Most artifacts are classified according to purpose or functionality. Looking around my desk area, I see scissors, a pad of lined paper, a coffee mug, and a tea tin. Above, there is a painting that my sister-in-law did in art school. The scissors are for cutting, the pad of paper is for writing things down, the tin keeps moisture away from bags of tea, and the mug holds hot beverages. Each of these objects can be used for other purposes, too. I've used both my mug and my scissors as a temporary bookmark. Yet most of us will understand that these are non-standard uses, and that bookmarking is not their primary function. In this section we will consider the strategy that defines art in terms of its unique, primary function. *Functionalists* regard this approach as the proper strategy for defining art. As Stephen Davies observes, "A functionalist on the matter of the definition of art will judge a definition to be adequate only if it explains the point of our distinguishing art from other things" (Davies 1991: 44).

So what about the painting that hangs on my office wall? What function distinguishes it from other kinds of artifacts? The painting certainly has a function: it decorates my office with vibrant color. But does that function make it an artwork? My desk scissors have a bright blue handle that contributes a splash of color to my office. However, that is independent of their function as a cutting instrument, the function relevant to classifying them as scissors. Typically, functional definitions of art assume that art's distinctive function is not that of being decorative or, to return to our earlier example, of attracting tourists. However, eliminating various functions as non-essential does not get us very far in resolving the serious and long-standing disagreement about which function is the relevant one. This disagreement is one of the primary reasons why philosophy of art is a distinctive area within philosophy and why there are no such areas as the philosophy of tables or the philosophy of scissors.

From Batteux until the middle of the twentieth century, functionalism was the only game in town when it came to defining art. Previous chapters of this book have already discussed a number of candidates for art's function, so you should have no difficulty in understanding the basic ideas in the following functional definitions of art.

- According to the mimetic theory, an artifact x is a work of art only if x succeeds in imitating some object, scene, or sequence of events. (See chapter 1.)
- According to the expression theory, an artifact x is a work of art only if x succeeds in expressing emotion. (See chapter 2.)
- According to the cognitive theory, an artifact x is a work of art only if x conveys new insights about the world. (See sections 3.3 and 9.7.)
- According to the aesthetic theory, an artifact x is a work of art only if x succeeds aesthetically. (See chapter 7.)

Although these schematic definitions do not attempt to provide sufficient conditions for art, they have two features in common. First, they preserve the usual requirement of originating in a human practice: an artwork is necessarily an artifact. Second, they agree in insisting that success in a particular function is a requirement for being a work of art. The theories differ only by disagreeing on what that function is. To the non-functionalist, this disagreement is relatively trivial.

There is an overwhelming objection to functional definitions. Different artworks are correctly valued for performing very different functions, and therefore there cannot be a unifying functional definition for art. Notice that the objection rests on being *correctly* valued. Most things are valued for multiple reasons, in part because most things can be used creatively, in novel ways. For example, you can remove a cork from a wine bottle by placing the bottom of the bottle into the heel of a shoe and then tapping the heel on a wall or door jamb. However, this does not demonstrate that handmade Italian leather shoes are correctly valued as substitutes for corkscrews. Similarly, classical music is sometimes played in and around stores in order to discourage teenagers from congregating there. The store managers value the music for reducing petty theft and nuisance loitering. However, J. S. Bach's *St. Matthew Passion* (1727) is not correctly valued for driving people away. The objection to functionalism is not based on unintended or highly unusual uses.

The objection to functionalism arises from the fact that we can specify at least two artworks that are correctly valued for performing completely independent functions. Bach's *St. Matthew Passion* is correctly valued for its expression of religious devotion, for its dramatic expression of human emotion, for its insights into the human psyche, and for its formal and aesthetic excellence. In sum, it performs all of the functions stipulated in the major functionalist definitions. However, Marcel Duchamp's *Fountain* (1917) performs only one of those functions, that of providing some level of insight, most notably into the nature of art (see section 1.4). The same holds true, perhaps, for conceptual art in general. At the same time, there are artworks that do not perform the function of providing new insights. The Italian Renaissance painter Raphael Santi executed more than two dozen portraits on the familiar theme of the Madonna and baby Jesus, and he was merely one of many painters churning them out. Say what you will about the best of them, it is not plausible to correctly value *The Madonna of the Pinks* (c.1506) for providing new insights. Likewise, the accusation of banality is commonly launched at all work that is formulaic, mannered, and overtly derivative. Yet a lack of fresh insight does not prevent such work from being art. Consequently, unless one is going to take the very bold step of denying that a good deal of what we recognize to be art is really art, functionalism appears doomed on the grounds that different artworks are regarded as art despite the fact that they are correctly valued in terms of completely different functions.

A second objection deserves attention. When we evaluate a functional artifact, we evaluate it relative to its primary function. A leaky umbrella is a bad umbrella, and so one might also contend – as many people do – that an ugly painting is a bad painting. However, if satisfying a specified function is a necessary condition for being art, then no evaluation of any artwork can ever dismiss it as genuinely terrible. If it receives a negative evaluation because it cannot perform its intended function, then it simply does not count as having satisfied the functional requirement. Since that means it is not art, it is incoherent to say that it is bad art. However, the objection continues, there is obviously a lot of very bad art in the world, and any theory that implies that we cannot give strongly negative evaluations is a misguided theory.

To fully appreciate this objection, let us return to Leo Tolstoy's version of the expression theory (see section 2.2). According to Tolstoy, expressivity requires a certain minimum of clarity. If the expression is too indefinite, then nothing is being expressed. On these grounds, Tolstoy argues that Beethoven's Piano Sonata No. 28, Op. 101 (1816) is too "obscure" in its expression. Therefore it is "an unsuccessful attempt at art," a charge that he extends to most of the music of Beethoven's "late" period (Tolstoy 1996: 135). Tolstoy has now deprived himself of any standard for saying what he really means, which is that Beethoven's Piano Sonata No. 28 is *bad art*, that is, ineptly conceived and executed art. We should therefore avoid functional definitions, because they inevitably confuse the issue of whether something is art with the independent question of whether it is worth our time.

However, is the no-bad-art objection really so damaging? Probably not. If you are designing voice-recognition software for a security system, but it fails to distinguish between a soprano voice with a thick German accent and a bass voice with a Louisiana Cajun accent, then you have simply failed to produce voice-recognition software. It is so bad that it doesn't deserve the classification. In contrast, voice recognition software that usually works, but has trouble distinguishing between siblings with similar voices, is functionally poor software. Analogously, it makes sense to say that complete failures – expressively, aesthetically, or however else – are not art. But most bad art does not fail completely, which leaves plenty of room for saying that some art is very bad art. Tolstoy has simply set the bar in the wrong place. His argument is that Beethoven's piano sonata lacks definite feeling, particularly when compared with folk songs, Bach's melodies, and much of Beethoven's earlier music. Tolstoy fails to make the case that the piano sonata is completely devoid of emotional expression, and so Tolstoy should classify it as very bad art, rather than dismiss it as "an unsuccessful attempt at art." (The fact that expression theorists can deny art status to expressively neutral art is a different matter. That is not the mistake that is alleged by the no-bad-art objection.)

Looking at this particular debate, you might extract a different lesson, which is to endorse a variation on the basic strategy of defining art functionally. Why not say that Beethoven *intended* to express emotion in the piano sonata, and that is the reason it is art? Unsuccessful paintings and music are artworks if they are intended to have the proper function. This appeal to intentions has the effect of allowing us to regard complete misfires as really terrible art, yet nonetheless art. Returning to the four functional definitions outlined earlier in this section, we get something like this:

- an artifact x is a work of art only if the person who produced x intended x to imitate some object, scene, or sequence of events
- an artifact x is a work of art only if the person who produced x intended to express emotion through x.

And likewise for the remaining functions.

Exercise: Make an "x" on a sheet of paper. Does this mark have the function of pictorially imitating a cow? If not, why not? Could the same mark on the paper pictorially imitate a cow by drawing it with the intention to look like a cow?

The appeal to intentions is frequently attacked as an appeal to artists' subjective and unverifiable mental states, turning attention away from the objective features of the artifacts. Due to a very influential article on literary interpretation by William Wimsatt and Monroe C. Beardsley (1946), appeals to artistic intention are sometimes dismissed without further comment as "the intentional fallacy." (Wimsatt and Beardsley are also discussed in section 5.1.) Their position denies that an author's intentions are relevant to understanding what a literary work means. They conclude that there is no point in appealing to intentions. The intentions are confirmed by the work, in which case we do not need to refer to the intentions, or they are not, in which case they are irrelevant. After all, Tolstoy seems to find evidence that Beethoven wanted to express emotion in the sonata, but he thinks Beethoven did a poor job of it. Unless Tolstoy's evidence is some letter or diary entry by Beethoven, Tolstoy must recognize the music's expressive function from some fact about the music itself, and so there is no need to appeal to Beethoven's intentions. Alternatively, we might deny that intentions are subjective and unverifiable mental states. We do not need to cite Beethoven's explicit pronouncements about his intentions. (And, if we had evidence of them, we would have to ask if the evidence was faked, an issue of genuine concern when it comes to the music of Soviet composer Dmitri Shostakovich.) To the extent that we need to appeal to intentions, human behaviors and the products of their activity offer adequate evidence of intentions. We will return to the topic of intentions below, in section 6.5.

6.4 Institutional definitions

The alleged major problem with citing intentions and purposes is that they are not observable. To put it another way, purposes and intended purposes are not *manifest* features of things. They are not available to the eye or ear. We are prone to overlook this fact because we seldom interact with artifacts without understanding their intended purposes, so an object's manifest features usually inform us of its purpose. However, consider an encounter with an unfamiliar artifact. Discovering such an artifact, two archeologists can disagree on its purpose. We don't have to look very far into the past for this effect. The television program *This Old House* features a reoccurring segment in which builders and contractors are challenged to classify nineteenth-century tools by sight alone. They are frequently baffled. (Have a look at Duchamp's *Bottle Rack* [1914] and guess at its original purpose.) Although the Paleolithic cave paintings of Altamira and Lascaux are featured in many art-history texts as examples of the earliest art, there is considerable debate about their specific purpose, beyond some vague notion of religious significance. Why, then, fasten on purposes? Perhaps some *other* non-manifest feature of fine art is the necessary condition around which to build our definition.

This insight was encouraged by the art experiments of the twentieth century, and by art galleries and exhibitions that presented strange new artifacts, musical works, and conceptual challenges. As it became increasingly clear that many modern artists were no longer bound by the traditional purposes of art, philosophers proposed that the *social and historical location* of an artifact might be more essential than its function. Perhaps Duchamp's *Fountain* was a sculpture rather than a mere plumbing fixture because he had an opportunity for exploiting institutional settings – an art exhibition and an avant-garde art magazine – that gave it that status. Instead of thinking that the Museum of Modern Art exhibited Walker Evans' photographs in 1938 because they are art and the museum was recognizing them as such, perhaps they are art because the museum exhibited them.

The result is the *institutional theory of art*. The basic insight derives from Arthur Danto's reflections on some of Andy Warhol's work in the early 1960s, particularly Warhol's imitations of Brillo boxes. (See section 1.4.) If two objects are visually indiscernible, yet one is an artwork and the other is not, then a non-manifest feature must explain the difference. Danto proposes that the difference is "an atmosphere of theory the eye cannot de[s]cry," meaning that a general, shared understanding of what is being accomplished by creating each object is the key to saying why only one of the two indiscernible objects is a work of art (Danto 1964: 580). Objects that arise from the theoretical commitments of a social network called the "artworld" are artworks. Objects that do not arise from those commitments are not. Danto later expanded on his idea in *The Transfiguration of the Commonplace* (1981), making it clear that the theoretical background of the artworld is merely one of several necessary conditions for art (see Carroll 1993). Greatly simplified, Danto proposes that something is a work of art if and only if it is an artifact, it is to be interpreted as offering a point of view about something, and its non-explicit message can only be understood by those who interpret it in light of its art-historical context.

For example, someone who approaches da Vinci's *The Last Supper* as a commissioned Renaissance religious work will reject the interpretation offered by the character Leigh Teabing in *The Da Vinci Code* (Brown 2003). Teabing says that the apostle John is missing from the painting, having been replaced by Mary Magdalene. But this "reading" treats it as a major deviation from the norms of the art-historical context of the Italian Renaissance.

Teabing interprets it as the personal expression of da Vinci. However, the assumption that da Vinci is making a unique, personal statement about the topic is anachronistic, for it draws upon an art-theoretical principle of a later age. It downplays the extent to which an orthodox Christian message emerges from the painting's heavy reliance on standard Renaissance symbolism. The artworld conventions of fifteenth-century Milan clarify the identity of each of the thirteen figures in *The Last Supper*, revealing that the apostle John is present. Similarly, the fact that Duchamp's *Fountain* is a scathing social commentary derives from the surrounding "atmosphere" of his time and place. If you do not understand the concept of an open-admission art exhibition – something that did not exist in the Renaissance – then you cannot hope to understand Duchamp's rhetorical gesture in submitting a urinal, much less its humor.

Danto's reference to artworld institutions is a small part of his theory, reminding us that socio-historical circumstances are always relevant to the correct interpretation of art. In this way, Danto retains communication as art's essential function. However, there seem to be many decorative artworks that do not say anything about anything, such as the leaded glass windows that architect Frank Lloyd Wright designed and installed in the Bradley house in Kankakee, Illinois (1900). Some of these windows have been removed and sold to art collectors, yet no one claims that they "say" anything about anything. Danto's theory falls prey to the standard problem faced by other functional definitions. For any unifying function we identify, there seem to be some artworks that do not have that function.

A less elaborate institutional definition arises if we minimize the function condition. George Dickie offers this definition:

> A work of art is an artifact of a kind created to be presented to an artworld public. (Dickie 1984: 80)

The Last Supper, *The Madonna of the Pinks*, and the *St. Matthew Passion* all share the same function, which is to support the Christian faith. However, that is not why they are artworks, for they do not share this function with Warhol's Brillo boxes or Duchamp's *Fountain*. Now add the decorative leaded glass windows that Frank Lloyd Wright designed for the Bradley house, and we have a group of objects that share no function beyond the minimal one of presentation to an artworld public. For Dickie, this shows that the essential nature of art does not place restrictions on what art must do. Different artists have distinct reasons for creating the art that they do. What do these reasons have in common? Nothing but the minimal function of presentation to an artworld public. To know whether something is a work of art, then, one must know whether it was created for this purpose, and whether its medium of presentation is one that is "of a kind" for presentation to an artworld public at that time and place. This latter requirement assumes that we understand the ideas of a public and an artworld (Dickie 1984: 81–2).

- A public is a set of persons whose members are prepared in some degree to understand an object which is presented to them.

- The artworld is the totality of all artworld systems.
- An artworld system is a framework for the presentation of a work of art by an artist to an artworld public.

If someone creates something that conforms to prevailing practices of presentation, we can assume that the person intends to present a work to an artworld public, which is just what Duchamp did in submitting *Fountain* to a juried show, and what Warhol did by offering the Brillo boxes for sale in a commercial art gallery.

Dickie's definition is highly unusual in being circular. The explanations of the key terms of the definition make use of other terms that are present in the definition itself and in other parts of the explanation. Although it wouldn't do to use the word "red" when defining "red," Dickie flaunts the circularity of this definition. It is justified, he argues, because art status depends on a complex relationship between agency, artifactuality, and public. Art-making is a self-reflexive activity. Although an artist does not have to stipulate "I intend this object to be regarded as art," art status cannot arise in the absence of awareness of existing art practices. Hence, the definition must be self-reflexive, too, and so the circularity of the definition cannot be a reason for rejecting it.

Depending on what a definition of art is meant to accomplish, Dickie's institutional definition is either blessed or cursed by his insistence that art has no essential function beyond presentation to the appropriate public. Blessed, if you think that it is a virtue of a definition to be value-neutral, so that art status does not imply that the object in question is *worth* presenting to an artworld public (Dickie 1984: 13–14). Cursed, if you think it a problem that the definition of art gives no guidance concerning the question of why art matters so much to so many people. Derek Matravers regards this supposed virtue as a genuine problem for institutional or "procedural" definitions, because the definition does not explain why we have the practices and procedures that we currently have. However, the activity of presenting objects to a public within an established presentational framework invites a justification of our framework. The institutional approach goes wrong in denying that the prevailing practices of the artworld stand in need of justification (Matravers 2000: 250).

Defenders of a value-neutral classificatory definition reply that the word "art" is frequently used to praise things that are clearly not artworks. It makes perfectly good sense to say, of a particular restaurant, "The Exchequer Pub makes a pizza that's a work of art." This merit-conferring use of "art" can be interpreted as non-classificatory and merely honorific. To view genuine art, one will have to travel two blocks over from the Exchequer Pub to the Chicago Art Institute. Therefore "art" has two distinct uses, a merit-conferring use and a value-neutral, strictly classificatory use. Definitions of art attempt to capture the latter. However, this argument can be turned on its head. The evaluative use of "art" for non-artworks is not mere happenstance. Praising a pizza as "art" implies that it is valuable in one or more of the ways in which art is valuable, which implies that classifying anything as art presupposes that it has some degree of value.

The institutional approach faces another serious problem. How does it deal with "outsider" art and indigenous non-Western art? For example, The Smithsonian American Art Museum in Washington, DC, displays a set of objects known as "The Throne of the Third Heaven of the Nations' Millennium General Assembly" (*c.*1950-64). Constructed from junk by James Hampton, a custodian, the dazzling assemblage is, as the title indicates, a throne room intended for God's use at the end of days as foretold in the book of Revelation. Hampton certainly did not intend to create an artifact for presentation to an artworld public, and he would most likely have been astounded at the artifact's prominence in an art museum. Yet it is commonly recognized that Hampton created "outsider" art – art that does not arise from formal training or within existing artworld institutions. Similarly, all known cultures produce objects that Western art publics regard as works of art. Most societies have done this without developing distinctive "artworld systems." Consider the Aboriginal rock paintings of Namadgi National Park, Australia. These paintings derive from religious practices, not "artworld" institutions. How, then, do we recognize that these cultural achievements are art? Do we have a universal standard for recognizing artworld systems? Institutional theories provide no such criteria.

6.5 Historical definitions

In chapter 3 we examined the question of whether creativity can be understood ahistorically, without reference to what comes before and after it historically. We examined G. W. F. Hegel and Karl Marx as proponents of the position that creativity can only be understood by reference to historical circumstances. (See section 3.4.) Similarly, some philosophers agree with Dickie that art is a self-reflexive activity, subject to the qualification that it is a *historically* self-reflexive activity. Looking closely at Dickie's institutional theory, it appears to have been designed to capture the idea that art is a historical development. The appearance of a new artworld system constitutes an evolution in the standard for being an artwork. The concept of art is malleable, changing over time. Batteux's definition of art does not recognize *Fountain* and the Brillo boxes as art because he is explaining how fine art is understood in 1746. As Danto says, "certain artworks simply could not be inserted as artworks into certain periods of art history" (Danto 1981: 44). As other cultural practices have changed, the prevailing "artworld systems" have also changed, opening the door to some artworks while closing the door on others. Consequently, an adequate *definition* of art should reflect art's historical malleability. Historical definitions highlight this point.

Jerrold Levinson defends a historical definition, specifically that an artwork "is an object that a person or persons, having the appropriate proprietary right over [it], nonpassingly intends for regard-as-a-work-of-art, i.e., regard in any way (or ways) in which prior artworks are or were correctly (or standardly) regarded" (Levinson 1990: 8–9). In other words, Duchamp had proprietary rights over the urinal, because he bought and thus owned it. Then he took the trouble to enter it into an art show, which indicates that he intended it for regard in some ways that prior artworks were standardly regarded. *Fountain* is linked historically to earlier works of art in a way that makes it an artwork, too.

Notice that Levinson's definition does not say that the person intends the thing to be art. The "artist" can intend something else, which, if that something else makes it subject to 'regard-as-a-work-of-art', makes the new object an artwork, too. So the definition confers art status on artifacts not consciously intended to be art. There are several hundred thousand Aboriginal rock carvings in Australia. Most of them predate the arrival of European immigrants and they were created for religious purposes, so it is safe to say that most of them were created without any intention to create art. Like Hampton's "The Throne of the Third Heaven," Aboriginal rock art counts as art under Levinson's definition. Hampton's throne room is art because he obviously intended it to be regarded in ways that other religious objects (e.g., chalices and decorated altars) have been traditionally regarded, as impressively beautiful artifacts. Because beautiful, meaningful artifacts have long been collected and displayed as works of art, Hampton's creation satisfies the requirement of having been intended to be regarded in a way that prior works of art are correctly regarded. Similar intentions are evidenced by Aboriginal rock artists. Their status as art is ensured if we agree that intentions do not have to be manifest, that is, intentions that the participants would confirm as guiding the activity if they were asked about those intentions. According to Denis Dutton (1977), stylistic consistency and standards of value are often implicitly intentional. The Zuni people of New Mexico created pottery with a distinctive style, yet the first anthropologists to report on them found that Zuni potters could not articulate their stylistic principles. Some anthropologists concluded that the designs were the unintentional result of culturally shared practices. In contrast, Dutton thinks that this interpretation would be as silly as concluding that inarticulate people who cannot describe their driving skills are unintentionally successful at navigating congested highways. Actions that consistently contribute to a culturally distinctive human achievement are intentional. The aesthetic success of Zuni pottery and Aboriginal rock art demonstrates implicit intentions, and those intentions are present even if they are denied by the artists during a discussion of their creative process. Adopting Dutton's account, it is clear that many artifacts and social rituals of traditional non-Western societies are the result of implicit intentions that are consistent with standard intentions for artworks. Dutton's criterion for implicit intentions has the additional benefit of dealing with the standard objection that intentions are too hard to know.

Exercise: Explain the difference between intending to write a limerick and intending to write a five-line poem. Explain how you can succeed in doing the former while only intending to do the latter. Then explain how this point parallels Levinson's proposal.

Levinson's proposal has the advantage that it recognizes outsider art and non-Western art. Unfortunately, Levinson's definition can be criticized for conferring art status on the basis of completely trivial relationships to other works of art. As observed earlier, being a Parisian tourist attraction painted by da Vinci is sufficient to be an artwork, yet that is not *why* the paintings are artworks. In contrast, the Eiffel Tower (1889) was intended to be a Parisian tourist attraction. The Eiffel Tower is among those architectural works that are indisputably artworks. However, *that* fact implies that the same holds for the Eiffel Tower replica in Las Vegas, because it was intended to be regarded in one of the ways that the Eiffel Tower is correctly regarded – simply as a tourist attraction. Worse yet, it seems that all tourist attractions created as such after 1889 are works of art, for they are all intended to be regarded as the Eiffel Tower is correctly regarded. Levinson's definition falls prey to the criticism that it extends art status to many things that are probably not art. Furthermore, we cannot save the definition by further specifying and limiting what counts as a relevant regard-as-a-work-of-art. Doing so would cut off future paths of artistic evolution. Unprecedented artistic gestures would not qualify, thus denying the possibility of avant-garde art.

So far, the discussion has ignored Levinson's proprietary thesis as a needless complication. Taking notice of that requirement produces another problem. The definition denies that something is a work of art whenever artists fail to own or appropriately control relevant aspects of their final product. Because Warhol did not have the right to use the design that he put on the Brillo boxes at the time he made them and offered them for sale, Levinson's definition seems to deny that they are artworks. A parallel problem can arise for original designs. Keith Haring's early work included graffiti in the New York subway. Lacking permission to put it there, Haring did not have the appropriate proprietary right over what he created, so it was not art. Identical designs, executed on someone else's property with their permission, would be art. Although we need something like the proprietary requirement in order to determine whose intentions are relevant, it appears to generate the problem that technicalities concerning ownership can be the only thing that prevents one of a pair of indiscernible objects from being an artwork.

Finally, historical definitions have a problem with the possibility of the first art. If an artifact is an artwork by virtue of having the correct relationship to some previous artwork(s), then when did the history of art begin? Wherever and whenever we locate art's historical beginning, the definition says that these artifacts require the correct relationship to previous art. Because the first art cannot be art through a relationship to earlier art, there cannot be first art. The historical definition undercuts the historical bedrock upon which all subsequent art status rests. There is consensus, shared by Levinson, that the only plausible answer is that the earliest stage of art is art for some reason that cannot be required for subsequent art-works (Levinson 2006: 18). Stephen Davies argues that this reason is almost certainly a fundamental human interest in aesthetic properties. (For more on this topic, see chapter 7.) Aesthetically rich artifacts made at the dawn of any culture's history count as art, and a backward-looking chain of influence is only required for subsequent art. Although a human concern "with achieving aesthetic effects is *historically* necessary" (to get art started), this concern is not *logically necessary* for subsequent artworks (Davies 2000: 209). Following the lead of Duchamp's *Fountain*, many artists have created artworks that do not prioritize aesthetic effects.

The first art problem reveals that historical definitions are ultimately *disjunctive* definitions. The definition must permit artifacts to be artworks for either of two reasons. More than one set of properties must be available, *either* of which must be sufficient for being a work of art. If a Paleolithic cave painting cannot be art according to the historical definition, then it must be art for a second reason. Robert Stecker therefore proposes that something is art either because it is intended to function as art has functioned at an earlier time, or simply because it fulfills some function that is a standard function some art has (Stecker 1997: 50). However, this solution is subject to the same criticism that haunts any definition that does not spell out the relevant functions. Many cities and even countries support their arts communities, theatre districts, and art museums because the arts attract tourists. Tourism is now a central function of art. So the replica of the Eiffel Tower in Las Vegas is again granted the status of an artwork, as is every other human creation that attracts tourists. In accommodating both first art and avant-garde art, the disjunctive strategy is simply too permissive.

6.6 The cluster account

As a result of philosophical debates that have no direct bearing on philosophy of art, philosophers have recently become open to the possibility that some of our words convey *cluster concepts*. A famous example in anthropology illustrates the peculiarity of cluster classifications. The Australian Aboriginal language of Dyirbal explicitly assigns all things to one of four basic categories. (This strategy of fundamental division broadly echoes the ancient Greek assignment of things to the four basic categories of earth, air, fire, and water.) One of the four Dyirbal terms is "balan." No other language has a term that corresponds to it, so its scope of reference is puzzling and counterintuitive to non-Dyirbal-speakers. Very broadly, an object is "balan" if it is female, or involves fire, or involves water, or is a dog or a scorpion, or is a particular species of snake or fish or bird (Lakoff 1987: 92). Native speakers take it for granted that these things are properly grouped, even though another of their basic terms, "bayi," refers to all animals not understood to be "balan," and so includes most species of snakes and fish. Because most fish are "bayi," many water-related items that are related to fishing are "bayi" rather than "balan." Furthermore, the animal species associated with "balan" do not strike Dyirbal speakers as exceptions to their use of "bayi." They accept these seeming misclassifications as readily as the average English speaker classifies tomatoes and cucumbers as vegetables – despite the fact that tomatoes and cucumbers fit our standard definition of fruit, not vegetable. Classifying tomatoes and cucumbers as vegetables derives from our cultural practices in preparing and eating various foods, which are independent of our botanical criteria for identifying fruit. And we might then notice that *all* fruits count as vegetables within the cultural context of sorting into "animal, vegetable, or mineral" at the start of a game of "Twenty Questions."

Exercise: Ludwig Wittgenstein, one of the twentieth century's most important philosophers, maintains that there is no single thing in common among all the things we call "games." "I mean," he says, "board-games, card-games, ball-games, Olympic games, and so on. What is common to them all?" (Wittgenstein 1953: 30). Can you specify anything common to all games?

"Balan" is a relatively simple case of a cluster concept, clustering things together based on culturally established connections among alternative sets of relevant properties. Several philosophers have recently proposed that "art" is a cluster concept, too. As such, unrelated features of objects and events might be sufficient, either alone or in groups, for placing objects in the extension of the concept. Notice that the very distinction just made, between objects and events, already suggests that fundamentally different entities will satisfy our definition. Therefore our attempt to define art should highlight the *differences* involved in grouping these very distinct kinds of things:

- Beethoven's Op. 101 (1816) (a sequence of tones intended to be executed on a piano).
- *The Last Supper* (a painted wall in Milan).
- Constantin Brancusi's *Bird in Flight* (1923) (abstract sculptures in various media that the United States Customs Office denied were art in 1926).
- Emily Dickinson's poem "Essential Oils – Are Wrung" (*c.*1863) (an oddly punctuated word sequence).

Next, recall the conclusion that there is no single function performed by every artwork (above, section 6.3), and supplement this diversity of function with the point that first art, "outsider" art, and a great deal of non-Western art does not arise from artworld institutions. So perhaps it is best to bite the bullet and admit that "art," like "balan," involves reference to any number of combinations of independent properties that lack a unifying thread. However, unlike the disjunctive strategy discussed at the close of section 6.5, these properties are to be specified with some level of detail.

Two cluster accounts of art deserve attention. There is considerable overlap between the accounts of Berys Gaut (2000) and Denis Dutton (2006). They agree that there is at least one property that is common to all art. It is the same one that was identified above as a necessary condition in other definitions: art is always produced by human action (Gaut 2000:

29; Dutton 2006: 369). Although that is the *only* thing that is common to all art, that is clearly not sufficient to provide a definition – mass-produced paperclips are products of human action and yet they are not artworks. This single necessary property can be supplemented by multiple properties and groupings of properties that, in conjunction with it, are sufficient to classify something as art. Different groupings of these properties are relevant in different cultures and even for particular artistic movements.

Here, simplified, is Dutton's list of characteristics that, added to artifact status, are relevant when deciding whether an object or performance is an artwork (Dutton 2006: 369–73):

1. it is valued as a source of immediate experiential pleasure, and/or
2. its production involves specialized skills, and/or
3. its form displays style, and/or
4. it is valued for displaying creativity, and/or
5. its appreciation makes it the object of critical discussion, and/or
6. it represents a real or imaginary experience, and/or
7. it is distinctively special and marked off from everyday, routine objects and events, and/or
8. it expresses the individuality of its creator, and/or
9. it is pervaded by expressive properties, and/or
10. it challenges our intellectual and perceptual capacities, and/or
11. it has some historical precedent in an established artistic form, and/or
12. it provides an imaginative experience for both producer and audience.

Some works, such as *The Last Supper*, satisfy all twelve criteria. Duchamp's *Fountain*, on the other hand, satisfies very few.

Gaut's list is very similar (2000: 28). However, he is more concerned with defending the strategy than with defending a particular list. All the same, it is interesting to see that his example of a cluster definition explicitly adds two items that Dutton omits, namely the possession of aesthetic properties and being made with an intention to be art. Dutton replies that there is no need for a criterion of possessing aesthetic properties, because these are the source of the immediate pleasure (the first criterion) and they are themselves dependent on combinations of other properties in this list. (For the plausibility of this view, see section 7.2.)

There is another, more significant difference between Gaut and Dutton. This difference concerns the use of the list. Gaut denies that this approach furnishes a definition. At best, we can say that something is art if it satisfies all the criteria. But that's about as far as we can go. A staggering number of distinct combinations of properties can be generated from a list of just ten properties, and for most of those combinations we have no plausible method for deciding which sets are always sufficient and which are never sufficient. Furthermore, there is no way to prioritize the items in the list, nor any good reason to set a minimum number of criteria that must be satisfied. (Some pairs of criteria might be sufficient, while other pairs are certainly not.) The absence of any of the criteria counts against something's being art, and the presence of any one of them counts in favor of its being art. The total number either way is a very strong indicator, but not decisive, and so an object or practice that satisfies five or six of the criteria is going to strike us as a borderline case of art. Gaut offers that the food prepared by good cooks is such a case. Scholarly writing by philosophers will satisfy an equal number of these criteria. Yet Danto's book *The Transfiguration of the Commonplace* is not an artwork. The cluster approach justifies too many different ways to be art to consider it a definition.

Exercise: Can you select a pair of criteria from Dutton's list that would not be sufficient to indicate that an artifact is a work of art? Can you select a set of four?

Gaut recognizes the natural, yet unjustified, tendency to prioritize which-ever criteria are most characteristic of highly familiar art. Therefore the absence of representation, expressive properties, and immediate experi-ential pleasure encourages many people to deny that *Fountain* is a work of art. Granted, signs of the individuality of its creator are minimally present with *Fountain*, in Duchamp's joke of signing it. However, the complete absence of such signs from "Sherrie Levine after Walker Evans" goes a long way toward explaining why audiences have trouble accepting Levine's photos as art (see section 1.4). Gaut's point is that these *are* artworks, yet at the same time their failure to satisfy criteria on the list counts against grant-ing them that status. In some periods of history, these would be decisive reasons to deny that a particular artifact is an artwork. In some cultural contexts, such as the New York art scene of the 1950s, representation counted against a painting's status as an artwork. In comparison, Raphael's skillful representations of the Madonna are minimally creative and fail to challenge our intellectual and perceptual capacities. Context matters, and therefore we have no reason to stipulate that the presence or absence of any of the criteria should be prioritized over any of the others. Finally, Gaut suggests that we might develop new criteria in the years to come. He regards the list as open-ended, which is another reason to deny our ability to universally prioritize any of the criteria. Since we are not in a position to say which of the numerous combinations of criteria are necessary, or to narrow down the combinations that are sufficient, the cluster account does not provide a definition. Yet it's what we have.

Dutton replies that there is no reason to believe that the list is genu-inely open-ended. Furthermore, some of the criteria are naturally more important than others. We can prioritize some of them, and the presence (or absence) of clusters of the more important criteria are sufficient for the presence (or absence) of art status. So we do know that some sets of prop-erties will be jointly sufficient to apply the concept of "art." Specifically, Dutton claims that the imaginative experience criterion is "one of the most important items on the list" (2006: 376). He appears to hold that any artifact or performance is art if it involves imaginative experience plus any one other property on the list. Alternatively, any artifact or performance that does not stimulate and reward imaginative experience would have to sat-isfy virtually all of the others. Therefore, our inability to enjoy professional sporting events imaginatively, as a creative display of style and yet without concern for who wins and loses, is a perfectly clear reason why competitive sport differs from art.

Where Dutton thinks that the cluster approach makes it clear why a professional football game is not an artwork, Gaut thinks it is a strength of his approach that it does not settle contested and borderline cases. Instead, it explains *why* there are so many cases of this sort. For example, many people insist that mass-produced designer products and popular entertainment are not art, on the grounds that they fail to meet some favored criterion from the list. (For more on this debate, see chapter 8.) However, these objections assume that there is more than one necessary condition for being art, which the cluster account explicitly denies. Other people claim that, because their candidate for art satisfies a particular item on the list (e.g., it is creative, or expressive), it is art. These people are making the mistake of elevating a mere indicator to the status of sufficient condition. Dutton agrees that this point is a general strength of the cluster theory, yet he holds out hope that we can make progress in specifying multiple sets of properties that will be sufficient. For those who support the cluster approach, the choice between Gaut and Dutton largely turns on the question of whether to settle for Gaut's flexible criteria over Dutton's goal of settling on alternative sets of sufficient conditions.

Exercise: Suppose that there is a small group of viewers who regularly watch professional sporting events without any concern for who wins or loses. They watch the games as pure displays of skill that involve creativity, individual style, and expressiveness. In fact, the availability of commercial videos of Olympic-competition figure skating suggests that there are people who respond to that sport in this way. On Dutton's account, do videos of performances by figure skaters such as Sasha Cohen and Kim Yu-Na qualify as art? If so, is this an important difference in Gaut's and Dutton's versions of the cluster approach? Does the existence of these videos offer evidence for or against either approach?

Issues to think about

1. Explain the proposal that a philosophical definition seeks conditions that are *individually* necessary and *jointly* sufficient.
2. In April 2010, the film critic Roger Ebert used his Internet blog to argue that video games are not – and cannot be – art. Within a few weeks he received over 4,000 replies, almost all of which disagreed with him. (See http://blogs.suntimes.com/ebert/2010/04/video_games_can_never_be _art.html.) Do any of the philosophical definitions surveyed in this chapter provide evidence against Ebert's claim?
3. Suppose a child of four is taken to an art museum on a family outing. The child enjoys some Impressionist paintings of flowers. The next day, the child makes a crayon drawing of a bunch of flowers and then attaches it to the family refrigerator with a magnet. Does Dickie's institutional

definition classify this drawing as a work of art? Does Levinson's histori-cal definition do so?

4. Why do we want a philosophical definition of art? Is it a serious prob-lem with Gaut's cluster approach that it does not resolve debates about difficult and borderline cases?

5. Explain the difference between a disjunctive definition and a cluster concept.

6. If we adopt a disjunctive or cluster approach, should we add "being a Parisian tourist attraction that was painted by da Vinci" as an additional disjunct? If not, why not?

Further resources

The best general overview of the many problems involved in defining art is Stephen Davies' *Definitions of Art* (1991). Noël Carroll's *Theories of Art Today* (2000) is a solid collection of essays on the topic. Another recom-mended set of essays is *Art and Essence* (2003), edited by Davies and A. C. Sukla. The classic functional definitions have many sources. The core texts on the expression theory are Tolstoy (1996) and Collingwood (1938). Clive Bell emphasizes form in the first chapter of *Art* (1958 [1914]), after which the aesthetic account is closely associated with Beardsley (1982). Updated attempts to revive the aesthetic function are offered by Iseminger (2004) and Zangwill (2007). Although Danto is not explicit about the pre-cise formulation of his institutional definition, he develops and defends it in *The Transfiguration of the Commonplace* (1981). Dickie (1984) is the most famous exponent of the institutional account, but Matravers (2000) usefully explains that most recent definitions of art adopt core ideas from Dickie. Stecker contrasts his own proposal with other definitions in *Artworks: Definition, Meaning, Value* (1997). For an interesting set of reflections on the broader implications of our brief discussion of cluster concepts, see Foucault (2002).

Few films emphasize the topic of defining art. However, *Bomb It* (2007) makes the case that graffiti is art by appealing to the function of expression. It provides a test case of how definitions are applied to disputed cases. On the general importance of institutions and the socialization that informs our grasp of them, see *The Enigma of Kaspar Hauser* (1974), an explora-tion of a "wild" child who must come to grips with the non-manifest social relationships that others take for granted. Returning to art, Part I of *Andy Warhol: A Documentary Film* (2006) provides fascinating insights into the institutional barriers that separate commercial from fine art, and *The Cool School* (2008) offers further insight into the loose structures of artworld institutions in its examination of the development of the Los Angeles art scene of the 1950s and early 1960s.

7 Aesthetics

The examples of functional definitions of art in chapter 6 include an aesthetic definition. It was also noted that aesthetically rich artifacts from the distant past are always classified as art. However, no explanation was offered of either point. This chapter will address the topic of aesthetics and art.

The modern term "aesthetic" is an adaptation of the Greek term "aesthesis," referring to things perceived. It first appeared in 1735, in Alexander Baumgarten's analysis of poetry (Baumgarten 1954). The sound of a poem is its aesthetic dimension, which he opposes to its conceptual content. Generalizing, aesthetic judgments are judgments about how things appear to us. Beyond those points, there is surprisingly little agreement about the difference between aesthetic and non-aesthetic judgments.

Aesthetics – notice the pluralization – refers to the study of aesthetic phenomena and judgments. Aesthetics is often equated with investigation of beauty and ugliness. Today, that is only a small part of it. This chapter examines major proposals about the nature, range, and justification of aesthetic judgments. In particular, we will explore the idea that aesthetic responses are highly sensitive to our other judgments about an object, including judgments about relationships to culture and to other works of art. Because there is so much disagreement about which judgments are aesthetic, it is generally thought best to begin by discussing some unproblematic cases. For that reason, judgments about beauty and ugliness receive a disproportionate amount of attention. Once we understand them, we can try to extend a parallel analysis to other cases. For example, does someone make an aesthetic judgment when calling attention to the "sad" appearance of a weathered barn? When a wine critic dismisses a red wine as an unbalanced fruit bomb? Although beauty and ugliness are not involved, both of these cases are generally classified as aesthetic judgments. What, then, of the judgment that classical music is old-fashioned and boring? Of the judgment that some abstract paintings are profound? To decide on the status of such cases, and to see why that status might matter to us, we will begin with an example of a beautiful artwork.

7.1 Aesthetic judgments and properties

"Nature is a dull affair," opines Alfred North Whitehead: "soundless, scentless, colourless; merely the hurrying of material . . ." (Whitehead 1953: 412). This worldview has been discussed and debated since the sixteenth century, when many philosophers and scientists endorsed materialism, the doctrine that we interact with a world of purely material things. However, scientific findings convinced them that material objects do not possess most of the sensory features that we experience. The sweetness of honey and the blue of the sky are perceptual effects of our interactions with material objects. In itself, the physical stuff that we observe is matter in motion. The material stuff of honey is not sweet and the sky has no color at all. Material differences cause us to *experience* honey as sweet and the sky as blue. We have these experiences because we have sensory receptors that feed us information about our immediate environment – our various modes of sense perception translate physical differences into sensory differences. Tastes and smells are responses to chemicals that compose objects. Sight and feeling respond to the shape, location, density, surface texture, and movement of physical objects. Looking at a crisp clear autumn sky, I see the blue at the horizon as a lighter shade than the blue higher in the sky. When my dog looks up at geese flying overhead, his eyes also register information about the environment. However, a dog sees the same sky as shades of gray. Dogs do not have the visual receptors that translate wavelengths of light into experiences of colors. Humans see things differently from other species, but it does not follow that any species sees things more "correctly."

Notice that Whitehead makes an additional point. Stripped of its sensory richness, the world as described by science is a dull place. If it lacks sensory or perceptible properties, then it also lacks beauty, ugliness, and the additional sensory qualities that we experience as positive and negative aesthetic values. It is ironic, therefore, that scientific facts about a painting can reveal its true provenance by providing hidden information that, once revealed, alters our response to its sensory properties. (See section 4.4.) In a much-publicized case, a painting that was categorized as a reproduction of a painting by the Italian Renaissance painter Raphael Santi turned out to be the original. A canvas in a private collection in England was long classified as one of many sixteenth-century copies of *The Madonna of the Pinks* (*c.*1506). An art curator happened to see this "copy" in 1991 and noticed that it had an unusually expensive frame (McKie 2010). Intrigued, the curator arranged to subject the painting to infrared radiation. This non-intrusive process can reveal dark colors that lie under a layer of paint. In this case, infrared analysis revealed that the painting was created by first drawing an extremely detailed sketch of the work's two figures and surroundings. However, this sketch would serve no purpose when copying the image from another painting. More importantly, the sketch matches the style and level of detail of a drawing that lies under a painting known to be an authentic Raphael. The true provenance of *The Madonna of the Pinks* was then confirmed when small samples of paint were removed from a part of the canvas that is hidden by its frame. The bare canvas was initially prepared with a coat of white paint. However, it proved to be a mixture of three paints. They contained distinctive levels of lead and manganese, and comparison with an authentic painting by Raphael confirmed a match of the three paints combined for this "white" ground.

What is missing from all of this science is the further point that *The Madonna of the Pinks* is a visual representation. This pictorial dimension emerges from Raphael's skilled manipulation of the object's physical properties. In chapter 5 we touched on the hypothesis that *The Madonna of the Pinks* might *look* different to someone who shifts from thinking of it as a copy to thinking of it as the original. Is this a plausible claim? After all, the patches of color are exactly as they were before, and the representation shows just what it showed before: a woman with a blue skirt holding a baby boy. (The pinks of the title are the dianthus flowers he holds.) If there is some difference in how the painting looks, it is *aesthetic*: the woman now seems much more graceful and poised than in the painting's many reproductions. The copies have the same woman and baby, but they are comparatively less graceful and beautiful.

We have arrived at a distinction among five kinds of judgments about the same painting.

- There are scientific judgments, such as the claim that the undercoat contains manganese.
- There are historical judgments, such as the claim that it was painted by Raphael.
- There are judgments about its sensory appearance, such as the claim that there is a blue patch in the upper right corner.
- There are interpretive judgments, such as the claims that the painting shows a woman holding an infant boy and that these are Mary and Jesus.
- There are aesthetic judgments, such as the claim that the image of the woman is graceful.

The standard explanation of why we have different types of judgments is that they cite distinct sets or families of properties. We could go beyond these five. For instance, we could consult a sixth family of properties and make economic judgments about the painting. The painting's value on the open market is an economic property. (We will return to the distinction between economic and aesthetic value in chapter 9.)

Exercise: David Hume says the following about Euclid's geometry:

> *Euclid has fully explained every quality of the circle, but has not, in any proposition, said a word of its beauty. The reason is evident. Beauty is not a quality of the circle. . . . It is only the effect, which that figure produces upon a mind, whose particular fabric or structure renders it susceptible of such sentiments (Hume 1998b [1742])*

Select one of the performing arts and one of the non-performing arts, and then select a particular artwork from each. Use those examples to explain Hume's point.

7.2 Supervenience

By itself, it is not very informative to distinguish aesthetic judgments from scientific and interpretive judgments. We will also want an account of inter-relationships among the different families of properties. This issue is often handled by introducing a piece of technical vocabulary, the notion of *supervenience*. This concept is not unique to aesthetics. Supervenience is frequently discussed in philosophy of mind, where it is brought to bear on the problem of how mental properties relate to physical ones. A supervenience relationship is present if the existence of a property of one type depends on the presence of some property, or arrangement of properties, of a different type. In the aesthetic case, the thesis says that aesthetic properties, such as beauty and ugliness, depend on the presence of ordinary perceptible properties, such as colors, sounds, and textures. (Alternatively, it is often said that the aesthetic properties emerge from these other properties.) The core idea is that there cannot be a change in an object's aesthetic properties without a change in the non-aesthetic properties. If one painting is beautiful and another is not, then there must be a non-aesthetic difference that explains this aesthetic difference.

Because artworks possess many different sorts of properties, most artworks display multiple supervenience relationships. For example, Renaissance painters made their own paints, and Raphael's paints have a distinctive combination of chemical properties. This paint chemistry explains sensory properties. Employing the terminology developed in section 7.1, it appears that one family of properties serves as the basis of another. Notice that this is a metaphysical point, not an epistemological one.

- With metaphysical supervenience, one *property* depends on one or more others.
- With epistemological supervenience, one *judgment* depends on one or more others. (Epistemology is also known as the theory of knowledge.)

Metaphysical and epistemological supervenience do not always align. For example, chemical properties generate and thus explain perceptible ones. The parallel thesis in epistemology says that we cannot know which colors are present unless we also know which chemicals are present. But that is wrong. We do not have to know anything about chemistry to see the colors. We can just look and see them. Similarly, we just look and see that Raphael's painting shows a woman holding a baby boy. This example demonstrates that some of our interpretive judgments are epistemologically independent of our awareness of scientific and historical properties. At the same time, other interpretive judgments display epistemological supervenience. Even if Raphael painted from live models, his painting should not be interpreted as a portrait of the woman and baby he painted. It is a religious painting that portrays Mary and Jesus. This fact depends on its social and historical provenance. (This supervenience is metaphysical, involving supervenience of one property upon another.) In addition, some understanding of the Christian tradition is required before one can arrive at an appropriate *interpretation* of it. (This supervenience is epistemological.)

Let's return to *aesthetic* supervenience. The supervenience thesis says that each aesthetic property depends on one or more non-aesthetic properties, so that any two objects with identical non-aesthetic properties will have the same aesthetic properties. *The Madonna of the Pinks* possesses the aesthetic property of beauty because it possesses a particular, complex arrangement of non-aesthetic sensory properties. I suspect that you will agree that the painting's beauty would be reduced if we retouched it with fluorescent blues and greens. Likewise, the woman's pose would be far less graceful if Raphael had given her bulky shoulders, as would be the case if the line across to her neck was more horizontal. Since beauty and grace are paradigm cases of aesthetic properties, these examples support the position that aesthetic properties supervene on non-aesthetic sensory properties. These non-aesthetic properties are the *supervenience base* for the painting's aesthetic properties. The supervenience base of *The Madonna of the Pinks* includes the shape of the continuous line that forms Mary's shoulder and neck and the shade of blue that dominates the painting's sky area. Furthermore, some degree of epistemological supervenience holds between non-aesthetic sensory properties and the aesthetic properties. At the very least, *seeing* the beauty depends on *seeing* the ordinary sensory properties.

Be very careful not to turn things around backwards. The supervenience thesis does not postulate an identity between aesthetic and non-aesthetic properties. As we saw in our discussion of definitions of art, sufficiency does not imply necessity (see section 6.1). The supervenience thesis says that there cannot be differences in supervening properties unless there are differences in base properties. It tells us that a particular base property (or set of base properties) is sufficient to generate a particular aesthetic property. It does *not* say that that base is required to obtain that aesthetic property. Paintings have visual properties in their supervenience base. Music does not. Yet the aesthetic property of beauty is found in both visual art and music. Therefore no fixed set of base properties is ever necessary for any particular aesthetic property. This technical point has an important consequence. It implies that base properties can interact in unpredictable ways. In advance of perceiving the result, we never know whether a *new* combination of non-aesthetic properties will generate a particular aesthetic property. Minor changes in the supervenience base can produce aesthetic surprises. As Frank Sibley puts it, "It is always conceivable that, by some relatively small change in line or colour in a picture, a note in music, or a word in a poem, the aesthetic character may be lost or quite transformed" (2001: 35).

Exercise: Suppose that we retouch The Madonna of the Pinks *with fluorescent blues and greens. Does the supervenience thesis imply that these changes must reduce or destroy its beauty? Explain.*

7.3 Two complications

Agreeing that aesthetic properties supervene on some non-aesthetic properties opens the door to several interpretations of aesthetic supervenience.

- Does the supervenience base for aesthetic properties *require* sensory
  properties? If so, then non-perceptible objects do not possess aesthetic
  properties.
- Is the supervenience base for aesthetic properties *restricted to* sensory properties? If so, then the historical property of being an Italian
  Renaissance painting is completely irrelevant to the aesthetic properties of *The Madonna of the Pinks*.

If we answer "yes" to the first question, we get the *weak dependence
thesis* defended by Nick Zangwill (2001). It says that all aesthetic properties
depend, entirely or in part, on sensory properties. If we answer "yes" to the
second question, we adopt *aesthetic empiricism* (Currie 1989). It implies
that copies of Raphael's paintings are aesthetically deficient if they are not
exact copies. A perfect copy would duplicate the relevant supervenience
base of sensory properties and therefore would be exactly as beautiful as
the original, because no other properties would be relevant.

Aesthetic empiricism is so popular that it passes as common sense
(Davies 2003). Nonetheless, there are good reasons to reject it. Above all, it
undermines claims that play a central role in our previous discussions of forgeries and authenticity. Aesthetic empiricism undercuts these conclusions
by denying that non-sensory, art-historical properties contribute to the base
for aesthetic properties. However, consistency with favored doctrines is just
one test for accepting or rejecting a theory. Are there independent reasons
to deny aesthetic empiricism? There are, for there are strong reasons to
agree that the supervenience base includes non-sensory properties.

The most important argument is advanced by Kendall Walton, who calls
attention to the way that pianos make music by hitting their strings with
hammers. As a result, all piano music sounds percussive. Yet some piano
music has a delicate quality. It is delicate "for that particular medium"
(Walton 2008: 207). To illustrate Walton's point, listen to Claude Debussy's
La cathédrale engloutie [*The Sunken Cathedral*] (1910) and then listen
to the pounding piano in Jerry Lee Lewis's "Great Balls of Fire" (1957).
Debussy said that he was composing "hammerless" piano music (Le Huray
1990: 4). In keeping with this goal, *La cathédrale engloutie* suppresses
the percussive quality of the instrument. All the same, Debussy's piano
works have a merely *comparative* delicacy, dependent on their degree of
deviation from the norm. Aesthetic empiricism tells us that it is a mistake to
attribute delicacy to this music. However, the delicacy is apparent to suita-
bly knowledgeable listeners. Other counterexamples are cases in which the
historical order of two works results in an aesthetic difference. Very competent paintings by Raphael's imitators look tired compared to his bold, fresh
work. However, these are controversial points and we will explore aesthetic
empiricism at greater length in section 7.5.

Exercise: When an artist assigns a title to a work, is the title a sensory or non-sensory property of that work? Is it important to know the title before listening to a musical work such as Debussy's La cathédrale engloutie? *How do these points relate to aesthetic empiricism?*

What about the weak dependence thesis? Should we endorse it? One of its implications, stressed by Zangwill, is that it strips ideas of aesthetic properties. Many scientists and mathematicians talk of the beauty and elegance of scientific laws and mathematical proofs. Since laws and proofs have no relevant sensory properties, Zangwill denies that these things are literally beautiful or elegant. Applied to artworks, the weak dependence thesis implies that conceptual art has no aesthetic properties. Conceptual art manipulates ideas and concepts. Sensory objects are employed to convey those ideas, yet their sensory properties are never the point. Yoko Ono pioneered a mode of conceptual art that involved issuing instructions for producing tokens of her work. One of her "musical" works is "Earth Piece" (1964). It consists of the instruction, "Listen to the sound of the earth turning" (Ono 1970). For supporters of the weak dependence thesis, such examples prove that some art lacks aesthetic qualities. (See Binkley 1977.) However, the conclusion is not so clear cut. Much of Ono's work is fresher, funnier, and more elegant than work by many other conceptual artists. There is no reason to suppose that these terms are being used in a non-standard or metaphorical way when applied to conceptual art. Freshness, wittiness, and elegance are aesthetic properties. Therefore there appear to be aesthetic properties that do not include sensory properties in their supervenience base.

7.4 Aesthetics and nature

So far, we have examined aesthetic judgments and properties by discussing artworks – and why not? Aesthetics is frequently equated with philosophy of art. However, aesthetic judgments are not restricted to judgments about art. Nature provides many displays of aesthetic properties. This point will be apparent to anyone who has admired a sunset, a rainbow, or a bird in flight. In these cases, the aesthetic effect is independent of human intentions. These objects are not artifacts (in the weak sense of being the product of human activity; see section 6.1). Therefore, their aesthetic properties do not supervene on cultural provenance. How important is this fact?

The distinction between nature and artifact plays a prominent role in the aesthetics of Immanuel Kant. His "Critique of Aesthetic Judgment" (1987) is probably the most significant contribution in the development of philosophical aesthetics. In it, he derives basic ideas about aesthetic judgment from an analysis of the beauty of a rose. For Kant, natural objects such as roses, bird songs, and scenic views invite a pure, uncomplicated mode of aesthetic judgment. In contrast, aesthetic judgments about artworks are a special, "impure" case. Responses to an artwork should be sensitive to the artifact's intended communicative purpose. For example, *The Madonna of the Pinks* should be viewed with some understanding of its religious significance. It might also be evaluated for its display of originality and, perhaps, as an expressive gesture of an artistic genius. (See section 3.2.). All of these judgments require an awareness of cultural provenance. In contrast, flowers do not carry messages reflecting artistic intentions, so aesthetic responses to roses do not require the same base of judgment as responses to paintings and other artworks. For that reason, a number of philosophers follow Kant in thinking that the *basics* of aesthetic theory should be extracted from examples of natural beauty, not art.

Exercise: Locate images of three different, well-known buildings that were designed for three different basic purposes. (For example, a hotel has a different purpose from a museum.) Does knowledge of each building's intended purpose affect its appearance? Transfer the purpose of each building you selected to one of the others. How would you judge the appearance of each building if this newly assigned purpose was the intended one?

Kant's contrast of artistic and natural beauty demonstrates that the discipline of aesthetics is not identical with philosophy of art. Unfortunately, many readers take away a different message. His position on pure responses to nature is often misread as a position *about art*. In other words, Kant is frequently thought to recommend aesthetic empiricism for both art and nature. This mistaken interpretation should be resisted. The most influential proponent of aesthetic empiricism for art is Clive Bell rather than Kant. (Bell's theory is discussed in section 7.5.)

Kant's writings are challenging, but those who read carefully will see that he does not endorse aesthetic empiricism regarding the aesthetic dimension of objects and events with human origins.

> What do poets praise more highly than the nightingale's enchantingly beautiful song . . .? And yet we have cases where some jovial innkeeper, unable to find such a songster, played a trick – received with greatest satisfaction [initially] – on the guests staying at his inn to enjoy the country air, by hiding in a bush some roguish youngster who (with a reed or rush in his mouth) knew how to copy that song in a way very similar to nature's. But as soon as one realizes it was all a deception, no one will long endure listening to this song that before he had considered so charming. (Kant 1987: 169)

In another passage, Kant offers a parallel argument about a garden that contains artificial flowers (1987: 166). At first glance, it may seem that he is making the obvious point that our psychological response changes if we know that the sounds come from a boy rather than a bird, or that the flowers are artificial rather than real. However, Kant is actually making a *normative* point, recommending what to do when making an aesthetic judgment. It is the same general point that was made about *The Madonna of the Pinks* in the last section. Origins always make an aesthetic difference and people should take relevant information into account before making aesthetic judgments. (If Kant's examples of the nightingale and the flowers remind you of the discussion of indiscernible counterparts in section 1.4, you are perceptive. Kant is exploring the same theme.)

Environmentalism has led to a renewed interest in aesthetic judgments concerning nature. There is a rich and growing literature on environmental aesthetics that continues to explore differences and parallels between judgments about art and those about nature. This contemporary debate frequently discusses Kant's normative thesis. How much information should we take into account when making aesthetic judgments? Are there different standards for judging art and nature? Allen Carlson has differentiated ten distinct models for appropriate aesthetic appreciation of nature (Carlson 2000). Although there is no space to examine all of them here, two influential models are variations of Kant's proposal that people should be aware of what is human-produced and what is natural.

- A minimal position holds that acceptable aesthetic judgments of nature require awareness of what is human-produced and what is natural, but nothing more. The aesthetic appreciation of nature should proceed from some understanding of what it is to be a product of nature (Budd 2002).
- Scientific cognitivism sees a strong parallel between aesthetic judgments about art and those about nature. Acceptable aesthetic judgments of artworks require some understanding of the art-historical tradition informing their production. Analogously, aesthetic appreciation of natural things requires a minimal understanding of relevant natural-historical and scientific information (Carlson 2008).

These two positions agree in being *cognitivist* in their orientation. In this context, cognitivism says that certain kinds of thoughts must be present in order to validate the judgment. Minimally, anyone who appreciates a seashell or a redwood tree should be aware that it is a natural object and not a human artifact, and so it is not art. Scientific cognitivism adds a further requirement. To be acceptable, judgments of natural objects and environments must be grounded in what natural science tells us about the subject of the judgment. For example, it is tempting to admire Monarch butterflies both for their coloring and for the fragile, delicate appearance of their wings. However, Monarch butterflies are like ducks. They migrate long distances in order to spend winter in warmer climates. Some Monarchs migrate as much as 3,000 miles. Scientific cognitivism warns that an aesthetic judgment about Monarch butterflies that lacks awareness of these facts is subjective and without merit. For their size, their wings are neither fragile nor delicate.

Exercise: Suppose that someone sees a field of flowers and says that it is "pretty as a picture." Do these remarks suggest a failure to judge nature appropriately? Do they trivialize nature? Or is this response a valuable starting point for a more refined engagement with nature, as the great naturalist Aldo Leopold contends (2001)?

Emily Brady (2003) and Ronald Moore (2008) criticize scientific cognitivism. It mistakenly implies that most people fail to appreciate nature properly most of the time. Furthermore, Brady argues that the requirement of scientific understanding is too constraining. Aesthetic experience is exploratory in nature, but excessive reliance on the findings of science inhibits perceptual exploration of nature. Specifically, it can interfere with an imaginative engagement with nature, and it tells us to ignore mere "folklore" as a guide to it. Yet folklore about animals and natural phenomena can enrich our perception of them, and imaginative engagement can stimulate perceptual discoveries. Looking at a tree and thinking that its bark is like a person's skin can encourage us to imagine the life of a tree in fresh ways.

Yuriko Saito (1998) brings an interesting twist to the point that Carlson's scientific cognitivism tells us that few people appreciate nature correctly. When aesthetic judgment is based on scientific knowledge, all of nature will seem aesthetically good. Properly contextualized, no environment or aspect of nature will seem aesthetically dull or ugly. Experiencing a massive earthquake, we should regard it as a wonderful and inevitable natural process. Borrowing an example from Holmes Rolston III (1989), Saito considers the case of hikers who come across a dead deer in the woods. The carcass is rotting, stinking, and covered with maggots. Appreciation of the positive aesthetic value of this situation requires a superhuman suppression of ordinary human responses. Two problems follow. First, the situation's ordinary sensory properties become irrelevant to its aesthetic properties. We are asked to ignore the stench and the repulsiveness of the visual decay. However, this is a superhuman demand, for no one can be expected to aesthetically evaluate all natural threats in a positive light. Philosophers generally agree to the slogan "should implies can," meaning that if we should do something, then we can do it. Conversely, we cannot be faulted for not doing what is beyond our reach. Saito relates this principle to the implication of Carlson's position that we should do what we cannot do. "Should implies can" tells us that we should not view nature in this way. Second, Saito argues that an appropriate aesthetic response to nature should be informed by moral interests. We should not, for example, admire the mushroom cloud of an atomic explosion as it destroys a city. Similarly, we should not withhold our normal moral judgments in order to aesthetically appreciate all of nature. Some natural events are threatening and harmful, and it would be wrong to abandon our moral concern for human suffering in order to overcome our sense of fear or horror. In this case, the implications of a strong scientific cognitivism are questioned for telling us that we should do what we should not do. (Another version of Saito's objection would be to say that, although it is possible to separate aesthetic from sensory properties for conceptual art, it is hardly plausible as an account of the aesthetic dimension of nature. Facing nature, we cannot alienate ourselves from our human sensibilities to a parallel degree.)

Exercise: Locate any of Claude Monet's colorful paintings of the river Thames, London. Is their visual appeal reduced when you consider that Monet consciously sought to capture colors created by air and water pollution? Should it be? Should every aesthetic judgment of nature consider the degree to which environmental pollution affects what is seen?

Despite continuing debate about the cognitive stance that should be employed when making aesthetic judgments about nature, many philosophers endorse two points. First, aesthetic empiricism should be rejected because it encourages a shallow response to natural objects and environments. Second, judgments about the aesthetic properties of artworks should be informed by awareness that these properties are present by virtue of human intentions. As Michael Baxandall puts it, "Awareness that [a] picture's having an effect on us is the product of human action seems to lie deep in our thinking and talking about pictures" (Baxandall 1985: 6). By extension, natural aesthetic properties are not the product of human action, and this fact should also inform aesthetic judgments of nature.

7.5 Formalism and detachment

Having reviewed aesthetic empiricism in relation to the aesthetics of nature, we are now prepared to explore its implications for art. Let's review a central issue. Does it matter whether the audience for *Star Wars Episode I: The Phantom Menace* (1999) is aware that it was filmed many years after *Episode IV: A New Hope* (1977)? This historical fact was obvious to movie audiences in 1999, but it is not necessarily obvious to new viewers today. Psychologically, knowledge of this historical, non-sensory property tends to reduce enjoyment of *Episode I*. However, we are concentrating on philosophy, not psychology, and we are examining the normative dimension of the psychological effects of knowing about non-perceptible properties. *Should* non-perceptible properties be considered if they will influence our aesthetic judgments? Advocates of aesthetic empiricism think that aesthetic properties supervene on sensory properties and no others, and therefore we should not allow non-perceptible properties to influence our aesthetic judgments. In fact, this normative conclusion is the source of the theory's name. "Empiricism" is a technical term in theory of knowledge. It refers to the position that all knowledge depends on information gathered from sense perception.

Aesthetic empiricism has many implications for art. Taken at face value, it seems to place Chanel perfume, cheesecake, and India pale ale in aesthetic competition with Italian Renaissance paintings and Debussy's piano music. All of these things offer complex experiences of aesthetic properties. Furthermore, they are artifacts, and their aesthetic properties are present by human design. In fact, perfume and cheesecake might be better candidates for uninformed aesthetic response, because their aesthetic properties are more immediately agreeable. Yet perfumes, desserts, and beverages are not considered to be aesthetic rivals to paintings and musical works. Painting and composing are fine arts, but perfumery, baking, and brewing are not. This distinction is puzzling when we consider that there has been a long tradition of defining art in terms of its aesthetic function. According to Monroe C. Beardsley's version of such a definition, "[A]n artwork can be usefully defined as an intentional arrangement of conditions for affording experiences with a marked aesthetic character" (Beardsley 1979: 729). This description certainly fits Chanel No. 5, the world's best-selling perfume. Beardsley does not believe that perfume, cheesecake, and beer are art. At the same time, he thinks that non-representational visual art and instrumental music are art. What explains this difference? There is no immediate reason to think that non-perceptible properties make a difference here. To understand why an aesthetic definition of art might classify Debussy's *La cathédrale engloutie* as an artwork, but not Chanel No. 5 perfume, it helps to understand the *formalist* tendencies of aesthetic empiricism. To this end, we will examine the theory promoted by Clive Bell, an early twentieth-century art critic.

Bell defends the modern trend toward greater abstraction in art. People who dislike abstract art often complain that they do not understand what it is saying, what it shows, or what it is "about." Bell discredits these objections by arguing that they are completely irrelevant to art appreciation. In *Art* (1958), he advances the bold claim that sensory form is the only aspect of any artwork that should concern anyone who is making an aesthetic judgment about art. We must disentangle two distinct claims here, an aesthetic definition of art and a doctrine about aesthetic judgment.

1. An artwork is an artifact that supports a positive aesthetic judgment. (Bell sometimes talks of "aesthetic judgment" and sometimes of "aesthetic emotion," but this detail can be set aside.)
2. Sensory form is the only legitimate basis for a valid aesthetic judgment. As Bell puts it, "To appreciate a work of [visual] art we need bring with us nothing but a sense of form and colour and a knowledge of three-dimensional space" (1958: 28).

Bell defends these two points with a straightforward argument. He begins with the then-standard assumption that all art must have at least one common function. (See section 6.3.) Take any group of artworks about which you make a positive aesthetic judgment. Take any group about which someone else makes a positive aesthetic judgment. Although there may be no artworks that are common to both groups, there must be some property beyond artifactuality that they have in common. Using the visual arts of painting, sculpture, and architecture as paradigm examples of art, Bell notes that some visual art is not representational. Therefore representation is not the common property we seek. The same reasoning applies to expressive properties. However, one thing is true of every visual artwork. Each involves a formal arrangement of sensory properties. Sensory form is the one thing that is "common and peculiar" to objects about which we make positive aesthetic judgments (Bell 1958: 17).

Bell's theory invites the obvious objection that every artifact has form, and therefore his theory makes every artifact into an artwork – cheesecake, for example. He avoids this result by claiming that form is not sufficient. Instead, the form must serve as the basis for a particular aesthetic property.

He denies that beauty is the relevant property. Many aesthetically successful artworks are not beautiful. But if not beauty, then what? Paraphrasing his theory into the language employed in earlier sections of this chapter, Bell holds that formal configurations of sensory properties are the supervenience base for the only relevant aesthetic property, formal coherence. Every artifact displays form, but few artifacts display the desired formal coherence. Bell calls it "significant form."

Bell is frequently criticized for saying too little about the formal relationships that are appropriately significant. However, this complaint misses its target. Bell's vagueness is consistent with the thesis of aesthetic supervenience. The same property has very different sensory bases in the different arts. Bell offers examples of significant form in painting, music, sculpture, and architecture. Begin with his assumption that every artwork displays sensory properties. For example, the blue areas of Raphael's *The Madonna of the Pinks* are in the upper right corner and across the lower middle of the painting. These blue areas are simultaneously present to viewers. In contrast, music, dance, and literature are temporal arts. Their sensory properties are revealed sequentially in time. The formal structure of a painting is necessarily quite different from that of a poem or story about the same thing. Generalizing, each artform offers a distinctive range of opportunities for spatial and temporal relationships. Significant form in painting will be very different from significant form in architecture or instrumental music. Therefore Bell cannot be faulted for saying relatively little about the general conditions for the desired aesthetic property.

Bell becomes more helpful when he claims that each successful artwork possesses a unique, particular form. Suppose two artworks share the same general structure, as happens when there is a standardized form, such as the form that is common to Shakespearean sonnets, the three-line pattern of the Japanese haiku, or the musical progression that defines a twelve-bar blues form. That general form is not a significant form. Setting aside what the words mean, a blues song that begins, "Woke up this morning, empty bottle by my bed," is formally distinct from one that begins, "Woke up this morning, liquor bottle by my bed." The relevant form is the formal appearance that emerges from *all* of a work's sensory properties in their total interconnection.

Bell couples his formalism with a psychological thesis. Awareness of significant form triggers a distinctive psychological reaction, a thrilling suspension of time and a sense of freedom from all ordinary cares and concerns. Basically, he argues that the fact the forms of two very different works can trigger a common response is evidence that they possess the same aesthetic property. Bell also describes this response as a species of rapture or ecstasy. His name for this highly rewarding feeling is "the aesthetic emotion." Bell appears willing to recognize any artifact as an artwork if its formal appearance triggers this emotion in someone.

Exercise: Can you think of any experience with an artifact that was so immersive and object-focused that you had the "aesthetic emotion" that Bell describes?

Were these objects artworks? If a video-game player reports that she gets this emotion when playing Final Fantasy VII, *does Bell's theory indicate that* Final Fantasy VII *is an artwork?*

Finally, Bell derives an epistemological, normative conclusion from his formalism. It is a recommendation of *detachment*. Art is essentially an aesthetic enterprise. Because the relevant supervenience base is restricted to sensory forms, awareness of sensory form is the only thing that can be relevant to the process of making an aesthetic judgment about any artwork. Therefore the audience for an artwork should be motivated by an interest in its aesthetic dimension, and should engage with art while suspending or ignoring ordinary goals and concerns. Caring about the fate of young Anakin Skywalker during the pod-racing sequence in *Star Wars Episode I: The Phantom Menace* is a distraction from the movie's stunning visual achievement. Furthermore, aesthetically motivated art lovers will not care how the plot of *The Phantom Menace* relates to *Episode IV: A New Hope*, much less care about the order of their creation. The rewards of film viewing are aesthetic, not narrative or expressive. Bell goes as far as concluding that thoughts about historical provenance and the artist's intentions are irrelevant distractions. (See Bell 1958: 33.) These thoughts can interfere with and invalidate our aesthetic judgments. Expressive art is therefore highly suspect, for it sacrifices pursuit of the aesthetic emotion for an immersion in the emotions of ordinary life. Consequently, most people have an "impure" experience of most art, most of the time. The theory therefore invites the same objection that is directed against Carlson's scientific cognitivism, that it is implausible because it invalidates too many aesthetic responses.

Does Bell's version of formalism have merit? To a large extent, the answer depends on the merits of pure aesthetic empiricism. First, Raphael's *Madonna of the Pinks* has both representational and expressive properties. Are these completely irrelevant to any aesthetic judgment we make of it? Jenefer Robinson (2005) observes that there are many cases where our emotional responses are first steps in grasping "hotspots" in an artwork's form, especially in the case of instrumental music. Second, is it plausible to think that art has become culturally important because it sometimes facilitates "the aesthetic emotion" in some people? As the next section will explain, aesthetic theories of art have flourished because they have the potential to explain why all human cultures have invested energy in the production of aesthetically interesting artifacts and rituals. Given the limited appeal of non-expressive abstract form, Bell's theory invites us to wonder why art is central to human culture.

On a positive note, formalism has resources to explain why Chanel perfume, cheesecake, and India pale ale are not art. They appeal to the tongue and the nose, two sensory modalities that do not allow us to control form. Form is a byproduct of order, which requires some method of ordering that establishes spatial and/or temporal differences among sensory elements. Although tastes and smells allow for interesting combinations and interplay of sensory properties, they do not support sensory structure. As David Prall (1929) explains the idea, the addition of garlic to a dish of food alters the total taste and smell without adding any new structure. Beardsley agrees that taste and smell lack the "intrinsic relations" required to generate aesthetically interesting structures (Beardsley 1981: 98). Therefore, Beardsley can deny that Chanel perfume has emergent *formal* properties, which are the sort he has in mind when he defines art as artifacts intentionally designed to feature aesthetic properties. Formalism seems to draw the boundary between art and non-art in the right place.

7.6 Making special

Return, for a moment, to the earliest examples of philosophical definitions of art. Charles Batteux defined art as intentional representation that uses beauty to supply pleasure. (See section 6.1.) Like Bell's proposal about significant form, Batteux's definition emphasizes a single aesthetic property. Both of their accounts propose that awareness of this property provides a valuable mental state. Of course, they disagree on which aesthetic property results in which mental state. The history of aesthetics is littered with competing proposals on these two points. Many nineteenth-century philosophers and critics paved the way for Bell by building a theory of Romantic art around the property of sublimity and linking it to an awe-filled grasp of the world's underlying structures. Later in that century, the *aestheticist* movement returned to a defense of art as a source of pleasure for its own sake. As Leo Tolstoy notes in *What is Art?*, aesthetic accounts of art tend to cluster around these two schools of thought (1996: 41). Tolstoy dismisses the Romantic approach as unintelligible. The competing aesthetic account of art answers the question of what art is good for by saying that it is a source of personal pleasure or satisfaction (1996: 47). However, the capacity to give pleasure does not distinguish artworks from candy and perfume, and so Tolstoy rejects the aesthetic as a significant property of art. (For Tolstoy's recommendation of an expression theory of art, see section 2.2.) Tolstoy's challenge to aesthetic definitions of art merits a response.

In the late twentieth century, philosophers developed two new lines of thought about aesthetic judgment, both of which avoid Tolstoy's charges of subjectivity and trivialization. First, emphasizing beauty and pleasure does not assign art a trivial function. This line of argument is associated with Ellen Dissanayake (1995). Second, beauty and pleasure are classic examples of aesthetic properties and responses, but it is a mistake to define art's aesthetic dimension by concentrating on beauty and pleasure. This line of thought is discussed in section 7.7.

Dissanayake is one of several recent authors to note that art history is a narrow discipline that focuses on visual representations and aesthetically enhanced objects. However, these "artworks" were usually produced as elements of a social ritual. A comprehensive history of art should discuss this "art" in relation to the participatory activities of music and dance. Music, dance, and expressive visual representation are found in all pre-modern societies. They all involve conspicuous display of aesthetic features. Against Bell, Dissanayake proposes that aesthetic properties were originally exploited as a means to a further end. Pre-modern humans aesthetically enhanced artifacts and events whenever there was a social reason to enhance their status, power, or memorability. From this perspective, traditional aesthetic theory went wrong in *equating* art's aesthetic dimension with art's basic function. An analogous error would be the following. Suppose that you notice that both swords and shovels have handles. Should you conclude that their defining purpose is to be handled by a human hand? This analysis would be shortsighted, for it ignores the obvious fact that both artifacts have handles so that they can be gripped by a human hand in order to fulfill additional functions. Similarly, Dissanayake proposes that art's aesthetic function is a means to achieve the additional goal of "making special" (1995: 42). This phrase summarizes the idea that a prominent display of aesthetic properties calls attention to something while also setting it apart.

Beautifying an object or activity generally involves making it vivid and imposing a distinctive pattern. On the one hand, this aesthetic enhancement provides pleasure and gratification (1996: 55). On the other hand, it is a public sign of extraordinary significance. If you are thirsty, a plain earthenware cup and a goblet made of gold are equally good for holding water. So if someone possesses a golden goblet, there will be some further ritual use for it, or some special status signified by its use. Bell and other theorists who associate art with transcendence and rapture are partially correct. In many pre-modern societies, aesthetically significant form is used to create extraordinary states of mind, which can further the general purpose of making selected experiences more significant and memorable for everyone involved.

Exercise: Think of the modern ritual of the public wedding. Why does the bride wear a special gown? How is a wedding ceremony similar to a classical music concert?

Dissanayake is offering a corrective to aesthetic definitions of art. The art of any pre-modern society is co-extensive with the very wide range of objects and activities that are "made special" through aesthetic enhancement. Nonetheless, pre-modern artists did not produce aesthetic objects for their own sake, nor for the sake of pleasure. Compare this idea to Bell's claim that the representational and utilitarian dimensions of artworks compete with their aesthetic success, and to Tolstoy's complaint that aesthetics trivializes art by reducing it to a source of pleasure. Against both of them, Dissanayake argues that aesthetic success and pleasure are a means by which objects and social activities become marked off as especially significant. Furthermore, her theory addresses the first art problem. (See section 6.5.) She recognizes that modern art practices have evolved from pre-modern art. A great deal of modern art is anti-aesthetic because aesthetic success is no longer required to create significance. Yet modern artists continue to exploit institutional structures that mark out some events and objects as socially special. In this respect, conceptual artists are not so very different from Raphael and Debussy.

7.7 Pleasure and appreciation

Dissanayake focuses on aesthetic enhancements that are gratifying and pleasurable. This approach has the merit of being very traditional while addressing the first art problem. However, this emphasis is subject to the criticism that it focuses on an overly narrow range of aesthetic enhancements. The death of Old Dan in *Where the Red Fern Grows* (1961), a popular children's book, is neither gratifying nor pleasant. Yet it has an aesthetic function of contributing both tension and balance to the story. If you are not sure that a children's book is an artwork, consider the brutal images of war atrocities created by Francisco Goya in his *Los Desastres de la Guerra* print series – *The Disasters of War*, created in 1810–20. Other artists specialize in work that might best be described as warped and creepy, such as David Lynch's film *Eraserhead* (1976) and his television series *Twin Peaks* (1990–1). Yet these artifacts are aesthetically rewarding. We are therefore unlikely to get a satisfying, comprehensive account of aesthetic enhancement from a theory that begins with the assumption that aesthetic properties characteristically furnish pleasure. Many philosophers think that a broader range of properties and responses are involved in aesthetic judgments about art.

Philosophers often map the flaws of failed theories as a guide to achieving a better one. So how does the traditional "pleasure model" fail? Let's walk through its major claims. It is apparent that some sensory properties are natural causes of pleasure in human perceivers. The sweetness of sugar causes pleasure. Other pleasures depend on enculturation. The characteristic "new car smell" gives pleasure to car buyers, but it would probably not give pleasure to someone who does not understand how it signifies the cash value of the new car. Building on this model, a simple aesthetic definition of art tells us that an artifact is an artwork if its sensory properties are selected to cause pleasure, either naturally or through enculturation. Faced with counterexamples like *Eraserhead* and Goya's prints, the pleasure model must confront a dilemma suggested in the last paragraph. If they do not cause pleasure, they are not art. If they are art, then we must construct a complicated story of how pleasure is present despite their genuine unpleasantness. In the past, the second option was commonly defended by employing the normative doctrine of detachment. To achieve aesthetic judgment, you must disengage from the ordinary concerns of life. Viewed with psychological distance or disinterest, Goya's images of decapitated bodies will cause pleasure. (The eighteenth-century term "disinterest" can be misleading. It is not a lack of interest, but a narrowing of focus.) In short, if you do not get pleasure from weird, disjointed movies like *Eraserhead* and from graphically brutal drawings like Goya's *The Disasters of War*, the defect is in you, the viewer. Aesthetically sophisticated people enjoy their aesthetic properties as much as babies enjoy sugar.

Exercise: Ask a friend to select a favorite film comedy and a favorite film that ends unhappily. After they have made their selection, ask them whether the two films give them equal pleasure. If the two do not give equal pleasure, ask them to explain why they admire something that offers lesser pleasure.

Where does the pleasure model go wrong? First, sensory experiences of art and nature can be rewarding without being pleasurable. Should we say that these experiences do not involve aesthetic judgment, or should we broaden our account of aesthetic judgment to cover these cases? (Although both strategies have their defenders, we will pursue the second possibility.) Second, pleasure taken in sensory appearances does not distinguish art from cheesecake. Earlier, we saw that formalism offers a strategy for explaining why a limited number of pleasurable artifacts are artworks. A simple pleasure theory must be supplemented with formalism or with some other mechanism for preserving this distinction. Third, the model's complicated story about cause and effect lacks genuine explanatory power. In claiming that the causal relationship fails whenever people have the wrong mental state (e.g., when they are not disinterested), the model introduces another variable that is relatively independent of the object's own properties. The mental state does more explanatory work than the aesthetic properties. Presumably, everything is aesthetically gratifying to anyone who can sustain the correct mental attitude. Fourth, the theory appears to say that the expressive content of artworks is irrelevant to their aesthetic success. We have seen that Bell explicitly endorses this strange result. Others try to find a way around it. Edward Bullough advocates a famous version of the theory in which audiences must simultaneously care about the implications of the content of the work and yet, paradoxically, not care about it in a personal way.

Recall our discussion of Hamlet, Hecuba, and expression theory (in section 2.1). Bullough pursues the idea that responses to art begin with emotional identification with the represented content. (Writing in 1912, he only discusses representational art.) Personal engagement generates an emotional response, which is then altered by regarding that response impersonally, as another phenomenon for observation. Awareness of the lack of practical consequences encourages "psychical distancing" from the situation. We inhibit our ordinary responses in order to observe those responses. To demonstrate the importance of this psychological process, Bullough offers the case of a jealous husband who cannot enjoy William Shakespeare's *Othello* (1603) because the plot hits too close to home. The play reignites his feelings about his wife and he feels miserable. All around him, the rest of the audience enjoys the play, empathizing with both the fictional husband and wife while simultaneously treating their emotional responses as an additional element of the theatrical event. The jealous husband fails to obtain and maintain psychological distance. He cannot enjoy the feelings caused by the play because he does not treat those feelings as phenomena for appreciation. Critics doubt that this mental state of distancing is paradoxical and "peculiar," as Bullough maintains (1912: 88).

It appears so paradoxical that it is impossible. Furthermore, the parallel experience of feeling emotionally distant in real-life situations is seldom pleasurable. It is normally described as a sense of alienation.

What we desire, therefore, is an analysis of aesthetic judgment that explains why a positive judgment is frequently – perhaps *normally* – accompanied by pleasure. At the same time, the analysis cannot advocate a straightforward or direct cause-and-effect relationship between aesthetic properties and pleasure. Sugar's sweetness is immediately pleasurable, but most pleasurable artworks do not provide pleasure so directly. Unless you endorse Bell's pure aesthetic empiricism, you will want to build some knowledge about the world and about art practices into the process so that the aesthetic judgment gets connected to the artwork's base properties in a plausible way. Finally, the account must allow positive judgments to accompany unpleasant responses.

Jerrold Levinson provides a theory that explains how artworks can be aesthetically worthwhile without being pleasurable (1996: 12). Furthermore, he endorses the need to incorporate facts about artistic provenance or creative context into the supervenience base of an artwork's aesthetic properties. For example, suppose that you find Goya's war prints too horrific to enjoy. By learning about Goya's expressive purposes in relationship to the Spanish war of independence (1808–14), you can become better positioned to understand that the shock value of the images is a deliberate strategy to express moral and political outrage. Set beside Goya's earlier *Los Caprichos* or "Caprice" series (1796–8), the war prints deepen his ongoing exploration of the dark side of the human condition. Viewed with knowledge of their creative context, Goya's war prints merit a second-order or *meta-response*, which literally means that you respond to your own initial response. (Suppose you get angry and say something horrible to a friend in public, and then you feel ashamed about having become so angry. The shame is a meta-response to the anger.) Levinson proposes that aesthetic judgments are meta-responses, "involving reflection not only on appearances per se but on the constitution of such appearances and the interaction between higher-order and lower-order perceptions" (1996: 8). If what is pictured in a Goya war print horrifies you and then you reflect on Goya's circumstances and his point of view, you can then *appreciate* how the depicted content and its violent stylization work together to "constitute" or create your initial response. This appreciation of how the artwork generates the first-order response is a response to the initial response, and thus it is a meta-response. (Although it is not framed in this terminology, Bullough's theory of psychological distancing becomes more persuasive if we read it as an early meta-response theory.) When the first-order response involves sensory properties, the meta-response is an aesthetic judgment. Although a second-order response can be pleasurable, the case of shame demonstrates that meta-responses are not necessarily pleasurable.

Locating aesthetic judgment in a meta-response carries a price. Levinson's meta-response only happens when someone asks how something promotes a first-order response. A person who is not aware of why they admire an appearance does not make an aesthetic judgment. Suppose two people take pleasure in the sensory appearance of a non-representational sculpture. One person simply likes its color. The second person attends to and appreciates the artistic choices that were involved in creating its form, texture, and color. In this situation, only the second person makes an aesthetic judgment. Many people find this result counterintuitive. For related reasons, we cannot always tell whether another person's response to an artwork reflects aesthetic judgment. Suppose someone admires Goya's *Disasters of War* series but fails to say why. We will never know whether the admiration reflects a warped, inappropriate first-order response or a legitimate second-order response.

Exercise: You are probably aware of the clichéd expression, "I don't know much about art, but I know what I like." Does the meta-response account imply that anyone who says this about a work of art has failed to make an aesthetic judgment about it? Explain.

Two additional criticisms deserve attention. First, Levinson thinks that his account works equally well for aesthetic judgments of both nature and art. However, if a sunset does not reflect intentional design, then it is unclear how anyone can *admire* and *appreciate* its appearance in a meta-response. The first-order response is a response to sensory properties, but then what information would ever lead you to think that a naturally produced set of sensory properties does not merit the first-order response? The most plausible answer is that a better understanding of natural science could encourage this response, but then we seem to fall back into a scientific cognitivism that recommends all of nature as aesthetically admirable. (See section 7.4.)

The second problem is the now-familiar issue of the status of artifacts that appeal to taste and smell. Pleasurable perfume and food do not happen by accident. Perfume makers and cooks employ considerable skill (and sometimes a good deal of applied science) in order to achieve a pleasing combination of sensory properties. Suppose that you sample two slices of cheesecake and you enjoy the taste of one slice a little more than the other. You then learn that the better slice was made "from scratch." The other was made by adding cream to a packaged mix. Knowing more about the origins of the two slices, you take another bite of each. This time, the sensory differences are more apparent. Next, you have appropriate second-order responses. You appropriately admire the texture and flavors of the "from scratch" cheesecake and you think less of the other. Recall that an aesthetic definition of art embraces any artifact that supports a positive aesthetic judgment. Generalizing from our cheesecake example, the meta-response analysis of aesthetic judgment invites us to conclude that perfumes and cheesecakes are aesthetic rivals of artworks. If artworks are supposed to be special in being designed to be objects of aesthetic judgment, then the meta-response theory generates counter-intuitive boundaries for art.

I conclude with a caution against accepting or rejecting the meta-response theory before you understand how it compares to its main rival in contemporary aesthetics. However, this rival theory relies on the concept of valuing an experience in itself. That topic must be delayed until chapter 9, which explores artistic and aesthetic value.

Before we get to that issue, chapter 8 takes up another idea that has appeared in the arguments covered in this chapter. It examines the assumption that it is important to distinguish between artworks and non-artworks in a way that keeps cheesecake, Chanel perfume, and video games in the latter category.

Issues to think about

1. Explain the concept of a supervenience base. Next, select a short poem. Substitute synonymous terms for some of the words in the poem. Identify aesthetic changes that result from these changes in the supervenience base. Now consider the original poem again, but construct a false history of composition for it. Identify changes in aesthetic properties that might result from this change in its history of production.
2. Use the example of delicate, "hammerless" piano music as a guide to selecting another aesthetic property that is relative to the standard appearance of other objects of the same type. Do these cases demonstrate that aesthetic empiricism does not hold for some aesthetic properties?
3. Explain the thesis of aesthetic empiricism.
4. What is conceptual art? What would you say to someone who says that it has no aesthetic properties?
5. Explain and then evaluate the proposal that all natural objects and environments merit positive aesthetic judgments.
6. Debussy's *La cathédrale engloutie* [*The Sunken Cathedral*] is a piece of instrumental music with a descriptive title. What does Bell's formalism tell us about the relevance of the title to the listening experience? Evaluate this position.
7. Explain Dissanayake's theory of the connection between art and aesthetic judgment. How would this theory explain the fact that only a limited number of buildings are considered artworks?
8. Explain and then evaluate the proposal that there is a necessary connection between positive aesthetic judgments and pleasure.

Further resources

Contemporary debates about aesthetic supervenience begin with the influential suggestions of Frank Sibley's "Aesthetic and Non-aesthetic," which is collected with his other essays in *Approach to Aesthetics* (2001). Support for supervenience comes from Bender (1987), Currie (1989), Zangwill (2001), and Young (2005). Challenges are raised by Eaton (1994) and Tilghman (2004). For further discussion of the aesthetic dimension of conceptual art, see Schellekens (2007). Moore (2008) is a wide-ranging, book-length introduction to the aesthetic dimensions of nature. Carlson (2008) offers a sustained introductory treatment of the cognitivist/conceptualist position. An alternative view, more in keeping with Kant's theory of free beauty, is defended in Malcolm Budd's *The Aesthetic Appreciation of Nature* (2002). Contemporary formalism is best explained and defended by Zangwill (2001). Dissanayake first proposed the "making special" theory in *What Is Art For?* (1988). In many respects, her theory is an elaboration of ideas sketched by Nietzsche (1999) in the nineteenth century. The tradition of disinterestedness runs from Kant (1987) to Bullough (1912) and Bell (1958), and then to Stolnitz (1960). Dickie (1964) did a great deal to discredit this tradition, yet it lives on in Fenner (2008). Brady (2005) and Dutton (2009) discuss why aesthetics has tended to ignore smells and tastes. Feagin (1983) offers a contemporary account of the pleasure of tragic art that initiates the recent focus on meta-responses. Another influential meta-response theory is outlined by Walton (2008).

8 Beyond the Fine Arts

When Aristotle (1997) wrote about tragic theatre 24 centuries ago, he discussed plays written for presentation in outdoor amphitheatres during religious festivals. These festivals also presented comedies. Unfortunately, Aristotle's discussion of comedy was not preserved. The theatre in Athens may have held more than 15,000 spectators – an audience that far exceeds the number of movie seats available in a comparably sized modern city. Unlike most other public events, the Athenian festivals welcomed attendance by women, children, and slaves. We know, therefore, that Aristotle was discussing tragedies aimed at a cross-section of the population, and we know that the great playwrights of the time – Sophocles, Aeschylus, and Euripides – wrote for multiple levels of society. Although we are uncertain whether women attended comic theatre, the presence of adolescent males is mentioned in Aristophanes' rewrite of his comedy *Clouds* (419 BCE). The Greeks entered their plays into competitions, and *Clouds* originally took third place (out of three). In the rewrite, a character steps forward and speaks for the writer. He informs the crowd that although *Clouds* is his best comedy, it lost the competition because he made the mistake of writing it for the discerning intellectuals in the audience, instead of introducing drivel and slapstick to entertain adolescents.

Aristophanes' complaint articulates a perennial tension. Is it better to write for a small number of highly critical people, or to aim to entertain the broadest number? More to the point, shall we follow R.G. Collingwood (1938) and Theodor Adorno (2004) and say that the concessions required for popular success are incompatible with the aims of art? Framed in this way, this question would not have occurred to Aristotle and Aristophanes, for they employed a very broad concept of *technē* or "art" that included all skilled shaping of materials. Although Aristophanes' *Clouds* and *Wasps* both contain dialogue that recognizes a distinction between highbrow and lowbrow comedy, the playwright is not distinguishing between art and something that is opposed to art. Aristophanes is making a distinction *within* the domain of *technē*. As discussed earlier (in section 6.2), it was only about 300 years ago that European intellectuals began to insist on a strict distinction between fine art and craft. But once that distinction is in place, playwrights count as artists. Stonecutters and silversmiths do not. It then becomes very tempting to make a parallel distinction between artists and comedians.

Taken at face value, the definitions of art that we surveyed in chapter 6 do not imply that fine art and the popular arts are mutually exclusive categories, in the way that "never married" and "widowed" are mutually exclusive. Nor do those definitions explain why philosophical aesthetics has been so routinely hostile to the popular arts. Death-metal music is undeniably expressive of a certain range of emotion, and many flower gardens in suburban yards display, in their modest way, as much concern for aesthetically pleasing design as the formal garden at the Palace of Versailles. As such, the tradition of denying that these things are art is an interesting and important topic for examination in its own right.

8.1 Popular and mass art

Many accounts of art are motivated by the goal of "elevating" art and treating it as a privileged category of human activity. Fine art is praised as having an improving effect on its audience that does not arise from competing popular pursuits. The result has been a tendency to treat popular art and fine art as mutually exclusive categories. Writing at the very beginning of the modern period, Joseph Addison argues that art, particularly literature, is the best use of leisure time: "of all the diversions of life, there is none so proper to fill up its empty spaces as the reading of useful and entertaining authors" (Addison and Steele 1965 [1711–14]: Vol. I, 397). He contends that imagination is the source of our pleasure with the arts and with aesthetically gratifying views of nature. For those with enough cultural sophistication to grasp the arts, imagination is stimulated into "pleasing and agreeable motions" (Addison 1965: Vol. III, 539). Art is therefore better than science and philosophy as a leisure pursuit, for they tire – and generally bore – most people. And art is superior to other contenders for our leisure time, such as gambling and excessive drinking, which excessively arouse the emotions: "There are, indeed, but very few who know how to be idle and innocent, or have a relish of any pleasures that are not criminal: every diversion they take is at the expense of some one virtue or another, and their very first step out of business is into vice or folly" (Addison 1965: Vol. III, 538–9). Art provides "safe" and "innocent pleasures" that are conducive to our mental and physical health. Aside from the riot that broke out at the 1913 Paris premiere of Igor Stravinsky's *Rite of Spring*, art venues are far safer places than the bars, gambling dens, and dog fighting arenas of Addison's eighteenth-century London.

Addison's arguments illustrate that the project of defining art was inspired, at least in part, by a social distinction between uncultured pastimes and cultured, superior ones. Addison's discussion of the pleasures of the imagination was published three decades before the appearance of Charles Batteux's definition of art in 1746. However, both authors are examining the pleasurable diversions of the idle upper class and the increasingly prosperous merchant class. (See section 6.2.) In short, the goal of defining fine art arose within a social project of disentangling the proper enjoyments of the lower and upper classes. (See Shiner 2003a.) Popular pleasures, in the sense of pleasures available to a very broad spectrum of society, are easily attainable. Their inferiority is only evident to those who have had the fortune to become acquainted with fine art. David Hume, generally regarded as the most important philosopher writing in English in the eighteenth century, captures this attitude in his famous essay of 1757, "Of the Standard of Taste."

> A man, who has had no opportunity of comparing the different kinds of beauty, is indeed totally unqualified to pronounce an opinion with regard to any object presented to him. By comparison alone we fix the epithets of praise or blame, and learn how to assign the due degree of each. The coarsest daubing contains a certain lustre of colours and exactness of imitation, which are so far beauties, and would affect the mind of a peasant or Indian with the highest admiration. The most vulgar ballads are not entirely destitute of harmony or nature; and none but a person, familiarized to superior beauties, would pronounce their numbers harsh, or narration uninteresting. A great inferiority of beauty gives pain to a person conversant in the highest excellence of the kind, and is for that reason pronounced a deformity. . . . Thus, though the principles of taste be universal, and, nearly, if not entirely, the same in all men; yet few are qualified to give judgment on any work of art. (Hume 1998a: 144, 147)

Hume believes that most people – "the generality of men," in his wording – derive no pleasure or value from any particular artwork. He thinks that this failure is partially due to a lack of social access. Foreshadowing ideas that will re-emerge in institutional and historical definitions of art, Hume thinks that art appreciation requires extensive understanding of the social purposes that lie behind each artwork, which in turn requires considerable education and familiarity with each work's social and historical context. (See sections 5.1, 6.4 and 6.5.) In the context of the eighteenth century, philosophers could scarcely imagine a population with widespread literacy, much less ongoing exposure to artistic excellence. (Hume's examples are mainly literature rather than visual art or music.) Consequently, art belonged to the upper classes. The experiences and education that prepare someone to appreciate art were inseparable from what was expected of anyone prepared to attain a high rank in society. It is no coincidence that the distinction between popular and fine art is sometimes described as a distinction between low and high art (see Cohen 1999a; Shusterman 2002; and Shiner 2003a: 94–8).

Examining French society in the second half of the twentieth century, sociologist Pierre Bourdieu argues that the fine arts have retained this association with the educated upper class. More importantly, he argues that the continuing divide between popular art and fine art is a social mechanism for perpetuating class divisions in modern society. The various functions postulated by functional definitions of art are a smokescreen hiding its primary social function. As Bourdieu's most famous remark on this function puts it, "Taste classifies, and it classifies the classifier" (Bourdieu 1984: 6). By responding to various kinds of art and by revealing their likes and dislikes, individuals reveal their ranked position in the social hierarchy. Bourdieu offers the example of a theatre critic who dismisses on-stage nudity as a "box-office gimmick" (Bourdieu 1984: 6–7). This critic is a typical "art" lover, displaying class snobbery by disapproving of theatrical staging that is designed to increase ticket sales. Conversely, people secure social ranking, in some measure, by learning to engage in the patterns of "cultural consumption" appropriate to that social position. Philosophers, for example, must learn to appreciate the functionless art of Duchamp and Warhol if they intend to be taken seriously as knowledgeable about philosophy of art! So it is not surprising that philosophical aesthetics has generally ignored popular art. Taking it too seriously might undermine one's intellectual credentials by revealing a pattern of illegitimate cultural consumption.

Bourdieu is directing a serious criticism against the seeming neutrality of the philosophical project of defining art. The recent preference for value-neutral, classificatory definitions is not value-neutral if it concentrates on a class of objects with a particular cultural value. (See section 6.4 for the distinction between value-neutral and value-laden definitions.) Defining "art" is more difficult than defining "wombat" or "supernova." Wombats and supernovas are *natural kinds*. These classifications are based on biological and physical structures that we discover by examining nature. In contrast, fine art is a cultural kind. The boundary of the classification is constantly redrawn by the very activity of talking about that boundary. In concentrating on some activities and objects at the expense of others, our definitions of cultural kinds reflect and reinforce our cultural prejudices. Looking back, Hume's contrast of superior and "vulgar" (i.e., uneducated) beauty is a fairly obvious loading of the dice in favor of the preferences of the educated upper class. Is our current language any less loaded?

Exercise: Reflect on your own encounters with the various arts in your formal education. To what extent do 21st-century patterns of education perpetuate Hume's distinction between readily accessible "art" and less accessible, yet objectively superior, fine art?

Philosophers have become more sensitive to the degree that modern prejudices inform the language that is used to frame the contrast between art and other spheres of culture. We can talk about *popular art*, where the word "art" implies that there is an important continuity between, say, a music video and G. F. Handel's opera *Tamerlano* (1719), between square dancing and Agnes de Mille's choreography for *Rodeo* (1942), and between the graphic art of Albrecht Dürer and the graphic novels of today. Or we can talk about *popular culture*, and thus avoid the implication of continuity with fine art. Finally, the rise of processes of industrial production has generated the related category of *mass art* (or, again downplaying connections with art, *mass culture*). This last category intersects with the other two in interesting ways. Popular art is often discussed as if it divides neatly into the two camps of folk art and mass art (e.g., handmade Hallowe'en decorations are folk art, but decorations purchased from a retail store are mass art). As before, the distinction presumes a hierarchy of value, with mass art on the losing end.

Exercise: List your five favorite films. When that task is complete, list your five favorite "art" films. If your two lists are different, explain why "art" films are different from other movies. (If you think that your reading of this chapter has influenced your answer, ask a friend to produce the first list. When it is completed, ask for the second list and then proceed with the analysis.)

Noël Carroll's analysis of mass art is useful for cutting through this tangle of distinctions. Carroll's theory proposes that mass art is a subcategory of popular art. A mass artwork is an artwork that is designed for ease of comprehension and which is made available to large numbers of people through "reliance upon mass delivery systems" (Carroll 1998: 199). The virtue of this analysis is that it calls attention to two distinct ways that the concept of "mass" arises for mass art.

- Industrial, mechanical, and digital processes permit production of numerous copies, allowing interaction by massive numbers of people at multiple locations. Audiences interact with copies rather than a single original object. Mass artworks are multiple artworks (see section 4.1).
- Mass artworks are "designed to be easy, to be readily accessible, with minimum effort, to the largest number of people possible" (Carroll 1998: 192). They are to be understood "with minimal effort, virtually on first contact, for the largest number of untutored (or relatively untutored) audiences" (1998: 196), making the material accessible to massive numbers of people.

If an object meets both of these conditions and is art by virtue of being "descended from traditional art-forms" (1998: 197), it is mass art. In other words, if something is produced on a mass scale, is a type of thing that is like some recognizable art-form, and nothing about its design interferes with understanding by masses of people, then it is mass art.

One implication of Carroll's analysis is that use of a medium enabling mass reproduction is necessary but not sufficient for mass art. Anne Geddes and Ed Burtynsky are photographers. Glossy, mass-produced calendars featuring the photographs of Geddes are available at thousands of retail outlets. Burtynsky's "Tailings" series has not been so favored. Burtynsky's photos of industrial waste and blighted landscapes invite a complex visual, cognitive, and emotional response. Yet Geddes and Burtynsky work in the same medium. Carroll's accessibility requirement explains why Geddes – who specializes in photographs of cute babies in cute costumes – is engaged in the production of mass art, while Burtynsky makes fine art. Although Burtynsky makes his photographs available for viewing on his professional website, the "Tailings" series is not designed to be popular, and therefore his work is not mass art. This insight is important for understanding why only some movies, books, and other mass-produced artifacts are fine art, while others in the same media are mass art. The same divide can apply to the work of a single individual. David Lynch's *Dune* (1984) is mass art, but his film *Mulholland Drive* (2001) is fine art. Bob Dylan's recording of his song "Knockin' on Heaven's Door" (1973) is mass art and his recording of "Desolation Row" (1965) is fine art. (Notice the reference to recorded music. Music is not mass art unless it is distributed by an automated technology.) You might object that the analysis implies that when Dylan sings those two songs in the same concert, that concert is divided into fine art and popular art segments. However, this is not such a strange result. Historically, it might be the norm. During the 1806 concert at which Ludwig van Beethoven premiered his Violin Concerto in D Major, Franz Clement, the soloist, entertained the audience by improvising a fiddle tune with the violin held upside down.

Carroll's analysis is subject to criticism on the grounds that he does not adequately explain what counts as art, so his analysis begs the question in assuming that mass art is a subcategory of art. As will become clearer in the following section, many philosophers proceed from the assumption that popular art and mass art are not subcategories of art. Yet Carroll's analysis stipulates that an artifact must be popular art before it can be mass art, which requires employment of a popular form of an established artform. Given that early masterpieces of cinema often lasted under a minute, and given that Henri de Toulouse-Lautrec designed commercial advertising posters that are now recognized as fine art, it appears that we should regard television commercials as a mass art. Yet Carroll denies that they have this status. At the same time, he sees no problem in allowing that video games are artworks. So it is not clear how an appeal to traditional artforms is supposed to function here. A second criticism is that his criterion of accessibility to relatively untutored audiences is an audience-relative criterion (Irwin 2007: 45–6). Carroll draws the line between popular and fine art according to an artifact's level of accessibility at the time of its creation. This analysis assumes that popular art requires some interpretation, however minimal. As a result, small degrees of historical or cultural distance can pose interpretive challenges. For example, the title of the Elvis Costello song "Secondary Modern" (1980) is immediately understood by British listeners born before 1975, yet meaningless to almost everyone else. (The term refers to a particular kind of educational institution in the United Kingdom. Secondary moderns enrolled adolescents who were not being prepared for university studies. These schools were phased out during the 1970s.) So is Costello's recording of the song a case of mass art, based on its initial accessibility in England? Or is it fine art, based on its culture-bound, short-lived accessibility? Or do we allow that a single artifact can be both things at once? Style can pose another barrier. At the height of his popularity, Charlie Chaplin was one of the world's top movie stars. Today, his silent, black-and-white comedies seem unbearably slow-paced. Modern audiences find them all but unwatchable. Like Aristophanes' comedies, the popular entertainment of one time and place has become the fine art of another. Objects do not remain fixed in either category. Carroll owes us a better account of how and when they shift categories.

Richard Shusterman observes that the situation is additionally complicated by our tendency to ignore the concept of entertainment, which historically predates recognition of popular and mass culture. Philosophers have generally regarded entertainment as a trivial or even harmful element of culture, distracting people from better uses of their time and energy. Shusterman observes that modern, empirically-minded philosophers tend to regard entertainment and pleasure as passive and therefore trivial responses to external objects, as if the pleasure of watching a movie is the same as the pleasure of a steam bath (Shusterman 2007: 143). This common view is naïve. As Aristotle explains, pleasure is normally the result of engaging successfully in a project or undertaking. The entertainment value of popular art depends on interpretation – of narratives, of the medium employed, of the ideas in play. So there is considerable continuity between the popular and fine arts, so-called. They both give pleasure "in perceiving and understanding the particular work's qualities and meanings, where such pleasure tends to intensify our attention to the work in a way that aids our perception and understanding of it" (Shusterman 2007: 143).

Although it is clear that a great deal of popular entertainment requires interpretation and therefore provides pleasure for the same reasons that art does, objections continue to be raised. The next section of this chapter surveys them.

8.2 Standard criticisms of popular art

Most criticism of popular art derives from either or both of these two propositions:

- popular culture does not produce artworks;
- the social consequences of popular culture are generally undesirable.

These very broad claims take on many specifications. We will examine both of them in greater detail in this section and the next. However, before we discuss particular versions of either claim, it should be noted that they are logically independent of one another. The first claim can be understood using a value-neutral, classificatory account of art. (The distinction between value-neutral and evaluative uses of "art" is explained in section 6.4.) The second claim does not mention art. So the second claim is an important criticism even if popular culture does produce artworks, as is necessitated by Carroll's account of mass art.

The first of the two claims looks like an empirical claim, one that is subject to confirmation or refutation by seeing how things are in the world. It has the same structure as "Idaho does not produce cotton," which is an empirical claim. Nonetheless, it is frequently treated as a self-evident truth that follows from the meaning of the terminology. Adopted without argument, it becomes the first step in establishing the superiority of fine art. The next step is to assume that art is uniquely valuable. Nothing else is of value in the same way. (This pair of assumptions will be examined in chapter 9.) If it is true by definition that popular movies, pop songs, and video games are not art, then the claim about art's unique value proves that this other material cannot be of value in the same way that fine art is valuable. However, difference does not establish superiority. Why does the absence of that unique value render popular art undesirable? That one thing is not good in the way that another kind of thing is good is not yet a reason to condemn either of them. Swimming has cardiovascular benefits that one cannot get from playing bluegrass music on a banjo, but that is no argument against playing the banjo, or against swimming. The argument needs another premise, one that identifies a significant conflict between the two. For example, you might argue that one detracts from the other. Time invested watching Harry Potter movies or playing *Guitar Hero* videogames is time wasted, for that time could have been spent with art. Therefore extensive engagement with popular culture is engagement with something less than genuine culture, which in turn "prevent[s] the development of a cultivated mind which can regard things in their true worth" (Arendt 1993: 217). From this perspective, it is no accident that time spent with popular culture is so often described as "killing time," and we are right to regard it as a "guilty pleasure," for it involves a retreat into private pleasures at the expense of self-development. In the long run, the argument concludes, either widespread engagement with popular culture will encourage all new art to become as dumbed-down as mass art or art will become an increasingly elite enterprise that has little impact on most of society.

Since this argument assumes that popular and fine art are mutually exclusive categories, we must examine the plausibility of that premise. Here are three reasons advanced in support of the claim that popular culture cannot produce artworks.

1. In order to be popular, "low" or mass art must be relatively simple and formulaic. Therefore it lacks the creativity and/or aesthetic richness of fine art. A common variation of this argument says that the formulaic structure of "low" art is linked to audience passivity, which is contrasted with the more active engagement required by fine art.
2. The production of art is a historically self-reflexive activity, and to engage with an artwork is to engage with a cultural tradition. Designed for popular reception, popular art lacks the cultural depth of fine art.
3. In the world of late capitalism, "artists" are entrepreneurs, selling a commodity in the art market. Under these circumstances, art has integrity "only when it refuses to play along with communication" (Adorno 2004: 405). Everything about it, including its very appearance, must "renounce communication" and thereby challenge the status quo (2004: 310).

The problem with each of these claims is that we can easily produce counterexamples from the realm of popular art. We can also attack these arguments from the opposite direction, by identifying central examples of fine art that fit the descriptions of popular art found in these arguments.

For example, Shusterman (2000) argues that the best examples of African-American popular music are counterexamples to these arguments. He offers the 1988 recording of "Talkin' All that Jazz" by the hip-hop group Stetsasonic as a counterexample to all three arguments. Although Shusterman observes that we can find many examples of popular music that are more complex than this rap, "Talkin' All that Jazz" cannot be dismissed as simple. It is semantically complex, exploiting the title phrase and other verbal ambiguities to imply multiple meanings, and it is cognitively structured as an argument against rap's many critics. Secondly, the band's verbal and musical references to other musicians provide significant historical context and self-reflexivity. (Although Shusterman does not mention the band's video for this song, the imagery in the video provides additional historical grounding.) It is clear that a "passive" audience cannot understand "Talkin' All that Jazz." Thirdly (and, for Shusterman, most importantly), the primary stylistic practices of rap (e.g., the practice of musical sampling, the use of African-American slang, the "funky" beats) are calculated to celebrate black urban culture in open defiance of the American status quo.

However, Shusterman's argument invites the response that he has merely demonstrated that "Talkin' All that Jazz" is fine art. Like William Shakespeare's *Romeo and Juliet* (*c*.1594–5), "Talkin' All that Jazz" merely demonstrates that art and commercial motives are not necessarily in conflict. Some fine art employs mass media, some fine art becomes (relatively) popular, and some fine art does both of those things, as demonstrated by the continuing popularity of *Romeo and Juliet* and Jane Austen's novels. These examples are not counterexamples to the claim that fine art and popular art are mutually exclusive. They are not readily accessible to enough people to be popular art. But then what should we make of the popularity of Seth Grahame-Smith's *Pride and Prejudice and Zombies* (2009)? Is this book an example of mass art that satirizes high culture, or does it borrow so much of Austen's antiquated writing that it is not sufficiently accessible to be mass art?

We have arrived at an impasse. Perhaps we can move beyond it by looking at the shared logic that underlies the three arguments. As we saw in section 6.1, there is a certain logic involved in proving that a particular object does not belong in a particular category. A *logically decisive* exclusion requires identifying the necessary conditions for that category, then demonstrating that the particular object fails to meet one or more of those conditions. It is even trickier to prove that two categories of objects are mutually exclusive, which is what one must do if one is to contend that popular art is not "real" art – that is, not the sort of art that concerns philosophy of art. For example, suppose that I want to prove that no frying pan can be President of the United States, an example chosen for its simplicity. I would point out that only natural-born citizens of the United States can be the President. Since frying pans are made, not born, they cannot be "natural-born" citizens of any place, much less the United States. Case closed. Generalizing from this example, the proper strategy is to specify two properties, the first of which is a necessary condition for one sort of thing, and then a second property, which is a necessary condition for being the other sort of thing, where the first property ensures that the second will not be present. What, then, is the necessary condition for art that is excluded by a necessary condition for popular or mass art? In chapter 6, we observed that artifactuality is the only property that is widely recognized as a necessary condition of art. However, artifactuality is also a necessary condition for popular art and mass art, so artifactuality cannot be the relevant property. To succeed, we must specify another necessary condition for being popular or mass art, and then explain how it conflicts with a necessary condition of fine art. Although being designed to be accessible to large numbers of people is a plausible requirement for being "popular" (and, following Carroll's analysis, for being mass art), there is nothing in any plausible definition of fine art that would exclude this property. Were that the case, then Shakespeare's *Romeo and Juliet* and most of the religious art of the Middle Ages would not be art.

Exercise: Demonstrate your understanding of the underlying logic by providing a logically decisive explanation of why an oil painting cannot be either a pop song or a video game. Then examine properties of pops songs and video games that might be offered as evidence that they cannot be artworks. Are any of these logically decisive?

Lacking any positive evidence that the properties of fine art and the properties of popular art are mutually exclusive, we can deploy Ted Cohen's theory of bilateral design to reject the three arguments claiming that popular culture cannot produce artworks. Here is Cohen's central point: "There are many significant works of art that are 'bilateral.' Such a work appeals to two audiences, audiences that may have few if any members in common . . . [A] great deal of the finest art we know appeals to different constituencies in many different ways" (Cohen 1999a: 141). Cohen offers the examples of movies directed by John Ford and Alfred Hitchcock.

Ford and Hitchcock worked in the Hollywood system in an era when all films were made for the widest possible audience, before the creation of the current ratings system. Ford's *The Searchers* (1956) is a cowboy-and-Indian movie and Hitchcock's *North by Northwest* (1959) is an action-adventure film. Both films were highly profitable – helped, no doubt, by using John Wayne and Cary Grant in their lead roles, respectively – but neither film won any Academy Awards. Today, both are ranked in the 40 best American films by the American Film Institute. These two movies are artworks if any movies are, yet both count as popular and mass art, too. Therefore these categories are not mutually exclusive. The underlying point is that there are many different features to appreciate in such works, and different groups within the audience respond approvingly to these different features. (See also Shusterman 2000: 190–1). *The Searchers* and *North by Northwest* are both "chase" films with exciting action sequences, and their plots are easily understood by virtually anyone on first viewing. However, each film also involves its strong male lead in a complex psychological drama, and each plot contains political undercurrents that provide allegorical commentary on American values. Aesthetically, each film is beautifully crafted.

In short, the bilateral thesis allows that some (but not all) artifacts can by appreciated in multiple ways and on multiple levels, and some of these artifacts straddle the divide that otherwise distinguishes fine art from popular art. Popular culture can produce works of art without sacrificing anything from our usual understanding of art. If the undesirability of popular and mass art is inherent in their design, then some fine art must be equally undesirable.

8.3 Social consequences of popular culture

However one draws the line between fine art and popular culture, many intellectuals insist that popular culture is socially undesirable, particularly in the form of mass art. Three proposals dominate this discussion:

- Fine art challenges its audience, actively engaging both imagination and intellect. The ease of comprehension required of popular art is incompatible with active response. At any given time, only avant-garde art is genuine art. The rest invites unreflective, passive reception, and so leaves the audience mentally dull, encouraging cultural and social passivity and a lack of individuality (Adorno 2002 [1938]; Greenberg 2003 [1939]).
- As John Keats said, "Beauty is truth, truth beauty." Popular culture offers platitudes and clichés instead of truths. It offers formulaic repetition instead of beauty. On both counts, it lacks the liberating qualities of fine art (Adorno 2004; Ruskin 1985).
- Popular and mass art attract the audience by relying on emotional engagement that inhibits, rather than develops, emotional health and maturity (Collingwood 1938; Bloom 1987).

The first of these arguments is very similar to the second one. The important difference is that the first focuses on the mental responses that are distinctively associated with the two spheres of culture and the second focuses on the properties that trigger those responses. It should also be noted that each of these arguments can be taken in either of two ways. First, they can be taken to say that people are relatively worse off for time spent with popular culture. Popular art is undesirable because it competes with fine art, turning people away from the benefits of fine art. However, the arguments can also advance by adopting an objective standard of human perfection against which all activities should be judged. From this perspective, any time spent with popular art is undesirable, consisting of a failure to live up to our human potential. People who still enjoy the music of their adolescence twenty years after the fact should worry us.

Exercise: Think of an example of an artwork that satisfies the bilateral thesis, which holds that the same artifact can function as both popular and fine art. Would these arguments support the creation of such artworks?

In order to take these criticisms seriously, we must agree that the alleged consequences are unique to popular culture. If they also arise with fine art, then they are not of interest as criticisms of popular art. To understand why this point matters, consider a different complaint. Suppose that a "green" supporter complains that the widespread use of polypropylene (code #5 plastic) is an environmental threat. However, suppose that the same person is not concerned about the widespread use of plastic bags made from low-density polyethylene. If the plastic bags pose the same environmental problems, then the criticism of the first should be extended to the second. Otherwise the criticism is arbitrary and the critic is either short-sighted or a hypocrite. Turning back to the arts, suppose that the artifactuality of popular music is the source of some undesirable social consequence. If so, then the problem also arises for Beethoven's music, as well, because artifactuality happens to be the one thing that is generally accepted as a necessary condition of fine art. As a result, the burden of distinguishing all fine art from all popular art falls on critics of popular culture, and it must be handled in a way that restricts the criticism to popular art. So what is the relevant difference that will restrict the criticism to popular culture, without backfiring on all art? Section 8.2 reviewed and criticized the claim that fine art and popular art (and thus, by extension, mass art) are mutually exclusive categories. Despite doubts raised about the underlying distinction, let's suppose that the distinction is a sound one so that we can concentrate on the arguments for the thesis that fine art is generally superior.

You might skip over consideration of the arguments in order to offer a direct challenge to the thesis. You might think that their relative value is beside the point. If Bourdieu is correct, people who invest significant time with popular art do not visit art museums or read Emily Dickinson. The existence of "superior" art makes no difference to their lives. So why bother to compare them? However, this is a weak argument. If popular art harms people, then everyone stands to lose from the collective damage that results when large numbers of people are passive, ignorant, and emotionally stunted. Similarly, producing a limited set of counterexamples from the best of popular culture does not really defuse the arguments if they are accurate about the general tendencies of popular art.

Another objection observes that all three arguments against popular culture were originally formulated as attacks on fine art. Versions of the three arguments are found in Plato's criticisms of music, poetry, and visual representation (Plato 2004). Proponents of a historical definition of art can respond that fine art has evolved in ways that have rendered it immune to these criticisms (see section 6.5). Alternatively, proponents of the cluster account can respond that some fine art will remain subject to such criticism, but some art will escape it, where the difference depends on which of the many possible properties are present in a particular artwork (see section 6.6).

Plato is not the only major philosopher whose theories are cited as evidence in this debate. Carroll (1998) observes that these arguments are almost always rooted in a theory of artistic autonomy that borrows from Immanuel Kant's theory of aesthetic response. However, we have already seen that Kant's discussion of the autonomous, active play of imagination and intellect is not a theory of fine art. (See section 7.4.) His theory of natural beauty is merely a prelude to his account of fine art. (We also discussed

Kant's view of fine art in section 3.2.) In the absence of independent reasons to endorse the assumptions about fine art that bolster the modern critique of popular culture, that critique rests on a terrible historical distortion.

A third objection is that the supporting arguments propose that specific psychological and social consequences follow from the basic properties of popular art. The arguments therefore postulate a causal relationship between popular art and various outcomes. However, philosophers have long understood that causal relationships cannot be understood in advance of systematically observing the effects where the alleged cause is present and comparing those results with appropriate contrasting cases (i.e., a control group where the alleged cause is absent). In philosophical jargon, we say that causes cannot be identified a priori. There is no getting around the fact that it is an empirical hypothesis, subject to empirical testing. In the absence of properly controlled observations, it is impossible to know whether time spent with popular culture has more harmful effects than does time spent with fine art. What we have at this point is untested speculation. And, given that exposure to fine art is regularly associated with higher income, higher levels of education, and other variables that reflect social advantages, it will be extremely difficult to determine the answer. The jury, as the saying goes, is still out on this topic.

8.4 Gender and race

Some 2,400 years ago, Socrates was put on trial. Ironically, Socrates had been one of the targets of Aristophanes' *Clouds*. Aristophanes thought that some of his jokes went over the heads of much of his audience. We also know that Socrates complained that the play prejudiced his jury against him (Plato 1989: 81). Although he faced execution for his offenses against the city-state of Athens, Socrates provoked the 501 citizen-jurors by telling them that they owed him a pension for his service to the city. He explained the nature of his service with a crude analogy. The city was a large horse, "a horse grown sluggish because of its size and in need of being roused by a kind of gadfly. . . . But perhaps you are angry, as men roused from sleep are angry, and perhaps you will swat me, persuaded . . . that you might lightly kill" (Plato 1989: 93–4). For many philosophers, Socrates' willingness to risk death when criticizing his own society serves as the paradigm of rational detachment from social pressures. Sections 8.2 and 8.3 have suggested that philosophers have displayed a great deal of irrational prejudice toward popular art, which suggests that philosophers do not always live up to the Socratic ideal.

Where previous chapters have taken philosophers and their arguments at face value, philosophical hostility to popular art is so poorly grounded in the facts that it appears to be little more than an expression of dominant social values. Philosophers are not immune from social prejudices and philosophical theories are themselves the product of historical and social change. As a result, philosophy is sometimes *ideological*. That is to say, some philosophical positions are promoted solely because their adoption

will serve the interests of the ruling class. For example, most contemporary
philosophers are professional educators in higher education. Therefore it
is in their interests to promote aspects of culture that require higher education and to either attack or ignore aspects of culture that are accessible
without it. For the most part, philosophy of art continues to promote the
social and institutional frameworks that have informed it since the early
eighteenth century. Both the arts *and philosophical discourse about the arts*
continue to reinforce dominant patterns of social, economic, and political
subordination.

Exploration of this possibility can be found in the work of philosophers
who apply the insights of feminism and race theory to philosophy of art.
Feminist aesthetics (Eaton 2008) and philosophical explorations of racial
distinctions (Roelofs 2005; Taylor 2010) highlight the roles that representation, expression, aesthetic preference, and related topics play in forming
and policing gender and racial identity. To take the most obvious case,
critics of popular culture have traditionally argued that fine art encourages individuality and liberation while popular culture does the opposite.
Feminism and race theory redirect the argument by calling attention to
the degree to which the "art" of women and persons of color has been
systematically excluded from fine art by being relegated to the "popular"
and low art categories. However, this philosophical project should not be
confused with the work of showing that many artworks – frequently called
"masterpieces" – reflect and reinforce the misogyny and racism of the dominant culture. The latter task belongs to art historians, critics, and practicing
artists. The philosophical project examines the conceptual framework of
modernity as it applies to the arts in order to shed light on the ways in
which our conceptual superstructure contributes to this overall pattern.
Notice, for example, that "masterpiece" assumes the activity of an Anglo-
European male.

Consider the eighteenth-century doctrine that fine art combines imitative representation with beauty (see section 6.2). Was the doctrine applied
in a neutral manner to all artifacts of this era? Consider two pictures: one
consists of flowers embroidered on a linen apron and the second is a painting of livestock, such as Aelbert Cuyp's *Young Herdsmen and Cows* (c.
1665). Both objects appear to satisfy the requirements of fine art. However,
craft and fine art were understood to be mutually exclusive, and so the
embroidered representation was classified as a "decorative" element of a
functional object. At the same time, it is no coincidence that embroidery
was women's work. The crude opposition of "masculine" and "feminine"
spheres of culture aligns with the opposition of "important" and "not so
important," respectively (Korsmeyer 2004: 85). (For more on this topic,
see section 3.6.) Confronting these categories at the dawn of the modern
period, visual artist Rosalba Carriera (1675–1757) circumvented prevailing expectations by transforming the traditional "craft" of decorating snuff
boxes with miniature portraits into the new artform of "miniatures."
Carriera accomplished this transformation by executing her portraits on
small pieces of ivory rather than on the lids of snuff boxes (Johns 2003).

At thirty, Carriera was famous, wealthy, and honored: she was the first woman ever elected to the Roman academy of art, the Accademia di San Luca. Despite her professional success, Carriera's strong association with the new artform identified it as a feminine genre. It was presumed to lack genius, which was associated with men. (See Staniszewski 1995 and Shiner 2003a: 121–3.)

Gender discrimination within the arts is not unique to Western societies. If you know very much about Elizabethan theatre and Shakespeare's plays, you are probably aware that women were banned from performing on the public stage. In the original performances of *Romeo and Juliet*, the role of Juliet was performed by a pre-adolescent boy. Although the long-standing ban on actresses served a social function of controlling women, Elizabethan society was simultaneously suspicious of men playing as women. They were attacked as sinful cross-dressers and as incitements to homosexual lust (Blake 1998: 122). The interesting historical fact is that virtually the same practices and arguments were occurring in Japanese theatre at the same time. *Kabuki* theatre appeared in the city of Kyoto around the beginning of the seventeenth century. Combining narrative, dance, and music, *kabuki* arose from public dance performances by a woman, the priestess or ceremonial dancer Okuni. Her innovative performance style spread throughout Japan. In 1629, associations with prostitution led to a ban on women in *kabuki*. Women's roles were given to boys. In 1652, boys were banned on the grounds that their presence was linked to homosexual prostitution. Since then, *kabuki* theatre has been reserved for adult men. *Geisha* and other music and dance styles then developed as an alternative vehicle for women's performances (Hahn 2007: 25–6). An avant-garde practice by women has become codified and ritualized as a vehicle for displaying male skills, with many *kabuki* roles handed down inter-generationally from father to son.

Where European societies have wielded a complex doctrine about craft, decoration, genius, and fine art in order to marginalize women's art, the achievements of persons of color were devalued by a simpler, if no less dismissive, categorization. Opposing the complex historical developments of European civilization with "the Other," "Modernity has been built in part on the myth that black peoples have no culture or civilization, and on the related myth – embraced in different forms by anti-black racists and by anti-racists, of all colours – that whatever practices black people have are primitive, timeless and homogenous" (Taylor 2010: 4).

From the perspective of European modernism, it might seem that "primitive" art is highly valued. However, something else emerges when "primitivism" is combined with assumptions about inherent racial differences. The critical reception of jazz in the first half of the twentieth century offers an interesting illustration of this dynamic. Stark differences are found in American and French explanations of why jazz is a legitimate art. American intellectuals celebrated jazz by "whitewashing" it, ignoring the African-American musicians who invented the genre. In contrast, prominent French critics praised jazz as "Negro" music, at its best when it was racially pure and thus unburdened by the stifling conventions of civilized music (Gioia 1988). Great jazz is a spontaneous, pure expression of emotion. While that sounds like praise, particularly in light of expression theories of art (see section 2.2), it carries some less-than-flattering baggage. It says that great jazz arises from a lack of culture, a lack of training, a lack of intellectual content, and a lack of self-reflection. If jazz is timeless music and a universally accessible outpouring of emotion, that is because it is so primitive that there is no cultural barrier to penetrate. As Ted Gioia notes, "Presented in such terms, the jazz performance seems hardly a cultural event and more like a medical affliction, akin to epilepsy" (1988: 31). Unfortunately, this subtly racist pattern of discourse has been replicated in almost all subsequent discussion of jazz.

Exercise: Ask someone who is a fan of blues music to name ten great blues musicians, and ask a fan of country music to name ten great country musicians. Is there a gender and/or racial pattern to the resulting lists? Does the pattern change when the list is supplied by someone of a different gender and race? What do such lists imply about the idea that blues music and country music are distinctively American *artforms?*

This section has offered a glimpse into the philosophical project of investigating the ideological dimensions of our discourse and associated conceptual framework. In practice, this project is affiliated with a larger, multidisciplinary re-examination of how art and popular culture have perpetuated racist and misogynist thinking. However, it must be kept in mind that these are general cultural patterns. Admitting that there is merit in these critiques does not imply that *every* artwork and *all* philosophy of art is always an agent of oppression. Furthermore, admitting that Aristophanes' *Clouds* is a reactionary political document that helped convict and kill Socrates does not negate its very real value as comic theatre, and admitting that the Rolling Stones' "Brown Sugar" (1971) is both sexist and racist does not mean that we can dismiss it without further discussion. In keeping with the thesis of bilateral design, the complexity of such cases should be regarded as an opportunity to generate new questions about art's power, function, and value (Lorraine 1990). Likewise, admitting that there are misogynistic implications in Kant's theory of artistic genius is no reason to chuck the modern, Kantian aesthetic tradition out the window. However, it is an invitation to accept it with a lot less deference.

8.5 Everyday aesthetics

If we explore the artworld by identifying what is common among Beethoven's piano sonatas, Pablo Picasso's paintings, foreign movies with subtitles, and Shakespeare's tragedies, then we are likely to regard art as a rare and special thing. However, we are also likely to regard art as something that relatively few people understand or care about. So what happens if we expand our horizons to include aesthetic activity that does not involve art in the traditional and restricted sense of fine art? What if we focus on objects such as Stephen King novels and backyard flower gardens, and on activities such as dancing to recorded music in nightclubs, plastering a railroad boxcar with graffiti, recording a "cover" of a favorite song and posting it on YouTube, and designing and sewing a quilt? David Novitz proposes that emphasizing the continuities between fine art and everyday life will reveal that the language and concepts pertinent to art have a broader range and are "deeply integrated into everyday life" (Novitz 1992: 15).

Leo Tolstoy's expression theory is an interesting precedent. (See sections 2.2 and 6.3.) The assumption that artists are motivated to share their emotions leads him to conclude that art should be accessible to the widest possible audience. Therefore the best art is universally accessible, and creates a community of its audience:

> A real work of art destroys, in the consciousness of the receiver, the separation between himself and the artist – not that alone, but also between himself and all whose minds receive this work of art. In this freeing of our personality from its separation and isolation, in this uniting of it with others, lies the chief characteristic and the great attractive force of art. (Tolstoy 1996: 140)

Fine art, which is art of the upper classes, has a different effect. It bores and confuses most people, and (as Bourdieu more recently argues) it tends to accentuate and amplify class and cultural divisions. Tolstoy therefore points to folk art as the only genuine art. Although this doctrine might seem attractive as a correction to the problems discussed in section 8.4, his account remains narrowly focused on a single function: emotive expression. Although he criticizes fine art, Tolstoy remains firmly in the modern tradition of prioritizing communication at the expense of all else, and he continues to seek the essential discontinuity between artworks and other artifacts.

A competing philosophical tradition assumes that it would be better to concentrate on continuities rather than discontinuities. John Dewey, an American pragmatist, has been influential for his thesis that we will only understand art's purpose and value by first "recovering the continuity of esthetic experience with normal processes of living" (Dewey 2005 [1934]: 9). Dewey's primary insight is that art's historical origins in aesthetically pleasing objects and rituals point to a natural human capacity for a uniquely satisfying, embodied experience. According to Dewey, an aesthetic experience is simply a coherent and individualized experience, one in which an individual apprehends both unity and completeness. Dewey wrote before there was any talk of multiple intelligences. Nonetheless, we might paraphrase Dewey's emphasis on being "active through [one's] whole being" (2005: 18), so that "the whole creature is alive" (2005: 27), as the thesis that an aesthetic experience is a coherent, conscious experience that integrates our multiple intelligences. This aesthetic absorption might be triggered by hearing a song on the radio, by seeing the first poppies of spring blooming along the highway, or by completing a new level of the videogame *Call of Duty: Modern Warfare 2* (2009).

The *everyday aesthetics* movement pursues these ideas, but with an important alteration. Dewey argues that most of our ongoing experience of the world is fragmented and unconnected. Although most experiences will have some aesthetic element, a "dominantly" aesthetic response is relatively rare within the flow and flux of everyday life (2005: 44). Artworks are objects that are intentionally designed in order to facilitate this kind of experience. (Like Tolstoy, Dewey proposes that artworks are uniquely valuable, especially for establishing social connections and transmitting culture. Unlike Tolstoy, Dewey does not compartmentalize emotional, intellectual, and sensual response.) What happens, then, if we pursue Dewey's emphasis on continuity without treating it as a preliminary stage for arriving at a theory of art? Responses that are "dominantly" aesthetic might be far more common than he allows. Arnold Berleant, one of the key figures in calling attention to the importance of everyday aesthetics, emphasizes the degree to which every human environment "is a culturally constructed context" rich with meaning and with the potential for aesthetic experience (Berleant 2005: 25). The physical design of a toaster, the patterns that result from the zoning restrictions of a city, and even the distinctive "fit" of a brand of jeans are all occasions for the immediate experience of cultural messages and values.

Exercise: Select a category of merchandise. Next, list competing "chain" retail stores that sell that kind of merchandise. Identify at least one chain that caters primarily to women, and one that caters primarily to men. Try to describe the distinctive look and feel of each of these "brands." Given that these stores display carefully designed total environments, how do the aesthetic choices of the different environments create an inviting atmosphere for some groups of people while alienating others?

In stressing our complex experiences of human-made environments, the exploration of everyday aesthetics has obvious connections to the traditional concern for the aesthetics of nature. (See section 7.4.) However, a number of philosophers have noted that this parallel encourages many of us to fall back on questionable assumptions about nature appreciation. All too often, it is assumed that we appreciate an environment by *viewing* it from a particularly fine vantage point, and as a static, distanced object or arrangement of objects. In contrast, the full aesthetic effect of any environment depends on immersion in it and movement through it, using all of the senses (Carlson 2000: 34–5). Why, then, do philosophers emphasize sight and hearing at the expense of the other senses? Dewey, for example, mentions smell only once in *Art as Experience*, a book of nearly 400 pages.

When we examine philosophical arguments that prioritize seeing and hearing as "higher" senses, we tend to find some version of the view that they can operate at a distance and thus possess greater objectivity. As Carolyn Korsmeyer explains,

> vision and hearing are allied with the mind, leaving touch, taste, and smell
> in the realm of the body and its physical sensations. Therefore the potent

> traditions that elevate mind over body are also at play . . . [and] we need to ask whether concepts of masculinity and femininity are also at work in the hierarchy of the senses. (Korsmeyer 2004: 87)

It is important to recognize that scientific models of perceptual response offer no support for our stereotypes about sense perception. If smells and tastes are subjective, then so is vision. Furthermore, tastes and smells are manipulated for their expressive and cultural significance, both in the home and in "fine" dining. When we pursue continuities between art and other dimensions of life, we find that the preparation and consumption of food is a rich arena of aesthetically rewarding, culturally significant activity. These admissions do not require arguing that food is fine art. Furthermore, they offer another opportunity to reconsider a sphere of activity that is routinely undervalued as feminine and therefore unimportant (Korsmeyer 2004: 96–103).

Issues to think about

1. Explain the proposal that mass art is a subcategory of popular art.
2. Explain the core idea of the thesis that fine art and popular art are mutually exclusive categories. Which response to that thesis is stronger, the ordinary method of producing counterexamples or the bilateral thesis?
3. What does it mean to say that philosophical hostility to popular culture is ideological? Is this a plausible response to standard criticisms of popular culture?
4. Explain the difference between saying that certain *artworks* are racist and misogynist and saying that basic ideas *in philosophy of art* have supported racism and misogyny. Does the first claim support the second? Does the second claim support the first?
5. What are the primary assumptions of the everyday aesthetics movement? How do they distinguish between an aesthetically successful humanly made environment and one that is a failure?

Further resources

Aesthetics generally ignores comedy and humor, but Cohen (1999b) demonstrates that jokes and joke-telling are philosophically interesting without privileging them as fine art. Kaplan (1966) provides an accessible overview of the major criticisms of popular and mass art. A longer and more sophisticated treatment is Horkheimer and Adorno (2002 [1947]). An influential nineteenth-century precedent is Ruskin (1985). Addison's defense of literature's superiority has been revived by Nussbaum (1992) and Carey (2006). Carroll's *A Philosophy of Mass Art* (1998) contains sustained discussion of many issues involving popular and mass art. Carroll's critics include Fisher (2004, 2005) and Novitz (2005). Bourdieu (1984) has been highly influential; for criticisms, see Gracyk (2007). Multiple critiques of unjust gendering in our intellectual tradition are brought together in Brand and

Korsmeyer (1995). Several of the essays grapple with race and racism. Piper (1996) assembles a series of powerful essays on issues that she faced as an African-American conceptual and performance artist in the American artworld. The "everyday" implications of Dewey's pragmatism are explored in Sartwell (1995). The best introduction to "everyday aesthetics" is the set of essays collected in *The Aesthetics of Everyday Life* (Light and Smith 2005). Saito (2007) provides a cross-cultural analysis of some of the same issues while emphasizing their moral dimension.

Baz Luhrmann's film *Romeo + Juliet* (1996), featuring Leonardo DiCaprio and Claire Danes, preserves much of Shakespeare's dialogue in a contemporary restaging and thus offers an interesting test case for the bilateral thesis. The sexual politics inherent in the Elizabethan theatre's ban on women is the central issue of two entertaining movies, the Oscar-winning *Shakespeare in Love* (1998) and the arguably superior *Stage Beauty* (2004). For more information on Burtynsky's photographs, see the video *Edward Burtynsky on Manufactured Landscapes* (2006). It is available online: http:// ca.ted.com / index.php / talks / edward_burtynsky_on_manufactured_land scapes.html. Many films explore the aesthetics of food, but *Babette's Feast* (1987) is particularly rich in its exploration of the intersection of gender, food, and the cultural implications of the humanly made environment. Jean Michel Basquiat worked on the border between high and low art as it existed thirty years ago. *Downtown 81* (2001) offers a glimpse of that art scene. Although the biopic *Basquiat* (1996) takes liberties with many facts, the film is not afraid to explore the topic of racism in the artworld.

9 Artistic and Aesthetic Value

In the summer of 1965, rock musician Bob Dylan visited the Factory, Andy Warhol's Manhattan studio. Warhol was branching out into filmmaking and invited Dylan for a screen test. (In Warhol's hands, these "tests" were really short, silent films, rather than screen tests in the traditional sense.) Accounts differ about what happened at the conclusion of Dylan's short time before the camera. Either Dylan surprised Warhol by indicating that he expected payment in the form of an original Warhol, or Warhol spontaneously made a gift of a canvas when Dylan admired it. In either case, the visit ended with Dylan and friends securing a silkscreen portrait of Elvis Presley to the roof of their station wagon. The canvas was *Double Elvis* (1963, a.k.a. *Silver Elvis*), which features grainy, overlapping larger-than-life impressions of a publicity photo from Presley's 1960 Western movie, *Flaming Star*. A few years later, married and starting a family in upstate New York, Dylan traded the silkscreen to his neighbor and business manager, Albert Grossman. He got a sofa for it. After Grossman's death in 1986, his widow sold the Warhol for $75,000. Ten years later, a *Double Elvis* print sold at auction for just short of half a million dollars. The whereabouts and value of the sofa are unknown.

9.1 Three kinds of value

If nothing else, the story of Dylan's Warhol demonstrates an important distinction concerning three kinds of value. First, there is exchange value. The economic or monetary value of a *Double Elvis* print and many other artworks is entirely a matter of how much money someone is willing to exchange for it at a given time. Warhol died in 1987, so there are no new original Warhols. The exchange value of his authenticated works has soared as museums and private collectors compete to own one. Dylan probably knew that his Warhol would be worth a lot of money someday. So why would he trade it for a sofa? Because exchange value does not align neatly with two other competing spheres of value. There is also an object's utility or use-value, which is its objective value relative to some activity of using it. When a vending machine sells two brands of cola and very few consumers can taste the difference, then the two products have objectively equivalent use-value as carbonated beverages. If their cost of production is also the same, then their exchange value should be the same, too. However, if consumers are regularly willing to pay more for one brand, there might be some additional real use, such as communication of social status that occurs when people use the product. Then, one brand may sell for more.

Third, there is subjective value, which is the value that something has to a particular individual. Subjective value can be radically at odds with the other two kinds of value. Needing a sofa, someone who has no immediate use for a very large piece of art might ignore its escalating exchange value and trade it for a sofa. Given that Dylan was wealthy and not motivated by the issue of long-term exchange value, there is nothing particularly irrational about the swap. There is a traditional saying in Latin, *de gustibus non est disputandum*, which means that there is no disputing about personal tastes. Taste preferences play an unpredictable role in establishing exchange value. Tastes make us choosy, and therefore two things that seem to have the same use-value will differ in price. If enough people share the same taste, and the means to satisfy that taste are scarce, then a relatively specialized taste can produce wildly inflated exchange values. For example, there is enough desire for sashimi in Japan – raw, fresh seafood – for bluefin tuna to be very expensive. As that species of fish becomes rarer and threatened with extinction, it is increasingly more expensive. Despite its high price, a great many people dislike sashimi and would not eat raw bluefish tuna even if it were given to them for free. In summary, subjective value explains why some commodities have prices that appear to be out of line with their use-value. Robert Rauschenberg's career has many parallels with Warhol's. But if more people like Warhol's work, then mediocre Warhols can cost more than the best Rauschenbergs on the open market. Exchange value, or price, is not always a reliable measure of success for a shared use-value.

Exercise: Given that a high-quality poster reproduction of Double Elvis *can be purchased for about 10 dollars, what objective use-value justifies the current exchange value of an authenticated original print?*

The remainder of this chapter focuses on use-value as a basis for objective evaluations. In order to say that Dylan made an objectively bad swap, we must be able to assign a use-value to the Warhol. Within the context of philosophy of art, this determination is a decision about its use-value *as a work of art*. So what is the use-value of art? This is not a new question for us. We have encountered it in previous chapters. Use-value is simply the idea of an object's unique function. Sofas and paintings clearly have different functions. If we can assign a comparative ranking to these different functions, then we will have a non-commercial basis for saying that one sort of thing is more valuable than another. If art plays a more significant role in life than sofas, then it was foolish for Dylan to swap a Warhol for a sofa. (Dylan, incidentally, later admitted that he regretted his trade.)

At this point, you are probably primed to challenge the assumption that all art has the same function. Do we assign the same use-value or function to the Diego Rivera mural in the Pacific Stock Exchange Building in San Francisco (1931), the Lady Gaga song "Poker Face" (2008), Yoko Ono's conceptual work "Earth Piece" (1964), and my paperback copy of J. D.

Salinger's *The Catcher in the Rye* (1951)? If so, is it expressive value? Is it aesthetic value? Or is it something else? Our inability to adopt a functional definition of art casts doubt on a genuinely common function. (See section 6.3.) One way around the problem is to say that different artworks have different use-values, yet some of these uses are *unique* to art. Another way around it is to say that some use-values are *typical* of art. While these strategies force us to admit that some particular artworks might lack the typical or unique values of art, we would gain a general understanding of how art is valuable. That might not be a bad concession. After all, the possibility of a mediocre Warhol was mentioned two paragraphs back. We *want* a theory that will admit that some artworks fail to fulfill any of the functions that are unique to or typical of artworks. We might classify these things as artworks because they reflect an *intention* to satisfy such a function, or because they are the kind of thing that typically satisfies such a function. (Recall Robert Stecker's disjunctive definition of art in section 6.5.) By allowing for the possibility that some artworks fail to achieve their intended or typical use-value, we can allow that art is valuable even if some artworks lack this value.

9.2 The uniqueness thesis

The previous section plunged us into questions of *axiology*, the philosophical subfield that examines value judgments and basic values. This section will examine the axiological thesis that art can be valuable in a way that nothing else is valuable.

At first glance, the uniqueness thesis appears to conflict with another idea that many people endorse about art. Many people support the additional thesis that each artwork is unique. Therefore, each artwork is uniquely valuable. However, if each artwork is uniquely valuable, then how can we claim that a particular use-value is typical of artworks? Notice the tension in affirming both of the following positions.

- What is valuable about Emily Dickinson's "Essential Oils – Are Wrung" is what is valuable about Warhol's *Double Elvis*. Only artworks are valuable in this same way.
- "Essential Oils – Are Wrung" is uniquely valuable. So is *Double Elvis*. Therefore what is valuable about Dickinson's "Essential Oils – Are Wrung" is not what is valuable about Warhol's *Double Elvis*.

Let's walk through an explanation of why the two proposals are in conflict. If two things have the same use-value, we should be able to say which, if either, does a better job relative to a specific function. All other things being equal, two DVD copies of Akira Kurosawa's film *The Hidden Fortress* (1958) have the same use-value. However, if one DVD is badly scratched and the other is in good condition, one of them is superior to the other. However, this comparison of two *copies* of *The Hidden Fortress* only succeeds because film involves multiple artworks, where multiple objects can be instances of the same work. (See chapter 4.) What if, instead of two copies of *The Hidden Fortress*, we compare the film with a singular artwork, such as Leonardo da Vinci's *Last Supper* (*c.*1498)? Assume that every artwork is valuable in the same way. But *The Last Supper* is badly damaged. It seems to follow that the damage makes it inferior in value to a good copy of *The Hidden Fortress*, the way that a damaged copy of *The Hidden Fortress* is inferior to a good one. Many people reject this conclusion. But why? If we can compare two copies of the same work, why doesn't the same logic extend to two different artworks? The answer is that, damaged or not, *The Last Supper* is a unique thing, offering a unique experience.

A moment's reflection reveals that this argument does not go through to its conclusion. The two DVD copies of *The Hidden Fortress* are also unique objects. (After all, if they were identical in all respects, there would only be one of them.) Their minor differences explain why, by reference to a shared use-value, one DVD is objectively better than the other. But if there are no *relevant* differences, then they have the same use-value. Therefore, saying that each artwork is unique is not enough to provide the desired conclusion that each artwork is uniquely valuable.

The argument for the unique value of each artwork is normally developed and strengthened by emphasizing art's aesthetic dimension. Although there might be some artworks that do not offer an aesthetic experience, they are the exceptions. Most artworks have aesthetic properties, and these contribute to artistic value when they are present. As Malcolm Budd puts it, "For you to experience a work with (full) understanding your experience must be imbued with an awareness of (all) the aesthetically relevant properties of the work – the properties that ground the attribution of artistic value and that constitute the particular forms of value the work exemplifies" (Budd 1995: 4). It is worth pausing to consider the term "experience." It implies that knowledge is gained through direct acquaintance with something, as opposed to knowledge that is gained through description, or by inference. The primary value of Dickinson's poems is the experience of reading them. The primary value of looking at Leonardo da Vinci's works is the experience of looking at them. By extension, the primary value of video games is the experience of playing them. Budd makes the additional point that each artistic medium generates aesthetic values in a unique way. One way to understand Budd's point is to see that the supervenience base for the aesthetic properties of each artistic medium is different. As a result, audiences encounter a distinctive range of aesthetic properties in film, literature, dance, and so on for all the arts. (See section 7.2.) Furthermore, each artwork in each artistic genre offers a distinctive, particularized aesthetic experience. Therefore, each artwork is valuable for its capacity to provide experiences which *only it* can provide.

Here is a different version of the crucial step in the argument:

> If aesthetic experience is always directed at and structured by the object experienced, then the particular experiences of reading a Shakespeare sonnet, hearing a Beethoven sonata, or viewing a Rothko painting cannot be had by other means than perceiving these specific objects; no pill or injection of mind-altering chemicals can provide the specific aesthetic experiences of appreciating these works. This argument may establish

that artworks have irreplaceable value as the objects of the aesthetic experiences they generate and structure. (Shusterman 2006: 221)

Richard Shusterman goes on to note that an irreplaceable value can also arise for those who misunderstand an artwork. Shusterman and Budd are offering an important reminder that some experiences lack an objective basis in the artwork. For the remainder of the chapter, we will assume we are talking about cases where a work is correctly understood. Given that restriction, we now have reasons to think that each artwork offers a unique, irreplaceable experience. George Lucas acknowledges that *The Hidden Fortress* inspired the main characters and some of the storyline of *Star Wars Episode IV: A New Hope* (1977). Yet watching *A New Hope* cannot substitute for watching *The Hidden Fortress* any more than watching *Star Wars Episode I: The Phantom Menace* (1999) can substitute for watching *A New Hope*. And no film can substitute for *The Last Supper*.

9.3 Value empiricism

We have now arrived at an empiricist axiology of art. It is the thesis of *value empiricism*. It is the standard explanation of how every artwork has the same kind of value, yet each is uniquely valuable. Each artwork is valuable for its capacity to provide an experience that cannot be gained in other ways. The tension outlined at the start of the last section is now removed by spelling out what we mean by the expression "what is valuable." The first of the two bulleted claims is making a point about a unique *kind* of value. Artworks are typically designed to be occasions for aesthetic judgment. The second claim says that the artistic or aesthetic value of each artwork is nonetheless unique. Each artwork offers a different experience and so each artwork is uniquely valuable.

- Dickinson's "Essential Oils – Are Wrung" and Warhol's *Double Elvis* are valuable in the same general way, as opportunities for valuable experiences.
- "Essential Oils – Are Wrung" is uniquely valuable. Because the valuable experience involves attention to and appreciation of its unique properties, the same experience cannot be derived from another of Dickinson's poems or from any other artwork.

A word of caution is in order here. You might recall our earlier discussion of aesthetic empiricism. It says that artistic provenance is irrelevant to aesthetic judgment. (See section 7.3.) Many value empiricists endorse aesthetic empiricism. However, they are independent positions. You can reject aesthetic empiricism while endorsing value empiricism. For example, you might think that provenance is relevant to aesthetic judgment on the grounds that some aesthetic properties supervene on a set of base properties that includes historical properties. Therefore you reject aesthetic empiricism. Furthermore, you might think that the experience associated with a properly informed aesthetic judgment is what is essentially valuable about that artwork. Therefore you endorse value empiricism. This particular combination of positions has come to be called "enlightened empiricism" (Davies 2006). For the remainder of this chapter, the arguments and examples presuppose enlightened empiricism.

Exercise: Suppose that two museum visitors arrive at Warhol's Double Elvis. *One does not know anything about Warhol's art and does not recognize that Elvis Presley is depicted. The other admires Warhol's work and knows who Elvis is. Are the two viewers equally prepared to get whatever this piece has to offer? What does the aesthetic empiricist say about this case? What does the enlightened empiricist say?*

Although value empiricism is very widely endorsed, James Shelley (2010) argues that it does not provide a satisfactory explanation of artistic value. For any particular artwork that provides a unique experience, what is valuable about that experience? The answer cannot simply be that it is valuable as the experience of that artwork, for that is what is in need of explanation. It must either be some content or other within that experience, or it must be the pleasure that is offered by the experience. In chapter 7, I observed that many important artworks are not designed to furnish pleasurable experiences, so pleasure is not a satisfactory explanation. (Furthermore, the goal of furnishing pleasure is not unique to art.) Pleasurable or not, Shelley observes that there is no good reason to say that two different experiences cannot possibly have the same value. For example, someone who intends to have a valuable experience by listening to Antonio Vivaldi's Concerto for Violin in G Minor (RV 319) might be equally well served by listening to his Concerto for Violin in G Minor (RV 328). A lot of Vivaldi's music sounds pretty much the same. But if the value of one piece of music is interchangeable with the value of another, then the same might be true of two paintings, two poems, and so on with all other types of art. A failure to rule out these possibilities invites a radical hypothesis. Although the experience of an Emily Dickinson poem is very different from the experience of a Vivaldi concerto, there is no good reason why someone who intends to have a valuable experience by reading a Dickinson poem could not derive an experience *with that same value* from a Vivaldi concerto.

Shelley's primary complaint against value empiricism is that it views artworks as a species of tools – artifacts with a function and a use-value. Given this perspective, why would anyone claim that every artwork is uniquely valuable? Imagine two hammers of the same brand and model. They sit side by side in a hardware store. However, one hammer is priced at twice the cost of the other. Using price as one measure of value, does this pricing strike you as reasonable? Would you be willing to pay twice as much for one hammer when you cannot tell the difference? Or would you assume that something has gone wrong here? (In the absence of evidence that artworks are uniquely valuable, a great many people question the stratospheric price tags on singular artworks by "name" artists.) Evaluated as tools, two different brands and models of hammers might have identical use-value. Analogously, identical use-value might hold for two artworks in different media when we evaluate them as opportunities for aesthetic experience. Shelley is correct to insist that value empiricism requires another supporting argument before we can conclude that each artwork has a unique use-value in providing an irreplaceable experience.

9.4 Instrumental value

The irreplaceability hypothesis is often bolstered by a traditional separation of values into two broad categories, instrumental value and intrinsic value. This new distinction is best understood by focusing on an example. Two hammers have the same use-value because they have the same *instrumental value*. An object's instrumental value is its value in furnishing something else of value. The exchange value of money is a classic example of instrumental value. In its basic use, money is valuable only to the extent that other people will accept it in exchange for other things. Most of these other things also have a use-value that turns out to be a merely instrumental value. Yet it is easy to lose sight of this deferment of value. Suppose you purchase a hammer. So long as it functions in its normal usage, it is virtually invisible to you – you are unlikely to think about it as you use it to drive nails (see Heidegger 1962). Driving nails, in turn, has another instrumental value, which varies from use to use. Someone might need to put new shingles on a garage roof, so that the garage stays dry when it rains. The same hammer can be used to build a fence. And so it goes with many other actions and objects, one thing serving as a tool for achieving some other purpose, which in turn serves as a means to another. What is the end point of this process? What do we ultimately gain from our engagements with tools and other things that possess purely instrumental value?

Aristotle (1999) argues that happiness is ultimately the one thing at which all our activities aim. The claim that happiness is the only such thing has been extensively debated, but it is not the point that concerns us here. Aristotle proposes that human activities do not make sense unless their consequences are intended to terminate in reasonable goals. Following Aristotle's lead, it has seemed obvious to many people that we cannot have an endless chain of instrumental value. The chain must terminate somewhere. In contrast to instrumental value, reasonable end goals are traditionally described as possessing *intrinsic value*. They are also said to be valuable for their own sake (i.e., not "for the sake of" something further). The argument, then, is that if nothing is valuable for its own sake, then there is no objective instrumental value.

Justice, human dignity, and wisdom have often joined happiness on lists of candidates for things that are intrinsically valuable. Value empiricism supplements this list with experiences of artworks. Asked to explain why we look at paintings, listen to music, and so on, the value empiricist says that there is no *further* goal to these activities. Artworks are immediately valuable. Tools are not. We don't manufacture hammers so that people can hammer things for the sake of hammering them. Therefore good artworks are not a species of tool. Suppose you travel to Milan, Italy, with the specific purpose of seeing *The Last Supper*. You arrive, you wait in line, and then you enter and experience it. Assuming that you satisfy the enlightened empiricist's requirement that you have a proper understanding of what you are experiencing, your purpose is achieved. Then you travel to Florence in order to view the relief sculptures of Lorenzo Ghiberti. This cultural tourism would be silly if these objects are not unique. In experiencing a work's objective properties, "the valuable qualities of a work are qualities *of the work*, not the experience it offers," and therefore the value of the work is intrinsic to the work (Budd 1995: 5). This is just another way of saying that *The Last Supper* and Ghiberti's sculptures are valuable for their own sake.

The thesis of art's intrinsic value is one way to understand the slogan of "art for art's sake." Some of its advocates cite it as evidence that instrumental value is irrelevant to artistic value. Yet this argument is weak. Art is valuable for securing and measuring social position, for "making special," and as a tool for reshaping society. (For these proposals, see sections 8.1, 7.6, and 3.4, respectively.) Some art is also useful as an investment, that is, as a tool for making money. We can reconcile these uses with "art for art's sake" by observing that these uses make little or no sense unless there is an independent reason why people experience art. To use art in these ways, people must want to interact with it. The best explanation of why people want to interact with art is that its aesthetic dimension has intrinsic value. (The special case of "anti-aesthetic" art can be handled by saying that it is not really valuable as art, or by endorsing the theory discussed below in section 9.6.) Consequently, instrumental value and intrinsic value are not mutually exclusive for the same property or object. There is no contradiction in saying that art belongs to the class of objects that is both valuable for its own sake and valuable for the sake of achieving something else of value. If this reconciliation of instrumental and intrinsic value is puzzling, consider the value of friendship. Aristotle (1999) notes that true friendship requires us to desire and pursue the happiness of another person without concern for any instrumental value we might gain. Happiness is intrinsically valuable, and therefore we desire it for others and not just ourselves. Yet friendship is reciprocal. Our friends desire and pursue what is good for us, in turn. Therefore friendship is instrumentally valuable, too. The lesson is that intrinsic value and instrumental value are not mutually exclusive. Art's intrinsic value is compatible with value empiricism.

Returning to Shelley's concerns, does recognition of art's intrinsic value support the thesis that *every* artwork has its own unique value? Here is one way to proceed to that conclusion. Like all other things that have intrinsic value, successful artworks "have their goodness in any and all circumstances" (Korsgaard 1983: 171). This point implies that the creation or destruction of any intrinsically valuable thing changes the amount of objective value that is present in the world. Is this plausible? Consider Rauschenberg's *Erased de Kooning* (1953). It was created by literally erasing a pencil drawing by Willem de Kooning. (Visually, the artwork is a piece of paper with some smudges on it. The museum that owns it classifies it as a drawing, but you might want to classify it as a piece of conceptual art.)

Normally, the creation of a new artwork increases the amount of artistic value in the world. But this case invites us to ask whether one work can replace another. Although the world was enriched by its creation, *Erased de Kooning* is visually uninteresting. Therefore there was less aesthetic value in the world once Rauschenberg started to erase de Kooning's drawing. The creation of Rauschenberg's work does not really compensate us for this loss of intrinsic value. The obvious explanation of the loss is that the Rauschenberg is aesthetically different from the de Kooning. This case supports the conclusion that the intrinsic *aesthetic* value of each artwork is unique and irreplaceable. The same cannot be said of other modes of *artistic* value.

Exercise: During World War II, the Germans looted many European art treasures from the countries that they occupied. Toward the end of the war, the retreating Germans hid many of these artworks in salt mines near Magdeburg. Suppose that one of these mines was lost and forgotten, and that several paintings by Claude Monet and Berthe Morisot are still there. Is there more value in the world because they exist unseen than would be in the world if these paintings had been destroyed?

A second argument proceeds by appeal to artists' intentions. If the aesthetic properties of artworks are not intrinsically valuable, then it is irrational for artists to individualize them to the degree that they do. Furthermore, if art possesses merely instrumental value, then audience experiences are all-important. However, if that is the case, then we are hard-pressed to explain our present artworld, in which "artists often do not care what others think" (Zangwill 2007: 158). Artists aim to produce something that has intrinsic value. However, their efforts would be pointless if they were simply replicating existing achievements. Therefore, successful artworks are uniquely valuable things.

Let's take stock. Our search for a demonstration of the unique value of each artwork led to the distinction between intrinsic and instrumental value. The process of exploring this distinction provided us with a better understanding of value empiricism. However, it did not really demonstrate that artworks provide a unique kind of value. After all, nature is an independent source of aesthetically valuable experiences. Nor is it clear that artworks are unique among artifacts, for value empiricism puts them in the company of perfume and chocolate éclairs. Finally, value empiricism offers little support for the thesis that each artwork is uniquely valuable. If you want to defend that thesis, you are better off defending art's intrinsic value and then arguing that an artwork's capacity to furnish valuable experiences derives from its intrinsic value. Yet the value of the experience is not the intrinsic value. There is a distinct possibility that the experiential differences offered by two artworks will be so minimal as to make no difference.

9.5 An alternative analysis

Christine Korsgaard (1983) has shaken up axiology by arguing that the traditional distinction between instrumental and intrinsic value is confused. Intrinsic value is the opposite of extrinsic value, and instrumental value is the opposite of what is valuable for its own sake. If we adopt her analysis, then any argument that rests on the opposition of instrumental and intrinsic value is untrustworthy and must be reconsidered. Korsgaard offers the following analysis.

- Instrumental value is how valuable something is for getting us something else that is of value. We also refer to such value as "a means to an end."
- Value for its own sake is a value that is independent of getting us something else that is of value. We also refer to such value as "an end in itself."
- Intrinsic value is a value that an object has, independent of its relationships with other objects.
- Extrinsic value is a value that an object has due to its relational properties, that is, due to its relationships with other objects.

This analysis provides a straightforward way of understanding the four value classifications. However, it undermines the idea that intrinsic value aligns with whatever is valuable for its own sake. This analysis undercuts the major claims of axiological empiricists. An artwork might be valuable for its own sake, yet lack intrinsic value. Furthermore, if artistic value is not intrinsic, then a valuable artwork might not retain that value in any and all circumstances. An artwork's value might vary according to changing social and historical circumstances (see Silvers 1991).

Given this understanding of "intrinsic," we must re-examine the thesis that aesthetically valuable artworks possess intrinsic value. Enlightened empiricism allows that some artworks have aesthetic properties that depend on non-perceptible base properties. Examples of such properties include historical facts that make something the culturally embedded object that it is. These are relational properties. If an artwork's aesthetic value depends on these properties, then its aesthetic value is an extrinsic property of that object. Therefore many artworks lack intrinsic value. An even stronger conclusion is defended by Monroe Beardsley (1965) and Jerrold Levinson (2006). They deny that any artifact has intrinsic value. Nothing possesses the property of artifactuality if it is the only object in the world. Yet the fact that something is an artifact is relevant to how it is experienced. (See section 7.4.) Therefore the aesthetic value of every artifact is an extrinsic value. And, of course, artworks are artifacts.

Although artworks are like tools in possessing extrinsic value, you might maintain that artworks are not mere tools. Hammers and food processors are never of value for their own sakes, yet artworks can be good or bad for their own sakes. To understand artistic value, we must understand which extrinsic goods are good for their own sakes and which are *merely* of instrumental value (i.e., for achieving some additional extrinsic value). Artworks are among the few things that fall into the category of extrinsic goods that also possess a "final," non-instrumental value, as an end in itself (Korsgaard 1983: 184–5). However, even this concession might be claiming too much for culturally embedded artifacts. Robert Stecker (1997) contends that art is always instrumentally valuable. An artwork's properties are one thing. Our experiences of those properties are something else. The artwork is a means to those experiences. If this is not a description of instrumental value, what is? Furthermore, the centrality of aesthetic properties is not unique to art. Stecker observes that the same thing holds for beds and cigars, which are designed with combinations of objective properties that allow them to serve as a means to providing very particular experiences. Jokes are not artworks, yet they strike me as another candidate for this general category. (You might add Dylan's sofa to this list, and then recall the discussion of perfume and cheesecake in chapter 7.) Being designed to furnish experience of aesthetic properties does not distinguish artworks as having a unique kind of value among human artifacts.

Exercise: Select two very similar artworks and explain the thesis that they are not valuable for their own sake. Distinguish it from the thesis that they possess extrinsic value.

It is plausible to conclude that artworks are in the same general category as cigars and well-designed cars. They are instrumentally and extrinsically valuable, but not intrinsically valuable or valuable for their own sake. However, you might resist this conclusion. You might insist, with Budd, that our lack of any *further* motivation to use them allows us to remove them from the category of what is instrumentally valuable. Against Budd, it seems that we can locate artworks that are not uniquely valuable for their own sake. Their value is purely instrumental. *Erased de Kooning* looks to be a good candidate. In order to create it, Rauschenberg asked his friend and mentor for a drawing. Suppose that de Kooning drew something just for this purpose. Furthermore, suppose that instead of whatever was actually there, de Kooning produced a very different drawing, *Intentionally Lousy Drawing*. This substitution would have made no difference at all for Rauschenberg's project. It simply does not matter what de Kooning's drawing looked like. Therefore de Kooning's drawing is of value *only* instrumentally, as a way to bring about Rauschenberg's artwork. It is good or bad to the extent that de Kooning's piece is good or bad. More generally, an aesthetically weak artwork that supports an admirable social change might be of value *only* instrumentally, by supporting an admirable goal. Artistic value does not consist in a thing's being valuable for its own sake. Therefore artworks can possess value without being valuable for their own sake. It appears that a clean distinction between the *kinds* of value exemplified by artworks and tools is not sustainable.

9.6 Appreciation

Gary Iseminger defends a distinctive version of enlightened empiricism. He rejects the assumption that everyone who has an informed experience of an artwork has more or less the same experience. As we discussed in chapter 7, many accounts of aesthetic judgment propose that it involves a pleasurable mental state. Iseminger is among recent philosophers who reject the assumption that every artwork is intended to furnish pleasure. Furthermore, human experiences are complex. Two people can have radically different total experiences in response to a common object or event. Edward Bullough offers the example of a theatre performance of William Shakespeare's *Othello* (*c*.1603), a tragedy about a jealous man who murders his wife.

> Suppose a man, who believes that he has cause to be jealous about his wife, witnesses a performance of *Othello*. He will the more perfectly appreciate the situation, conduct and character of Othello, the more exactly the feelings and experiences of Othello coincide with his own . . . In point of fact, he will probably do anything but appreciate the play. In reality, the concordance will merely render him acutely conscious of his own jealousy. (Bullough 1912: 93)

Bullough goes on to offer a complicated psychological account of why the rest of the audience appreciates the tragedy when this man does not. Iseminger sidesteps the need to offer a complex psychological explanation of this difference. His account of aesthetic response is refreshingly bare-bones.

Iseminger proposes that a positive aesthetic judgment centers on a respondent's *appreciation* of an experience. A single insight about axiology is then sufficient to account for the value of art's aesthetic dimension. Experiencing is distinguished from finding value, and "appreciation" is then defined as any mental state that involves both (Iseminger 2004: 36):

> Appreciating is finding the experiencing of a state of affairs to be valuable in itself.

The analysis focuses on a respondent's *belief* about her own particular experience. The presence of an experiential requirement is sufficient to make it an account of *aesthetic* value.

A note on terminology is in order here. A state of affairs is a thing's having a particular property. Yoko Ono's authorship of "Earth Piece" is a state of affairs. So is the smudged appearance of Rauschenberg's *Erased de Kooning*. However, there is an important difference between these two cases. You can *experience* the smudge, but I am not so sure that we can experience Ono's authorship, which took place five decades ago. (And I'm quite sure we cannot experience the sound of the earth turning, as "Earth Piece" stipulates!) Some properties are available for inspection during an experience, and some are not. For Iseminger, the presence or absence of sensory properties is sufficient to account for the difference between aesthetic and non-aesthetic appreciation. So what is the difference between an appreciative experience of the play *Othello* and the jealous husband's experience of it? After all, both responses involve experiencing it with understanding. For Iseminger, the crucial difference is the total state of mind. All other things being equal, the jealous husband would rather not have had that experience of that play. If it was a good production, most of the other theatre-goers found the experience to be valuable in itself. That is, they valued experiencing the play, whether or not there was anything else to be gained by having seen it. In that case, they aesthetically appreciated it.

This account has four clear virtues. The first virtue is that it is completely indifferent to the task of identifying common properties that are shared by all of the objects and events that we appreciate. The value is not restricted to a narrow range of properties, as it is, for example, with formalism; nor does it characterize the experience as detached, disinterested, or otherwise special. (See section 7.5). Appreciation is a question of the value of the resulting total experience. Second, there is no need to supplement the account with an analysis of the elusive concept of aesthetic experience. A third virtue of the analysis is that it makes it clear that successful artworks have instrumental value for offering an experience that audiences find valuable. The question of whether artworks possess intrinsic value is irrelevant. Fourth, it gives us a plausible theory of why art is held in such high regard. Typically, artworks are objects *intended* to be experienced and appreciated. Many experiences of art are found valuable for their own sake, and thus our chain of reasons for having art terminates in the fact that artworks are instrumentally valuable in providing something that is not of merely instrumental value. People who have appreciated *Othello* know that the play has value, for in appreciating it they have already found the experience of it to be valuable for its own sake.

Exercise: Many people who value painting and film appreciate the paintings of Claude Monet and the films of Martin Scorsese. Is it possible that these people are mistaken about the states of affairs that make their experiences valuable? Explain this thesis, and then contrast it with the possibility that people can be mistaken about the value of their own experiences when they appreciate paintings and films.

Compare Iseminger's theory of aesthetic appreciation with Jerrold Levinson's account of aesthetic response. (See section 7.7.) Like Levinson's account, Iseminger's "appreciating" is a second-order response. It begins with a response to a state of affairs. The response involves direct perception of aspects of the state of affairs. Then there is an additional response, which involves believing that that experience is worthwhile. (Step one is to have an experience. Step two is to find it valuable in itself.) Their two models agree that pleasure might be present, but it is not required. Yet Iseminger's model is much simpler than Levinson's proposed meta-response. Unlike Levinson, Iseminger does not require any understanding of how a particular artwork achieves the response that it does. Against Levinson, I am not confident that the majority of viewers of Lucas' *Star Wars* films are aware of how he integrates film editing, camera angles, Wagnerian music, and archetypes extracted from comparative mythology in order to arrive at specific content, themes, and meanings. I think that most people understand what Lucas is getting at without actually reflecting on that content "in relation to the structural base on which it rests" (Levinson 1996: 6). Yet I am unwilling to say that most fans do not appreciate these movies. Iseminger's account does not face this problem.

Although Iseminger's analysis has the advantage of being much simpler than Levinson's theory, Iseminger's account faces a serious criticism. As formulated, his account says that you are not engaged in appreciation if you fail to find the experience of the state of affairs to be valuable in itself. The jealous husband watching *Othello* is sorry he went. Suppose, therefore, that an art critic goes to a gallery opening of an up-and-coming painter. She thinks that the art is boring. It's not particularly bad, but then again it's not interesting. Did the critic appreciate the art? If we adopt Iseminger's analysis, then she did not appreciate it, and she did not have an aesthetic response. That result is clearly wrong. Furthermore, there are countless cases where people intially take things for granted. Suppose that a wealthy student attends college at a "ritzy" school and attends classes in architecturally impressive classrooms. The student notices the relevant states of affairs, such as the rich wood paneling, the thick carpets, and the comfortable chairs, but takes these things for granted. In this case, the individual is "tracking [states of affairs] without appreciating" (Iseminger 2004: 103). On Iseminger's account, these people are "tracking" and experiencing without finding the experiences to be valuable for their own sake. These responses do not satisfy the conditions for having an aesthetic state of mind. However, many findings of value occur later, through comparison. Suppose the wealthy student attends a conference at an urban public college and, noticing the concrete-block walls, the linoleum floors, and the uncomfortable plastic chairs in the classrooms, recognizes that the experience of being in these rooms is far less satisfying than the experience offered by the classrooms back "home." Is this student appreciating the experience of the classrooms with the concrete-block walls – or appreciating the classrooms at the "home" school?

Exercise: Suppose someone is "killing time" between classes and watches some Internet videos. Among them is Beyoncé Knowles's video for "Single Ladies (Put a Ring on It)" (2008). The experience is pleasant. However, under these circumstances, the person does not think about whether the experience is valuable for itself. Did this person appreciate the video?

These examples suggest that the central term, "appreciating," has several distinct meanings. Iseminger relies on one of them. It implies a finding of positive value. However, the art critic's informed response seems to be a genuine case of art appreciation. We merely have to allow that "valuing" can recognize negative values, too. Appreciating can include a belief that an experience has negative value when considered as valuable for its own sake. By extension, the belief can be a finding of neutral value, as when one can "take it or leave it." It seems that our art critic found the experiencing of the state of affairs to be of relatively *neutral* value on the continuum of value. She was genuinely engaging in art appreciation. However, if we interpret the situation in this way, a new objection arises. If you find the experience of a concrete block wall to be uninteresting, our revised interpretation of "appreciating" implies that you appreciate it. In supplementing positive value with neutral and negative degrees of value, we might as well say that we find each and every one of our experiences to be valuable in itself. In that case, every experience is an aesthetic, "appreciative" response. However, it is unlikely that we are engaged in aesthetic appreciation, all of the time. Furthermore, art is no longer special. Art furnishes occasions for aesthetic appreciation, but so does everything else.

My suggestion is to preserve the general advantages of Iseminger's account of appreciation while shedding these problems. This move requires recognition of yet another meaning of "appreciating." It can mean that one made an effort to evaluate something. One can say, "I appreciate the pie you baked for me, but I found the taste of the rhubarb overpowering and could not eat it." In this example, one "appreciates" the pie by having an experience of a state of affairs and *consciously* deciding how good the experience is. The mental act of *evaluating* the experience is what differentiates appreciating from Iseminger's "tracking without appreciating." In light of this example, we should modify Iseminger's key phrase, "is finding the experiencing of a state of affairs to be valuable in itself." It becomes:

> Appreciating is evaluating the experiencing of a state of affairs as valuable in itself.

According to this amended analysis, the only times we do not have aesthetic experiences are those times we do not ask how we value an experience. And, of course, there are many such times, not all of them related to art. To borrow an insight from an influential defender of modern art, Clement Greenberg, the lesson is that "anything that can be experienced at all can be experienced aesthetically" (Greenberg 2002 [1971]: 129). Yet not everything is appreciated, because many experiences are not evaluated. By exploiting standard institutional settings, artists indicate to audiences that they offer something with the understanding and intention that any experience of it will be evaluated for its own sake. Bored while waiting in a long line of stalled traffic, you are certainly free to evaluate the experience. But you're not likely to do so. Attending a movie or an art gallery or a music concert, you are very likely to do so. Appreciating is a more common activity with art than with other experiences, so we are primed to evaluate our experiences of art when we encounter it.

9.7 Cognitive value

Very few people think that aesthetic value exhausts artistic value. *Cognitivism* holds that art's aesthetic value is supplemented by various cognitive values. A painting should do something for the intellect and not just the eye. In other words, art is typically valuable for the ways in which it engages with and improves our thought processes.

A cognitivist axiology assigns instrumental, extrinsic value to art. Furthermore, cognitivism does not assume that art yields value through appreciative evaluation. An individual might receive cognitive benefits from an artwork without personally finding it to be valuable. The value is located with the effect on the audience, not with the experience itself. Repeated exposure to Cubist paintings might alter your ideas about spatiality without your being conscious that this cognitive change has taken place. This theory is particularly attractive as a way to explain the value of the many modern and post-modern artworks that have limited aesthetic merit. For example, critics presuppose a cognitivist perspective when they validate *Erased de Kooning* as an exploration of the ideas of authorship, ownership, and property – an intellectual exploration that is also attributed to Sherrie Levine's photographs of other photographs, except that her work is cognitively enriched through its exploration of further topics, particularly gender. (See section 1.4.) Finally, artworks that have limited experiential value might have significant cognitive value, simply by serving as embodiments and thus reinforcers of a culture's traditional values (Levinson 1996: 12). The French flag is an artwork of this type.

Despite its plausibility, cognitivist axiology of value faces an obstacle that we discussed in relation to aesthetic accounts. In addition to being *typical* of artworks, the relevant type of value should be *uniquely* advanced by artworks. Cognitivism must demonstrate that the artworld makes an indispensible contribution to processes of discovery, thinking, and learning. As such, cognitivism faces distinctive obstacles. The most obvious one is that it appears to place science and art into direct competition, with art the likely loser. Scientists, not artists, taught us that many diseases are caused by bacteria, viruses, and inherited conditions. Scientists, not artists, are going to determine whether a global climate change is being caused by human activities. Worse yet, many great artworks are full of lies. Bram Stoker's *Dracula* (1897) is a fine novel, and Francis Ford Coppola made a good film from it. But if we left it to artists, people with the inherited enzyme disorder of porphyria would still be classified as vampires and their "treatment" would consist of a stake through the heart. Or consider John Prine's song "Angel from Montgomery" (1971), which opens with an autobiographically false claim, "I am an old woman named after my mother." Cognitivism must explain how fictions teach valuable truths.

The cognitivist's first line of defense is to appeal to the value of imaginative engagement. As the character Hamlet says in Shakespeare's play of that name, "There are more things in heaven and earth . . . Than are dreamt of in your philosophy" (*Hamlet*, Act 1, Scene 5). Art, and narrative art particularly, invites imaginative engagement that makes us vividly aware of possibilities that would not otherwise occur to us. Artworks present situations and states of affairs that one would not ordinarily encounter, and therefore it can encourage audiences to entertain new possibilities. For Berys Gaut (2007), the most important aspect of fiction is that imaginative processing allows you to project yourself into the position of someone very different from yourself. That is what Prine did in writing "Angel from Montgomery," and it is what the audience does when listening to it. Gaut makes the point that this process depends on psychological common-alities among people. By imaginatively experiencing the situations and emotions of others, we obtain genuine understanding of what it is like to be in those situations, how others experience them, and even how others see us, in return. For example, the Academy Award-winning film *All Quiet on the Western Front* (1930) opened the eyes of Americans to the possi-bility that World War I propaganda might not be true, and that not every German soldier was a brutal, rampaging "Hun." As this example implies, cognitive values can be extended to include the ethical or moral dimen-sions of human life. Fictions can encourage new moral judgments. Ethical education occurred if narrow-minded Americans watched *All Quiet on the Western Front* and realized that the infantrymen in the trenches might not be responsible for the horrors of that war. Similarly, Robert Altman's *M*A*S*H* (1970) encouraged a later generation of movie-goers to think more critically about the then-current war in Vietnam. Yet Vietnam is never mentioned in Altman's film. The particular "facts" we learn from art are far less important than the mental modeling it provides. Although the film *One Wonderful Sunday* (1947) has nothing to do with earthquake survivors, watching it may enable people outside of Japan to empathize with what people there were experiencing as they reconstructed their lives in the wake of the devastating earthquake of March 2011.

Moral understanding is sometimes put forth as *the* cognitive value that distinguishes art from entertainment and other pleasurable experiences. You can appreciate a roller-coaster ride, but it is not designed to encourage ethical learning. Martha Nussbaum defends a strong version of the view that we should value art for what it teaches. She proposes that literature is *uniquely* suited to teach us ethical lessons, because "certain truths about human life can only be fittingly and accurately stated in the language and forms characteristic of the narrative artist" (Nussbaum 1992: 5). *All Quiet on the Western Front* and *M*A*S*H* were novels before they were adapted as screenplays. Nussbaum's position entails that, with respect to ethical enlightenment, the novels are cognitively more valuable than the films. On the face of it, this position seems to overstate the case for literature. Does Nussbaum seriously mean to say that watching a film cannot have the same effect? To understand why she does mean this, return to the idea, introduced above in section 9.2, that each artistic medium is formally and aesthetically distinct. Different media permit different forms and stylistic combinations of elements. Each novel takes many hours to read, providing an extended examination of characters, their thoughts, and their choices. Each film lasts about two hours. Beyond immersion time, the most impor-tant difference is that an author's *writing style* assigns moral significance and controls audience attention in a way that cannot be true of mere dia-logue and a series of visual images. Good literature is more nuanced than the best film, at least in showing how thought processes can work through difficult moral issues and arrive at ethically sound results. Ultimately, Nussbaum is claiming that a predominantly visual narrative is less philosophical than a strictly linguistic one.

A growing body of work in philosophy of film challenges the cognitive superiority of literature. For example, Murray Smith (1995) contends that film viewing requires an active cognitive construction of plot and character. At the same time, film offers spectators a perspective that is more like that of ordinary experience, and so it fully engages the cognitive processes that are ordinarily employed in ethical decision-making. Watching *All Quiet on the Western Front*, an attentive viewer must track representations of multiple characters, some of whom undergo considerable change. We track the characters in relation to multi-sensory information that furnishes plot. Finally, we ethically evaluate the characters and their choices. Our cognitive and ethical responses are not gratuitous. They are controlled by the construction of the artifact, including its cinematic style. Why isn't this engagement better than a more literary, philosophical one as an instrument of ethical exploration and learning? Given their greater accessibility, the film versions of *All Quiet on the Western Front* and *M*A*S*H* might be better instruments for encouraging subversive ethical thinking than are the respective novels.

Ethical sensitivity is merely one example of art's alleged cognitive value. Similar debates arise for each of the other cognitive functions that are assigned to the various arts. Suppose it is the case that some arts possess greater instrumental value relative to some cognitive ends. Does a dispersal of cognitive value undermine the claim that cognitive value is an important artistic value? It might seem to be a problem on the grounds that no one cognitive value will unify the arts. However, we can minimize the objection by adopting a historical perspective on cognitivist axiology. Different artforms are important at different times. New artforms arise and develop whenever an existing artform is no longer useful for carrying out its instrumental role. For example, the history of painting includes a long tradition of portraiture, including a tradition of multiple copies of the same portrait. (Recall the discussion of Hans Holbein the Younger in section 4.3.) Portraits have an obvious cognitive value in providing information about what someone looks like. However, the development of photography made painted portraiture less valuable for this purpose. Can you imagine sitting for a painting in order to secure a likeness for your passport? As photography *replaced* painting as a way of creating likenesses, painters explored other cognitive purposes. Painted portraits became far more expressive, and representational practices became more creative.

This strategy makes cognitivism more pluralistic. This point is consistent with the fact that most cognitivists already endorse *value pluralism*, the position that the answer we seek will not be located in only one kind of value. You are a value pluralist if you agree that artistic value embraces both aesthetic and cognitive value. The historical version of cognitivism merely fragments cognitive value into additional distinctive types. This broadened pluralism has the additional advantage of justifying our tendency to understand art by employing broad categories such as Renaissance humanism, Romantic individualism, and post-modernism. This familiar approach assumes that distinctive ideas develop across several arts simultaneously. Post-modern artists, for example, are said to endorse skepticism and nihilism and to value the particularity of interaction over the modern ideal of the autonomous individual. Many are thought to be engaged in exploration of cyclical and figural, rather than linear, approaches to time structure. These broad descriptions are thought to apply to arts as different as architecture and dance, and they are thought to help explain the emergences of new media, such as video and then computer art. In the present context, the point is to note that a pluralistic cognitivism makes sense of this general approach. Without it, it hardly makes sense for an art critic to assert that the themes of fragmentation and nihilism are present in both Frank Gehry's Guggenheim Museum Bilbao (1997) and the dance choreography that William Forsythe has developed for the Frankfurt Ballet and for his own dance company, such as *Decreation* (2003). This approach to art criticism and history weakens Nussbaum's hypothesis that specific cognitive achievements are reserved for specific uses of a single artistic medium.

If you have learned anything by now, it will be that philosophy looks at both strengths and weakness. You will not be surprised to find that we are ending on a critical note. An overly pluralistic version of cognitivism has its disadvantages. If it is going to be a general theory of artistic value, then every major art form will display cognitive value. (It will not be necessary for each and every artwork to possess cognitive value. As with aesthetic value, we must be prepared to say that some artists fail in their efforts to impart cognitive value, while others will simply not pursue that species of artistic value.) However, Immanuel Kant (1987) was one of the first philosophers to emphasize that one of the major artforms appears to lack cognitive value. Instrumental music teaches us nothing. It explores no ideas. It does not make us better people. Therefore, if Vivaldi's Concerto for Violin in G Minor (RV 319) is *typical* of instrumental music in failing to possess cognitive value, then cognitivism fails as a general theory of artistic value. You will not be surprised to learn that the philosophy of music is littered with attempts to show that the great instrumental composers deliver more than mere aesthetic value (e.g., Young 2001). Some philosophers fall back on the view that music represents emotions, but then you might recall our difficulties in explaining that idea in chapter 2. Peter Kivy (2009) argues that no theory has yet addressed Kant's great challenge. There is a distinct tradition of "absolute music" that is merely music, including many of the greatest works of Haydn, Mozart, and Beethoven. Although their work displays jaw-droppingly brilliant complexity, there is no plausible explanation of how they provide more cognitive value than the non-pictorial visual complexities of a Persian rug. The value is purely aesthetic, and we seem to have a major artform that is unlike all the rest. In order for cognitivism to succeed as a general theory of artistic value, it appears that someone will have to provide a more compelling account of the cognitive value of absolute music.

Issues to think about

1. Define "axiology."
2. Select two artworks in two different art media. What does axiological empiricism say about their value? How does enlightened empiricism modify this account of their value?
3. Explain the distinction between instrumental and non-instrumental value by explaining how a university education possesses both kinds of value.
4. Select an artwork that you value. Using it as a focal point, explain Korsgaard's distinction between saying that it is intrinsically valuable and saying that it is valuable for its own sake.
5. Why does anyone deny that two very similar artworks might be valuable in exactly the same way and in the same degree?
6. Explain Iseminger's analysis of "appreciating" art and contrast it with two other analyses of "appreciating."
7. Explain the concept of value pluralism.
8. Outline the strengths and weaknesses associated with adopting a historical perspective on cognitivist axiology.

Further resources

For further discussion of the relationship between economics and the arts, see the collection of essays assembled by Klamer (1996). It includes an interesting essay on Warhol. The principle of *de gustibus non est disputandum* is the subject of David Hume's classic essay, "Of the Standard of Taste" (Hume 1998a); the topic is pursued in Schellekens (2009). There is a rich literature on intrinsic value. Start by comparing Moore (1903), Beardsley (1965) and Budd (1995), and then review the challenges launched by Stecker (1997) and Levinson (2006). Despite important differences, Iseminger's *The Aesthetic Function of Art* (2004) and Zangwill's *Aesthetic Creation* (2007) represent something of a renaissance for the position that aesthetic value is art's primary value. This thesis is vigorously opposed by Carroll (2010). Goodman (1978), Young (2001), and Gaut (2007) defend cognitivist axiology, whereas Stolnitz (1992), Lamarque (1996), and Posner (1997) pose strong challenges. Carey (2006) offers the most recent defense of the superiority of literature. An overview of ideas about the cognitive value of film is available in Wartenberg and Curran (2005).

The Art of the Steal (2009) is a documentary that examines the fate of an important collection of modern and post-Impressionist art in the decades following the owner's death. The film explores conflicts between economic value, social value, and artistic value in contemporary America. *Howl* (2010) draws heavily on court transcripts to replicate the competing arguments about artistic value when an allegedly obscene poem went on trial in 1950s America. It presents an interesting case study of the idea of art for art's sake. *Dirty Pictures* (2000) focuses on a parallel case, the 1990 trial of a museum director who exhibited photographs by Robert Mapplethorpe.

10 Conclusion

Having reached the end of this survey of topics in contemporary philosophy of art, you may feel that you have just visited a smorgasbord of ideas. You may be wondering why the cook offered so much pickled herring and was stingy with the smoked salmon. You sampled a little of this topic and a little of that topic, you found your plate loaded with second and third helpings of a few core ideas, and perhaps you watched some of the recommended films as your dessert course after reading the chapters. Did it leave you hungry for more?

I will not be offended if the smorgasbord analogy fits your experience of reading this book. In inviting you to sample from here and there, I may have given the impression of proceeding with minimal pattern or plan. After all, I started by suggesting that you could read almost any chapter without concern for what happens in the other chapters. So why did I proceed in this way? My approach reflects my experience of contemporary philosophy of art as a vibrant and expanding field. If it is to be true to its subject matter, an introduction cannot focus on any one topic or philosophical position. Therefore, I rejected an approach that would suggest that learning philosophy of art means learning *the* answers to *the* questions that reflective people raise about art. Instead, I have tried to show that philosophy of art deals with a wide range of questions and that these questions have developed over the course of time. One consequence is that some very interesting topics received limited attention. Another result is that some topics, while interesting in their own right, have little or no connection to topics in other chapters.

If I have done my job in introducing you to philosophy, however, you will appreciate that philosophers expose and challenge underlying assumptions. To the degree that you endorse this critical model of philosophizing, you will not rest content with my claim to have produced an introduction that reflects the diversity of the discipline. You should find yourself questioning my assertion that this book reflects the field that it surveys. You will want to know more about my underlying assumptions and reasons. Fair enough.

Antiquity offers the idea of nine sisters, the nine muses, most of whom inspired writers and performers – and two of whom inspired historians and astronomers. According to modern classifications, this model is mistaken. Our modern "common sense" says that painters and sculptors need creative inspiration, but not historians and astronomers. Even video game designers seem more deserving of a dedicated muse than do modern astronomers. Moving beyond this metaphor, my literal point is that differ-ent cultures can – and do! – endorse slightly different alignments of creative, intellectual, and culturally enriching activities and objects. Yet I can locate no reason to suppose that our modern, Western grouping is more rational than the grouping of ancient Greek mythology. And I'm not persuaded that "we" have any one definitive grouping, either. In some conversational contexts I find myself interested in the fine arts, in which case video games and garden gnomes are not art. In other contexts, I find that they count as art. These fluid boundaries of art do not derive from confusion about the concept, nor do they arise from the permissive attitudes that "anything goes" and "it's all subjective." They arise from a very common tendency to use a single term to capture a constellation of contextually differentiated concepts. Language, however, does not function if its application to things in the world is arbitrary. If anything goes, then the *things* we are discussing play no role in our discussion. (See Wittgenstein 1953: 100.) I have tried to show that consideration of particular artworks often makes a difference in how we should make sense of things. Those artworks are grounded in cul-tural traditions. Clearly, then, there are some cultural rules in place here. The great complication is that there are so many of them.

I conclude that the artistic activities of Emily Dickinson, Yoko Ono, Sherrie Levine, and Katsushika Hokusai are united by a messy, evolving structure of relationships. Although eighteenth- and nineteenth-century intellectuals had a clear idea of what they would achieve by defining art, I doubt that we have maintained a consensus about what we gain by treating the various arts (plural) as one thing, art (singular). In short, I'm skeptical about finding a grand, unifying theory that works for all cultures through-out all of history. At the same time, skepticism does not justify outright denial. It remains possible that an essence of art lies hidden beneath these layers of history and cultural difference. It is possible that a poem, a con-ceptual "piece," a photograph of a photograph, and a woodblock print are essentially the same thing. It seems to me, however, that we have exhausted the obvious candidates for that essence. Until another proposal arises, we will profit by thinking about art from a different perspective. I endorse Peter Kivy's call for more exploration of the philosophies of the different arts (Kivy 1997). The different arts present us with rather different puzzles, and these problems are as challenging and interesting as the traditional quest for a unifying definition of art. Puzzles about visual depiction do not arise if we think paintings and piano sonatas are the same thing. The possibility of self-expression in a piano sonata is not a pressing issue if we think piano sonatas and Navajo sand paintings are the same thing. Pursued piecemeal, these are fascinating topics, and well worth our attention.

There is another reason to emphasize and explore differences. Many puzzling and fruitful questions about art are difficult to formulate. Never mind the answers – the *questions* only become apparent with the help of philosophical concepts and distinctions. Encounters with art do not, in and of themselves, inspire people to wonder about the range of alternatives to the physical object hypothesis (chapter 4), or to consider the distinction between first-order and second-order responses to artworks (chapter 7), or to think about art as a cluster concept (chapter 6). Few visitors to the Louvre Museum or the Tate Modern will spontaneously arrive at the distinction between necessary and sufficient conditions. Without it, however, they will be hard pressed to make sense of the diversity of artifacts on display by asking whether historically necessary conditions are logically necessary, much less whether historically necessary conditions are sufficient for being art (chapter 6).

Philosophical questions arise when we consciously examine assumptions and doctrines that most people take for granted. Yet philosophical discussion of Andy Warhol's Brillo boxes, Marcel Duchamp's readymades, and Sherrie Levine's photographs can make it seem as if the artworks themselves generate the philosophical puzzles that we are addressing. In that case, artists should get the credit that I am assigning to philosophers. This conclusion should be rejected as hasty. It overlooks the fact, emphasized by Arthur Danto, that art is now surrounded by an invisible "atmosphere of theory." Some of that theory is *philosophical* theory. Finding Christian symbolism in medieval European cathedrals comes as no surprise to anyone who knows the history of Europe; the existence of philosophically provocative art in the contemporary artworld should come as no surprise, either. Very few artists are trained in secluded communities that keep philosophical theories at bay. I concede that some artists receive minimal exposure to philosophy. At the same time, it would be silly to downplay the degree to which the academic training of visual artists, musicians, writers, filmmakers, and even game designers is infused with ideas generated by philosophers. Philosophers and artists have engaged in dialogue for over two millennia. Now and then, it even happens that a philosopher infuses philosophy into art by becoming an artist. (Among my favorites are painter Robert Motherwell, filmmaker Terrence Malick, conceptual and performance artist Adrian Piper, and comedian/author/actor/filmmaker Steve Martin.)

I want to close by elaborating on a suggestion that I made in passing, three paragraphs back. The arts are united by a messy, evolving structure of relationships. As I suggested in chapter 5, artworks do not represent their originating cultures in a straightforward way. People often say that changes in art reflect changes in the culture. It would be more accurate to say that changes in art *are* changes in the culture. The arts are themselves a significant element of culture. To the extent that artworks reflect *ideas* that circulate in a particular culture, there is no reason to be surprised to find that *ideas about art* frequently influence the content and style of art. In some cases, this process is facilitated by the fact that artists also function as critics. Around 100 years ago, George Bernard Shaw was an extremely controversial playwright. He was also an influential art critic, reviewing music, literature, and visual art. He was an early champion of the artistic power of photography. His struggles to articulate his praise and criticism of other artists in clear language made him extremely self-conscious about his own art. More relevantly, his unfashionable public defenses of Impressionism,

Wagner's operas, and photography challenged both Victorian moralizing and the "art-for-art's-sake" movement. To the extent that many in the artistic avant-garde take it for granted that artistic experimentation is aligned with progressive politics, they are children of Shaw. Against Shaw, the painter James McNeill Whistler defended artistic autonomy and aestheticism in his famous "Ten O'Clock" lecture, a public talk he presented on a number of occasions prior to its appearance in print (Whistler 1998).

Shaw and Whistler are merely two examples of a widespread phenomenon. They belong to the ranks of artists who defend particular philosophies of art either directly, by explaining and defending their philosophical commitments, or indirectly, by working as art critics. Written for a broad public, such writings generally do more to popularize a particular philosophy of art than the writings of philosophers. And in the course of popularizing philosophy of art, artists often blend, supplement, and rework the ideas they adopt from philosophers, art critics, and from other artists. Then they do the same, again, in a different way, by making art that embodies and confirms those ideas. Philosophers, in turn, find themselves reformulating their philosophies of art in order to take account of new artworks and new artistic styles that reflect various artists' personal understandings of philosophy of art. To the degree that Shaw's plays and Whistler's paintings embody their philosophies of art, philosophers will find it hard to deny that some art is highly political and some art is not. There will be no straightforward answer to the question, "Is art politics by another name?" Sometimes it is, and sometimes it isn't, and it would be irresponsible to ignore art that fails to conform to our philosophical prejudices. When Arthur Danto was forty he was a full-time philosophy professor. He was also a visual artist (primarily producing woodblock prints) and an art critic. At that point he saw the original exhibition of Andy Warhol's Brillo boxes in New York City. This event forced Danto to reconsider just about everything he thought he knew about philosophy of art (Danto 2009: x). I imagine that this pattern of shock and adjustment has been replayed by many other people, and that it will be again. (Unlike Danto, I do not think that art has stopped evolving.)

I frequently teach philosophy of art to students who are majoring in art, graphic design, and film. Perhaps you are reading this book because you are an art student and you are trying to get some background on what philosophers say about art. Perhaps you came across an idea that infuriates you, and you'll challenge it with your next art project. And, perhaps, we'll have to rewrite the philosophy of art because of you. Philosophy of art evolves to keep pace with new developments in art, as well as in philosophy. Or perhaps you are a philosophy student exploring a new area within philosophy. If so, you should recognize that my "smorgasbord" represents many of the major subdisciplines of philosophy. We discussed value theory, philosophy of language, theory of knowledge, and environmental philosophy, as well as metaphysical debates about the nature of different types of properties and objects. To engage fruitfully in philosophy of art, you must understand and engage with a wide range of fundamental philosophical issues. Thinking about art is a wonderful stimulant to thinking about the full breadth of philosophy. And to the same extent that engagement with art is important in a well-rounded life, engagement with philosophy of art contributes to being a well-rounded philosopher.

References

Addison, J., and Steele, R. (1965 [1711–14]) *The Spectator* (ed. D. Bond). Clarendon Press.

Adorno, T. (1973 [1964]) *The Jargon of Authenticity* (trans. K. Tarnowski and F. Will). Northwestern University Press.

——(2002 [1938]) "On the Fetish-Character in Music and the Regression of Listening," in *Essays on Music* (ed. R. Leppert and trans. S. H. Gillespie), pp. 288–317. University of California Press.

——(2004 [1970]) *Aesthetic Theory* (trans. R. Hullot-Kentor). Continuum.

Appiah, K. A. (2006) *Cosmopolitanism: Ethics in a World of Strangers*. Norton.

Arendt, H. (1993) "The Crisis in Culture: Its Social and Its Political Significance," in *Between Past and Future: Eight Exercises in Political Thought*, pp. 197–226. Penguin.

Aristophanes (1998) *Aristophanes I: Clouds, Wasps, Birds* (trans. P. Meineck). Hackett.

Aristotle (1991) *The Art of Rhetoric* (trans. H. Lawson-Tancred). Penguin.

——(1997) *Aristotle's Poetics* (trans. G. Whalley). McGill-Queen's University Press.

——(1999) *Nicomachean Ethics* (trans. T. Irwin, 2nd edn.). Hackett.

Arnheim, R. (1957) *Film as Art*. University of California Press.

Ayers, D. (2004) *Modernism: A Short Introduction*. Blackwell.

Bacharach, S. (2005) "Toward a Metaphysical Historicism," *The Journal of Aesthetics and Art Criticism* 63: 165–73.

Baumgarten, A.G. (1954) *Baumgarten's Reflections on Poetry* (trans. K. Aschenbrenner and W. B. Holther). University of California Press.

Baxandall, M. (1985) *Patterns of Intention: On the Historical Explanation of Pictures*. Yale University Press.

Beardsley, M. C. (1965) "Intrinsic Value," *Philosophy and Phenomenological Research* 26: 1–17.

——(1979) "In Defense of Aesthetic Value," *Proceedings and Addresses of the American Philosophical Association* 52: 723–49.

——(1981) *Aesthetics: Problems in the Philosophy of Criticism* (2nd edn.). Hackett.

——(1982) *The Aesthetic Point of View*. Cornell University Press.

Bell, C. (1958 [1914]) *Art*. Capricorn.

Bender, J. (1987) "Supervenience and the Justification of Aesthetic Judgments," *The Journal of Aesthetics and Art Criticism* 46: 31–40.

Berger, J. (1977) *Ways of Seeing*. Penguin Books.

Berleant, A. (2005) "Ideas for a Social Aesthetic," in Light and Smith 2005: 23–38.

Binkley, T. (1977) "Piece: Contra Aesthetics," *The Journal of Aesthetics and Art Criticism* 35: 265–77.

Blake, A. (1998) "Boy Actors in Women's Roles," in *Shakespeare: Readers, Audiences, Players* (ed. C. Edelman and R. S. White), pp. 121–30. University of Western Australia Press.

Bloom, A. (1987) "Music," in *The Closing of the American Mind*, pp. 68–81. Simon and Schuster.

Boden, M. (2004) *The Creative Mind: Myths and Mechanisms* (2nd edn.). Routledge.

Bourdieu, P. (1984) *Distinction: A Social Critique of the Judgement of Taste* (trans. R. Nice). Harvard University Press.

Brady, E. (2003) *Aesthetics of the Natural Environment.* Edinburgh University Press.

——(2005) "Sniffing and Savoring: The Aesthetics of Smells and Tastes," in Light and Smith 2005: 177–93.

Brand, P. and Korsmeyer, C. (eds.) (1995) *Feminism and Tradition in Aesthetics.* Pennsylvania State University Press.

Brown, D. (2003) *The Da Vinci Code.* Random House.

Brown, L. B. (2004) "Marsalis and Baraka: An Essay in Comparative Cultural Discourse," *Popular Music* 23: 241–55.

Budd, M. (1995) *Values of Art: Pictures, Poetry, and Music.* Allen Lane.

——(2002) *The Aesthetic Appreciation of Nature.* Clarendon Press.

Bullough, E. (1912) "'Psychical Distance' as a Factor in Art and as an Aesthetic Principle," *British Journal of Psychology* 5: 87–117.

Callen, A. (2000) *The Art of Impressionism: Painting Technique and the Making of Modernity.* Yale University Press.

Carey, J. (2006) *What Good Are the Arts?* Oxford University Press.

Carlson, A. (2000) *Aesthetics and the Environment: The Appreciation of Nature, Art and Architecture.* Routledge.

——(2008) *Nature and Landscape: An Introduction to Environmental Aesthetics.* Columbia University Press.

Carroll, N. (1988) *Philosophical Problems of Classical Film Theory.* Princeton University Press.

——(1993) "Essence, Expression, and History: Arthur Danto's Philosophy of Art," in Rollins 1993: 79–106.

——(1996) *Theorizing the Moving Image.* Cambridge University Press.

——(1998) *A Philosophy of Mass Art.* Clarendon Press.

——(ed.) (2000) *Theories of Art Today.* University of Wisconsin Press.

——(2001) "Art, Practice, and Narrative," in *Beyond Aesthetics: Philosophical Essays*, pp. 63–74. Cambridge University Press.

——(2010) *Art in Three Dimensions.* Oxford University Press.

Cohen, B. (1982) "A Tale of Two Paintings," *Annals of the Royal College of Surgeons of England* 64: 3–12.

Cohen, S. J. (1982) "The Problems of Swan Lake," in *Next Week, Swan Lake: Reflections on Dance and Dancers*, pp. 1–18. Wesleyan University Press.

Cohen, T. (1999a) "High and Low Art, and High and Low Audiences," *The Journal of Aesthetics and Art Criticism* 57: 137–43.

——(1999b) *Jokes: Philosophical Thoughts on Joking Matters.* University of Chicago Press.

Coleman, E. B. (2005) *Aboriginal Art, Identity and Appropriation.* Ashgate.

Collingwood, R. G. (1938) *The Principles of Art.* Clarendon Press.

Colonnese, T. G. (2004) "Native American Reactions to *The Searchers*," in *The Searchers: Essays and Reflections on John Ford's Classic Western* (ed. A. M. Eckstein and P. Lehman), pp. 335–42. Wayne State University Press.

Currie, G. (1989) *An Ontology of Art.* St. Martin's Press.

Dadlez, E. M. (1997) *What's Hecuba to Him?: Fictional Events and Actual Emotions.* Pennsylvania State University Press.

Danto, A. C. (1964) "The Artworld," *Journal of Philosophy* 61: 571–84.

——(1981) *The Transfiguration of the Commonplace: A Philosophy of Art.* Harvard University Press.

——(1986) *The Philosophical Disenfranchisement of Art.* Columbia University Press.

——(1993) "Responses and Replies," in Rollins 1993: 193–216.

——(2009) *Andy Warhol.* Yale University Press.

Davies, D. (2003) *Art as Performance.* Blackwell.

——(2006) "Against Enlightened Empiricism," in Kieran 2006: 22–35.

Davies, S. (1991) *Definitions of Art.* Cornell University Press.

——(1994) *Musical Meaning and Expression*. Cornell University Press.

——(1997) "Contra the Hypothetical Persona in Music," in Hjort and Laver 1997: 95–109.

——(2000) "Non-Western Art and Art's Definition," in Carroll 2000: 199–217.

——(2001) *Musical Works and Performances: A Philosophical Exploration*. Clarendon Press.

Davies, S. and Sukla, A. (eds.) (2003) *Art and Essence*. Praeger.

Davies, S., Higgins, K. M., Hopkins, R., Stecker, R. and Cooper, D. E. (eds.) (2009) *A Companion to Aesthetics* (2nd edn.). Wiley-Blackwell.

Da Vinci, L. (1989) *Leonardo on Painting: An Anthology of Writings by Leonardo da Vinci* (ed. and trans. M. Kemp and M. Walker). Yale University Press.

Dewey, J. (2005 [1934]) *Art as Experience*. Perigee/Penguin.

Dickie, G. (1964) "The Myth of the Aesthetic Attitude," *American Philosophical Quarterly* 1: 56–66.

——(1984) *The Art Circle: A Theory of Art*. Haven Publications.

Dickinson, E. (1891) *Poems: Second Series* (ed. T. W. Higginson and M. L. Todd). Roberts Brothers.

Dilworth, J. (2005) *The Double Content of Art*. Prometheus Books.

Dissanayake, E. (1995) *Homo Aestheticus: Where Art Comes From and Why*. University of Washington Press.

——(1988) *What Is Art For?* University of Washington Press.

Dodd, J. (2007) *Works of Music: An Essay in Ontology*. Oxford University Press.

Duchamp, M. (2003) "The Richard Mutt Case 1917," in Harrison and Wood 2003: 252.

Dutton, D. (1977) "Art, Behavior, and the Anthropologists," *Current Anthropology* 18: 387–94.

——(ed.) (1983) *The Forger's Art: Forgery and the Philosophy of Art*. University of California Press.

——(2006) "A Naturalist Definition of Art," *The Journal of Aesthetics and Art Criticism* 64: 367–77.

——(2009) *The Art Instinct*. Oxford University Press.

Eagleton, T. (1990) *The Ideology of the Aesthetic*. Blackwell.

——(2002) *Marxism and Literary Criticism*. Routledge.

Eaton, A.W. (2008) "Feminist Philosophy of Art," *Philosophy Compass* 3: 873–93.

Eaton, M. M. (1994) "The Intrinsic, Non-Supervenient Nature of Aesthetic Properties," *The Journal of Aesthetics and Art Criticism* 52: 383–97.

Engell, J. (1981) *The Creative Imagination: Enlightenment to Romanticism*. Harvard University Press.

Evans, G. (1982) *The Varieties of Reference*. Oxford University Press.

Feagin, S. (1983) "The Pleasures of Tragedy," *American Philosophical Quarterly* 20: 95–104.

Fenner, D. (2008) *Art in Context: Understanding Aesthetic Value*. Oxford University Press.

Fisher, J. A. (2004) "On Carroll's Enfranchisement of Mass Art as Art," *The Journal of Aesthetics and Art Criticism* 62: 57–61.

——(2005) "High Art versus Low Art," in Gaut and Lopes 2005: 527–40.

Foucault, M. (2002) *Order of Things: An Archaeology of the Human Sciences* (trans. anon.). Routledge.

Freud, S. (1922) *Beyond the Pleasure Principle* (trans. C. J. M. Hubback, 2nd edn.). International Psycho-Analytical Press.

——(1997) *Writings on Art and Literature*. Stanford University Press.

Gaiger, J. (2008) *Aesthetics & Painting*. Continuum.

Gantefϋhrer-Trier, A. (2004) *Cubism*. Taschen.

Gaut, B. (2000) "'Art' as a Cluster Concept," in Carroll 2000: 25–44.

——(2007) *Art, Emotion, and Ethics*. Oxford University Press.

——(2008) "Opaque Pictures," *Revue Internationale de Philosophie* 62: 381–96.

Gaut, B. and Livingston, P. (eds.) (2003) *The Creation of Art: New Essays in Philosophical Aesthetics*. Cambridge University Press.

Gaut, B. and Lopes, D. (eds.) (2005) *The Routledge Companion to Aesthetics* (2nd edn.). Routledge.

Ginsberg, A. (1956) *Howl and Other Poems*. City Lights Books.

Gioia, T. (1988) "Jazz and the Primitivist Myth," in *The Imperfect Art: Reflections on Jazz and Modern Culture*, pp. 19–49. Oxford University Press.

Godlovitch, S. (1998) "Performances and Musical Works," in *Musical Performance*, pp. 81– 96. Routledge.

Goehr, L. (2007) *The Imaginary Museum of Musical Works: An Essay in the Philosophy of Music* (2nd edn.). Oxford University Press.

Goodman, N. (1976) *Languages of Art: An Approach to a Theory of Symbols* (2nd edn.). Hackett.

——(1978) *Ways of Worldmaking*. Hackett.

Gracyk, T. (1996) *Rhythm and Noise: An Aesthetics of Rock*. Duke University Press.

——(2001a) *I Wanna Be Me: Rock Music and the Politics of Identity*. Temple University Press.

——(2001b) "Who Is the Artist if Works of Art are Action Types?" *Journal of Aesthetic Education* 35: 11–24.

——(2007) *Listening to Popular Music: Or, How I Learned to Stop Worrying and Love Led Zeppelin*. University of Michigan Press.

Greenberg, C. (2002 [1971]) "Counter-Avant-garde," in *Marcel Duchamp in Perspective* (ed. J. Masheck), pp. 122–33. Da Capo.

——(2003 [1939]) "Avant-Garde and Kitsch," in Harrison and Wood 2003: 539–49.

Hahn, T. (2007) *Sensational Knowledge: Embodying Culture through Japanese Dance*. Wesleyan University Press.

Hamilton, J. R. (2007) *The Art of Theatre*. Blackwell.

Hanslick, E. (1986) *On the Musically Beautiful* (trans. G. Payzant). Hackett.

Harrison, C. and Wood, P. (eds.) (2003) *Art in Theory, 1900–2000: An Anthology of Changing Ideas* (2nd edn.). Wiley-Blackwell.

Harrison, C., Wood, P. and Gaiger, J. (eds.) (1998) *Art in Theory, 1815–1900: An Anthology of Changing Ideas*. Wiley-Blackwell.

Hegel, G. W. F. (1975) *Aesthetics: Lectures on Fine Art* (2 vols., trans. T. M. Knox). Clarendon Press.

Heidegger, M. (1962) *Being and Time* (trans. J. Macquarrie and E. Robinson). Harper and Row.

——(1971) "The Origin of the Work of Art," in *Poetry, Language, Thought* (trans. A. Hofstadter), pp. 15–87. Harper and Row.

Hjort, M. and Laver, S. (eds.) (1997) *Emotion and the Arts*. Oxford University Press.

Hopkins, R. (1998) *Picture, Image and Experience: A Philosophical Inquiry*. Cambridge University Press.

——(2006) "The Speaking Image: Visual Communication and the Nature of Depiction," in Kieran 2006: 145–59.

——(2010) "Sculpture and Perspective," *British Journal of Aesthetics* 50: 357–73.

Horkheimer, M. and Adorno, T.W. (2002 [1947]) "The Culture Industry: Enlightenment as Mass Deception," in *Dialectic of Enlightenment: Philosophical Fragments* (trans. E. Jephcott), pp. 94–136. Stanford University Press.

Hume, D. (1998a [1757]) "Of the Standard of Taste," in *Selected Essays* (ed. S. Copley and A. Edgar), pp. 133–54. Oxford University Press.

——(1998b [1742]) "The Sceptic," in *Selected Essays* (ed. S. Copley and A. Edgar), pp. 95–112. Oxford University Press.

Irwin, W. (2007) "Philosophy as/and/of Popular Culture," in Irwin and Gracia 2007: 41–63.

Irwin, W. and Gracia, J. J. E. (eds.) (2007) *Philosophy and the Interpretation of Pop Culture*. Rowman and Littlefield.

Iseminger, G. (2004) *The Aesthetic Function of Art*. Cornell University Press.

James, H. (1983) *Novels, 1871–1880*. Library of America.

Jameson, F. (1991) *Postmodernism or, The Cultural Logic of Late Capitalism*. Duke University Press.

Janaway, C. (1999) "What a Musical Forgery Isn't," *British Journal of Aesthetics* 39: 62–71.

Jensen, H. (1973) "Exemplification in Nelson Goodman's Aesthetic Theory," *The Journal of Aesthetics and Art Criticism* 32: 47–51.

Johns, C. M. S. (2003) "'An Ornament of Italy and the Premier Female Painter of Europe': Rosalba Carriera and the Roman Academy," in *Women, Art and the Politics of Identity in Eighteenth-Century Europe* (ed. M. Hyde and J. Milam), pp. 20–45. Ashgate.

Johnston, D. (1993) "Spiritual Seekers Borrow Indians' Ways." *New York Times*, December 27, 1993: A1.

Kandinsky, W. (1977 [1911]) *Concerning the Spiritual in Art* (trans. M. T. H. Sadler). Dover Publications.

Kant, I. (1987 [1790]) *Critique of Judgment* (trans. W. Pluhar). Hackett.

Kaplan, A. (1966) "The Aesthetics of the Popular Arts," *The Journal of Aesthetics and Art Criticism* 24: 351–64.

Keith, A. B. (1924) *The Sanskrit Drama: Its Origin, Development, Theory and Practice*. Oxford University Press.

Kelly, M. (ed.) (1998) *Encyclopedia of Aesthetics* (4 vols.). Oxford University Press.

Kieran, M. (ed.) (2006) *Contemporary Debates in Aesthetics and the Philosophy of Art* (Contemporary Debates in Philosophy). Blackwell.

Kivy, P. (1989) *Sound Sentiment: An Essay on the Musical Emotions, Including the Complete Text of the Corded Shell*. Temple University Press.

——(1993) *The Fine Art of Repetition: Essays in the Philosophy of Music*. Cambridge University Press.

——(1995) *Authenticities: Philosophical Reflections on Musical Performance*. Cornell University Press.

——(1997) *Philosophies of Arts: An Essay in Differences*. Cambridge University Press.

——(2001) *New Essays on Musical Understanding*. Clarendon Press.

——(ed.) (2004) *The Blackwell Guide to Aesthetics*. Blackwell.

——(2006) *The Performance of Reading: An Essay in the Philosophy of Literature*. Blackwell.

——(2009) *Antithetical Arts: On the Ancient Quarrel between Literature and Music*. Clarendon Press.

Klamer, A. (ed.) (1996) *The Value of Culture: On the Relationship between Economics and Arts*. Amsterdam University Press.

Korsgaard, C. (1983) "Two Distinctions in Goodness," *Philosophical Review* 92: 169–95.

Korsmeyer, C. (2004) *Gender and Aesthetics: An Introduction*. Routledge.

Kracauer, S. (1997) *Theory of Film: The Redemption of Physical Reality*. Princeton University Press.

Krausz, M. (1993) *Rightness and Reasons: Interpretation in Cultural Practices*. Cornell University Press.

Lakoff, G. (1987) *Women, Fire, and Dangerous Things*. University of Chicago Press.

Lamarque, P. (1996) *Fictional Points of View*. Cornell University Press.

——(2010) *Work and Object: Explorations in the Metaphysics of Art*. Oxford University Press.

Le Huray, P. (1990) *Authenticity in Performance: Eighteenth-Century Case Studies*. Cambridge University Press.

Leopold, A. (2001) *A Sand County Almanac: With Essays on Conversation from Round River*. Oxford University Press.

Levinson, J. (1990) *Music, Art, & Metaphysics: Essays in Philosophical Aesthetics*. Cornell University Press.

——(1996) *The Pleasures of Aesthetics: Philosophical Essays*. Cornell University Press.

——(ed.) (2005) *The Oxford Handbook of Aesthetics*. Oxford University Press.

——(2006) *Contemplating Art: Essays in Aesthetics*. Oxford University Press.

Light, A. and Smith, J. M. (eds.) (2005) *The Aesthetics of Everyday Life*. Columbia University Press.

Lopes, D. (1996) *Understanding Pictures*. Oxford University Press.

——(2003) "The Aesthetics of Photographic Transparency," *Mind* 112: 434–48

——(2006) "The Domain of Depiction," in *Contemporary Debates in Aesthetics and the Philosophy of Art* (ed. M. Kieran), pp. 160–74. Blackwell.

Lorraine, Renée (1990) "A History of Music," in Brand and Korsmeyer 1995: 160–85.

Lu, C. (2000) *Lu Chi's Wen Fu: The Art of Writing* (trans. S. Hamill). Milkweed.

Mancoff, D. (2008) *Van Gogh's Flowers*. Frances Lincoln.

Margolis, J. (1995) *Interpretation Radical but Not Unruly: The New Puzzle of the Arts and History*. University of California Press.

Marx, K. (1998) "Individual Production and Art," in Harrison et al. 1998: 341–5.

Matravers, D. (1998) *Art and Emotion*. Oxford University Press.

——(2000) "The Institutional Theory: A Protean Creature," *British Journal of Aesthetics* 40: 242–50.

McKie, R. (2010) "How the National Gallery Uses Science to Spot Fakes and Masterpieces," *The Guardian*. www.guardian.co.uk/theobserver/2010/jun/20/national-gallery-restoration-science (accessed May 26, 2011).

Moore, G. E. (1903) *Principia Ethica*. Cambridge University Press.

Moore, R. (2008) *Natural Beauty: A Theory of Aesthetics beyond the Arts*. Broadview.

Nahm, M.C. (1956) *The Artist as Creator: An Essay on Human Freedom*. Johns Hopkins University Press.

Neill, A. (1991) "Fear, Fiction and Make-Believe," *The Journal of Aesthetics and Art Criticism* 49: 47–56.

Nettl, B. (1983) *The Study of Ethnomusicology: Twenty-Nine Issues and Concepts*. University of Illinois Press.

Newton, I. (1959) *The Correspondence of Isaac Newton, Volume I: 1661–1675* (ed. H. W. Turnbull). Cambridge University Press.

Nietzsche, F. W. (1999) *The Birth of Tragedy and Other Writings* (ed. R. Geuss and R. Speirs, trans. R. Speirs). Cambridge University Press.

Nochlin, L. (1988) *Women, Art, and Power and Other Essays*. Westview Press.

Novitz, D. (1992) *The Boundaries of Art*. Temple University Press.

——(1995) "Messages 'In' and Messages 'Through' Art," *Australasian Journal of Philosophy* 73: 199–203.

——(2005) "Aesthetics of Popular Art," in Levinson 2005: 733–47.

Nussbaum, M. (1992) *Love's Knowledge: Essays on Philosophy and Literature*. Oxford University Press.

Ono, Y. (1970) *Grapefruit* (2nd edn.). Simon and Schuster.

Parezo, N. (1991) *Navajo Sandpainting: From Religious Act to Commercial Art*. University of New Mexico Press.

Parfit, D. (1984) *Reasons and Persons*. Oxford University Press.

Pater, W. (2010 [1877]) *Studies in the History of the Renaissance* (ed. M. Beaumont). Oxford University Press.

Peacocke, C. (1987) "Depiction," *Philosophical Review* 96: 383–410.

Piper, A. (1996) *Out of Order, Out of Sight, Volume I: Selected Writings in Meta-Art 1968–1992*. The MIT Press.

Plato (1989) *The Dialogues of Plato, Volume I: Euthyphro, Apology, Crito, Meno, Gorgias, Menexenus* (trans. R. E. Allen). Yale University Press.

——(1996) *The Dialogues of Plato, Volume III: Ion, Hippias Minor, Laches, Protagoras* (trans. R. E. Allen). Yale University Press.

——(1997) *The Dialogues of Plato, Volume IV: Parmenides* (trans. R. E. Allen, revised edn.). Yale University Press.

——(2004) *The Republic* (trans. C. D. C. Reeve). Hackett.

Posner, R. (1997) "Against Ethical Criticism," *Literature and Philosophy* 21: 1–27.

Prall, D. W. (1929) *Aesthetic Judgment*. Thomas Y. Crowell Company.

Radford, C. (1975) "How Can We Be Moved by the Fate of Anna Karenina?" *Aristotelian Society Supplement* 49: 67–80.

Radnóti, S. (1999) *The Fake: Forgery and Its Place in Art*. Rowman and Littlefield.

Rawls, W. (1961) *Where the Red Fern Grows*. Doubleday.

Ridley, A. (2003) "Against Musical Ontology," *Journal of Philosophy* 100: 203–20.

Robinson, J. (2005) *Deeper than Reason: Emotion and Its Role in Literature, Music, and Art*. Oxford University Press.

Roelofs, M. (2005) "Racialization as an Aesthetic Production: What Does the Aesthetic Do for Whiteness and Blackness and Vice Versa?" in *White on White / Black on Black* (ed. G. Yancy), pp. 83–124. Rowman and Littlefield.

Rollins, M. (ed.) (1993) *Danto and his Critics*. Blackwell.

Rolston, H., III (1989) *Environmental Ethics: Duties to and Values in the Natural World*. Temple University Press.

Roth, P. (1959) *Goodbye, Columbus*. Houghton, Mifflin and Co.

Rudinow, J. (2010) *Soul Music: Tracking the Spiritual Roots of Pop from Plato to Motown*. University of Michigan Press.

Ruskin, J. (1985) *Unto This Last and Other Writings* (ed. C. Wilmer). Penguin.

Ryle, G. (2000) *The Concept of Mind*. University of Chicago Press.

Sacks, O. (1998) *The Man Who Mistook His Wife For a Hat and Other Clinical Tales*. Simon and Schuster.

Saito, Y. (1998) "The Aesthetics of Unscenic Nature," *The Journal of Aesthetics and. Art Criticism* 56: 101–11.

——(2007) *Everyday Aesthetics*. Oxford University Press.

Sartwell, C. (1995) *The Art of Living: Aesthetics of the Ordinary in World Spiritual Traditions*. State University of New York Press.

Schellekens, E. (2007) "The Aesthetic Value of Ideas," in *Philosophy and Conceptual Art* (ed. P. Goldie and E. Schellekens), pp. 71–91. Oxford University Press.

——(2009) "Taste and Objectivity: The Emergence of the Concept of the Aesthetic," *Philosophy Compass*, 4: 734–43.

Shelley, J. (2010) "Against Value Empiricism in Aesthetics," *Australasian Journal of Philosophy* 88: 707–20.

Shiner, L. (2003a) *The Invention of Art: A Cultural History*. University of Chicago Press.

——(2003b) "Western and Non-Western Concepts of Art: Universality and Authenticity," in Davies and Sukla 2003: 143–56.

Shusterman, R. (2000) *Pragmatist Aesthetics: Living Beauty, Rethinking Art* (2nd edn., revised). Rowman and Littlefield.

——(2002) "Of the Scandal of Taste," in *Surface and Depth: Dialectics of Criticism and Culture*, ch. 5. Cornell University Press.

——(2006) "Aesthetic Experience: From Analysis to Eros," *The Journal of Aesthetics and Art Criticism* 64: 217–29.

——(2007) "Popular Art and Entertainment Value," in Irwin and Gracia (2007): 131–57.

Sibley, F. (2001) *Approach to Aesthetics: Collected Papers on Philosophical Aesthetics* (ed. J. Benson, B. Redfern and J. R. Cox). Oxford University Press.

Silvers, Anita (1991) "The Story of Art is the Test of Time," *The Journal of Aesthetics and Art Criticism* 49: 211–24.

Smith, M. (1995) *Engaging Characters: Fiction, Emotion, and the Cinema*. Clarendon.

Solomon, R. (2007) *True to Our Feelings: What Our Emotions Are Really Telling Us*. Oxford University Press.

Spiegelman, A. (1996) *Maus: A Survivor's Tale*. Pantheon.

Staniszewski, M. A. (1995) *Believing Is Seeing: Creating the Culture of Art*. Penguin.

Stecker, R. (1997) *Artworks: Definition, Meaning, Value*. Pennsylvania State University Press.

——(2003). *Interpretation and Construction: Art, Speech, and the Law*. Blackwell.

Stolnitz, J. (1960) *Aesthetics and the Philosophy of Art Criticism*. Riverside.

——(1992) "On the Cognitive Triviality of Art," *British Journal of Aesthetics* 32: 191–200.

Taylor, P. (2010) "Black Aesthetics," *Philosophy Compass* 5: 1–15.

Thomasson, A.L. (2006) "Debates about the Ontology of Art: What are We Doing Here?" *Philosophy Compass* 1: 245–55.

Tilghman, B. R. (2004). "Reflections on Aesthetic Judgement," *British Journal of Aesthetics* 44: 248–60.

Tolstoy, L. (1996 [1898]) *What is Art?* (trans. A. Maude). Hackett.

Vasari, G. (1991) *The Lives of the Artists* (trans. J. C. Bondanella and P. Bondanella). Oxford University Press.

Walton, K. (1978) "Fearing Fictions," *Journal of Philosophy* 75: 5–27.

——(1984) "Transparent Pictures: On the Nature of Photographic Realism," *Critical Inquiry* 11: 246–77.

——(1997) "Spelunking, Simulation, and Slime: On Being Moved by Fiction," in Hjort and Laver 1997: 37–49.

——(2008) *Marvelous Images*. Oxford University Press.

Wartenberg, T. and Curran, A. (eds.) (2005) *Philosophy of Film: Introductory Text and Readings*. Blackwell.

Whistler, J. M. (1998) "'The Ten O'Clock Lecture' 1885," in Harrison et al. 1998: 838–47.

Whitehead, A. N. (1953) *Alfred North Whitehead: An Anthology* (ed. F. Northrop). Macmillan.

Wimsatt, W. K. and Beardsley, M. C. (1946) "The Intentional Fallacy," *Sewanee Review* 54: 468–88.

Witkin, R.W. (1993) *Adorno on Popular Culture*. Routledge.

Wittgenstein, L. (1953) *Philosophical Investigations* (ed. G. E. M. Anscombe and R. Rhees, trans. G. E. M. Anscombe). Blackwell.

Wollheim, R. (1980) *Art and Its Objects: With Six Supplementary Essays* (2nd edn.). Cambridge University Press.

Wolterstorff, N. (1980) *Works and Worlds of Art*. Clarendon Press.

Woolf, V. (1998) *A Room of One's Own and Three Guineas*. Oxford University Press.

Yanal, R. (1999) *Paradoxes of Emotion and Fiction*. Pennsylvania State University Press.

Young, J. O. (1999) "Art, Knowledge, and Exemplification," *British Journal of Aesthetics* 39: 126–37.

——(2001) *Art and Knowledge*. Routledge.

——(2005) *Aesthetics: Aesthetic Theory*. Routledge.

——(2008) *Cultural Appropriation and the Arts*. Blackwell.

Young, J. O. and Brunk, C. G. (eds.) (2009) *The Ethics of Cultural Appropriation*. Wiley.

Zangwill, N. (2001) *The Metaphysics of Beauty*. Cornell University Press.

——(2007) *Aesthetic Creation*. Oxford University Press.

Films

All Quiet on the Western Front, dir. L. Milestone, 1930.

Amadeus, dir. M. Forman, 1984.

An Angel at My Table, dir. J. Campion, 1990.

Andy Warhol: A Documentary Film (a.k.a. *American Masters: Andy Warhol*), dir. R. Burns, 2006.

Archangel, dir. G. Madden, 1990.

The Art of the Steal, dir. D. Argott, 2009.

Art School Confidential, dir. T. Zwigoff, 2006.

Avatar, dir J. Cameron, 2009.

Babette's Feast, dir. G. Axel, 1987.

Basquiat, dir. J. Schnabel, 1996.

Batman Begins, dir. C. Nolan, 2005.

Battleground, dir. W. Wellman, 1949.

Beauty and the Beast, dir. G. Trousdale and K. Wise, 1991.

Be Kind Rewind, dir. M. Gondry, 2008.

Black Swan, dir. D. Aronofsky, 2010.

Blade Runner, dir. R. Scott, 1982.

Blade Runner (Ultimate Collector's Edition), dir. R. Scott et al., 2007.

Blowup, dir. M. Antonioni, 1966.

Bomb It, dir. J. Reiss, 2007.

Bride and Prejudice, dir. G. Chanda, 2004.

Bright Star, dir. J. Campion, 2009.

Cadillac Records, dir. D. Martin, 2008.

Clueless, dir. A. Heckerling, 1995.

The Cool School, dir. M. Neville, 2008.

The Dark Knight, dir. C. Nolan, 2008.

Der Untergang (*Downfall*), dir. O. Hirschbiegel, 2004.

Dirty Pictures, dir. F. Pierson, 2000.

Dogma, dir. K. Smith, 1999.

Downtown 81, dir. E. Bertoglio, 2001.

Dracula, dir. F. Coppola, 1992.

Dune, dir. D. Lynch, 1984.

Edward Burtynsky on Manufactured Landscapes, dir. unknown, 2006.

The Enigma of Kaspar Hauser, dir. W. Herzog, 1974.

Eraserhead, dir. D. Lynch, 1976.

Fahrenheit 451, dir. F. Truffaut, 1966.

The Fake, dir. G. Grayson, 1953.

The Gods Must Be Crazy, dir. J. Uys, 1980.

Hamlet, dir. L. Olivier, 1948.

Hamlet, dir. F. Zeffirelli, 1990.

Hamlet, dir. K. Branagh, 1996.

Harry Potter and the Sorcerer's Stone, dir. C. Columbus, 2001.

The Hidden Fortress, dir. A. Kurosawa, 1958.

Howl, dir. R. Epstein and J. Friedman, 2010.

The Hurt Locker, dir. K. Bigelow, 2009.

Juno, dir. J. Reitman, 2007.

La Belle et la Bête, dir. J. Cocteau, 1946.

The Lord of the Rings: The Fellowship of the Ring, dir. P. Jackson, 2001.

The Lord of the Rings: The Return of the King, dir. P. Jackson, 2003.

The Lord of the Rings: The Two Towers, dir. P. Jackson, 2002.

Lust for Life, dir. V. Minnelli, 1956.

Mansfield Park, dir. I. MacDonald, 2007.

M*A*S*H, dir. R. Altman, 1970.

Mulholland Drive, dir. D. Lynch, 2001.

Muse, dir. A. Brooks, 1999.

My Kid Could Paint That, dir. A. Bar-Lev, 2007.

My Own Private Idaho, dir. G. Van Sant, 1991.

North by Northwest, dir. A. Hitchcock, 1959.

One Wonderful Sunday, dir. A. Kurosawa, 1947.

Ran, dir. A. Kurosawa, 1985.

Rembrandt's J'accuse, dir. P. Greenaway, 2008.

Requiem for a Dream, dir. D. Aronofsky, 2000.

Romeo + Juliet, dir. B. Luhrmann, 1996.

The Searchers, dir. J. Ford, 1956.

Sense and Sensibility, dir. A. Lee, 1995.

Shakespeare in Love, dir. J. Madden, 1998.

Stage Beauty, dir. R. Eyre, 2004.

Star Wars Episode I: The Phantom Menace, dir. G. Lucas, 1999.

Star Wars Episode IV: A New Hope, dir. G. Lucas, 1977.

The Thomas Crown Affair, dir. J. McTiernan, 1999.

Throne of Blood, dir. A. Kurosawa, 1957.

Titanic, dir. J. Cameron, 1997.

Troy, dir. W. Petersen, 2004.

Twin Peaks (The Complete Series), dir. D. Lynch, 2007.

Unseen Cinema: Early American Avant-Garde Film 1894–1941, dir. B. Posner, 2005.

We Were Soldiers, dir. R. Wallace, 2002.

Who the #$&% Is Jackson Pollock?, dir. H. Moses, 2006.

Index